Jonathan Wiesel's
CROSS-COUNTRY SKI VACATIONS

Second Edition

A Guide to the Best Resorts, Lodges, and Groomed Trails in North America

John Muir Publications
Santa Fe, New Mexico

John Muir Publications, P.O. Box 613, Santa Fe, New Mexico 87504

Printed in the United States of America.
Second edition. First printing September 1999.

Library of Congress Cataloging-in-Publication Data
Wiesel, Jonathan.
    Jonathan Wiesel's cross-country ski vacations : a guide to the best resorts,
lodges, and groomed trails in North America. — 2nd ed.
              p.   cm.
    Includes index.
    ISBN 1-56261-484-3
    1. Cross-country ski trails—United States Guidebooks. 2. Cross-country ski
trails—Canada Guidebooks. 3. Ski resorts—United States Guidebooks. 4. Ski
resorts—Canada Guidebooks. 5. United States Guidebooks. 6. Canada
Guidebooks.   I. Title. II. Title: Cross-country ski vacations.
GV854.4.W53 1999
796.93'2'0973—dc21   99-26706
                                                              CIP

Editor: Dianna Delling
Production: Marie J. T. Vigil
Cover design: Marie J. T. Vigil
Typesetter: Melissa Tandysh
Maps: Susan Harrison
Printer: Publishers Press

Front cover: © David Madison (Royal Gorge Cross Country Ski Resort, California)
Back cover photos: *large*—© Don Portman (Sun Mountain Lodge, Washington)
                 inset—© David Madison (Royal Gorge Cross Country Ski
                         Resort, California)

Distributed to the book trade by
Publishers Group West
Berkeley, California

*The information in this book is subject to change without notice. We strongly
recommend that you call ahead to verify the information presented here before
making final plans or reservations. The author and publisher make no representation
that this book is absolutely accurate or complete. Errors and omissions, whether
typographical, clerical, or otherwise, may sometimes occur herein. All destinations are
included without charge to them. The resorts, lodges, or areas that have photographs
have paid a fee to help defray the cost of publication.*

Dedicated to Benjamin Wiesel, father and friend.
New Yorker, New Englander, physician, philosopher,
and grand parent, he invested his life with contagious
zest and grace. Dad was always supportive, usually
managed to restrain his hilarity at my ludicrous
enthusiasms (balding long-haired hippie in cowboy
boots definitely qualified), and never hesitated to
puncture my pomposities. He would be pleased by the
love and hopes that have inspired this book.

Contents

Foreword

As an alpine ski racer at McGill University in the 1970s, I had a very tough and very good physical training coach named Skip Sheldon. As part of our training, he suggested cross-country skiing. My introduction was on a typical sub-zero day north of Montreal, packing out a 10-kilometer loop in two feet of new powder. The wooden skis, lignostone edges, and bizarre waxing kits weren't much of an attraction. But I soon learned it was a sport that could transform; one that I could master, excel at, and enjoy. And so can you. Now the equipment is made of super-light, space age materials, and cross-country ski bottoms glide faster than those on alpine racing skis. From Sweden's Vasaloppet and Switzerland's Engadine to Canada's 100-mile marathon and Norway's Birkebeiner, nordic skiiing has become a fabulous way to see a world few of us can begin to imagine.

If you're already a cross-country skier, you know the sport's wide-ranging appeal: spectacular scenes of tall pines dusted with fresh-fallen snow; the exhila-rating feel of breathing in crisp, clean air; the fun of skiing with family and meet-ing new friends; and the serenity that comes with gliding through some of the most beautiful land you will ever see. Skinny skis let you experience places that others will never see. For example, California's Royal Gorge, the largest cross-country area in the world (a veritable Disneyland for nordic aficionados), offers the magnificence of high wooded forest, jagged mountains, and rolling Alpine meadows stretching into the backcountry.

The vacations in this book are even good for your health! (When was the last time you returned from a holiday more fit than when you began?) Aerobically, cross-country is the finest recreation you'll ever find. It builds muscles and lowers body fat—a single hour of moderately-paced skiing burns 800 calories, allowing you to enjoy delicious homemade food at the ranch, resort, or lodge of your choice. And it's a sport for all ages. Children as young as two can cross-country ski, while you'll also see people in their eighties out there smiling. Maurilio DeZolt is a perfect example of the fact that youth doesn't dictate ability. Maurilio was 43 years old when he led the Italian cross-country team to a gold medal at the Lillehammer Olympics in the 10-kilometer relay. He beat dozens of athletes in their twenties who had fathers his age.

I took my firstborn skiing on my back for his first two years. Now he's a teenager, and we love hitting the trails at Trapp Family Lodge in Vermont (owned by the von Trapp family of *Sound of Music* fame). I'm always finding something new about cross-country, whether it's cutting-edge equipment, technique refine-ments, or a new destination. But my favorite things remain the same: Working hard, burning out my lungs and clearing out my brain on the uphills, then tucking the downhills, trying to go as fast as I possibly can.

Whatever it is you like about cross-country, and even if you haven't tried it yet, here you'll find the perfect destination. Author Jonathan Wiesel is both extremely knowledgeable and passionate about skiing. He describes resorts and lodges ranging from rustic to five-star, and trails from semi-flat to world-class challenging. He shares the truly important information too, like whether the strudel is good and the staff friendly. There are vacations for families looking for fun, athletes in search of a good workout, and couples seeking a romantic getaway. My advice to you is this: Read the book, select a getaway, then go! And take an extra couple of strides and another bite of strudel for me.

Dr. Bob Arnot
NBC News Chief Medical Correspondent

Preface

Though the memory seems to fade into prehistoric times, I loved snow and cold long before I developed a passion for cross-country skiing. The first time I became truly conscious of this affection was as a self-consciously erudite 14 year old, reading a stanza of William Blake's "To Winter":

He withers all in silence, and in his hand
Unclothes the earth, and freezes up frail life.

Clearly, Blake was a summer person.

Perhaps it's related to a high metabolism, but, for me, warm weather induces allergies, physical lethargy, and mental sloth. Winter, in contrast, doesn't just stimulate, it sings with beauty, clarity, dimension, energy, creativity.

Fast-forward to February 1971: the setting, a small hill near the Kawishiwi River near Ely, Minnesota; the vehicles of destruction, a pair of wood Bonna 1800 nordic skis; the bruised ego, all mine. I had been a competent alpine skier for 15 years; intended to spend some months in Austria, where I swiftly racked up left ankle and knee thanks to a fall while wearing a French-made "wet-look" ski-suit; couldn't stomach the idea of a winter without snow play; signed up for an Outward Bound course in the far northern Midwest; and was abruptly introduced to a world of narrow boards, free heels, ankle-high leather "boots," and lignostone edges. The immediate results were blissful glide on the flats, encouraging pace on ascents, and downhill devastation. It took several dozen plunges and admirable self-restraint on the part of our instructor to convince me that, yes, controlled descent on skinny skis is entirely possible, but, no, leaning forward aggressively is not a clever way to initiate a turn unless you enjoy examining ski tips from snow level. (The noseplow is an effective way to stop but exceedingly hard on one's glasses.)

Suffice it to say that I fell in love with this sport, abandoned alpine, and still bring off the occasional photogenic faceplant. Millions of downhillers share this interest in cross-country—some with fervor, some mildly, some grudgingly by force of circumstance (a vacationing family commits to "sharing a little time together" on the slopes and tracks).

Over the past quarter-century, my affection for the sport has evolved but never ebbed. What began as a torrid affair with exercise, technique, and cold air has matured (or at least mellowed) into something both gentler and more sweeping: a deep appreciation of the season and the people who enjoy it.

The trail has led me from Minnesota to Montana, with snow stops along the way in 26 states and provinces and five European countries. (Ironically, I've not yet been to Scandinavia.) It still astonishes me that a bookworm born in New York, who grew up in Connecticut suburbia and older in Berkeley, California, and who studied Contemporary Latin American Military History became committed to a way of life as demented as the ski industry. (Our motto: "To make a small fortune in the ski business, start with a large fortune.")

This is not an "everything in one" introduction to skiing, nor another trail guide. It's not for ascetics, racers, technocrats, or people who dislike superlatives. You are about to encounter half a lifetime's highly subjective observations on sensational cross-country ski *destinations*—places fascinating not just for skiing but for *ambiance*, which ranges from the unorthodox to the elegant, broadening in both culture and girth.

Your choice of activities is as diverse as your selection of facilities: you may ski, dine, snowshoe, ride horses, hone your sense of beauty, be hyperactive or lazy, make love. . . . Prepare for sensory overload!

I hope results are as entertaining for the reader as this grand research project has been for the author. And if great places have been left out, please let me know for the next edition by e-mail at wiesel@imt.net.

A friend commented that the title should be *The Cross-Country Ski-in/Ski-Out Jacuzzi B&B Fine Dining Indoor Plumbing Dog Trail and Great Places Book*. That's a pretty good summation, though I (born with a full set of sweet teeth) still think of it as *Seconds on Desserts*.

Jonathan Wiesel
Bozeman, Montana

Acknowledgments

During the course of writing this book, I've been the undeserving recipient of courtesies that extend beyond the customary and friendships that exceed the conceivable. I would like to thank John Muir Publications, most patient guides and editors; the hundreds of ski area operators who endured hours of interrogation and generously provided lodging; editors for whom I've written, who coped with the shock of receiving articles early so I could concentrate on the revision of this opus; dear friends Kris Thomas and Bob Ekey, for shatteringly practical suggestions ("Jonathan, are you *sure* you want to say that?") and sharing daughter Madison and son Alex so we could test our pulk-sled; Chris and John Frado, for encouraging this mad enterprise despite a cumulative 40 years' experience in the ski business; Peter Hale, equipment mentor, countless-time chauffeur to Bozeman's Gallatin Field and certified care giver to Typo the Toyota (Kris and Bob share that title, too); State Farm Insurance, for an almost infallible road atlas that stood up to rain, snow, and crinkling in luggage; Pam and Bill Bryan of Off The Beaten Path, who lent smiling encouragement and sent me to scout exotic spots despite my sense of humor; Tourisme Québec, Ontario Tourism, and the Anchorage Convention & Visitors Bureau, for sponsorship and meticulous planning on three visits; Kim Brinkley and Monica Van Duzer, favorite zoo keepers and ardent Yellowstone skiers (Kim, are there truly winterized dung beetles?); Cody and Willie, Newfoundlands Extraordinaires and my immediate family, who forgave frequent temporary abandonment; ski-area-operator-turned-real-estate-mogul Bruce Simon, who taught me to "work smarter, not harder" (Bruce, why didn't you say years ago that an Apple laptop is a journalist's lifesaver?); the waitresses at Minneapolis Airport's late, lamented Garden Restaurant, who let me sit through long working meals without a sign of impatience; and Gene Kilgore, friend and inspiration, who politely argued it was Now or Never to write this tome before grey cells disappeared with the albino remnants of my hair.

Forever, thanks to the unsung historical figures who kept me going in all weathers—the inventors of hot showers, clothes dryers, desserts, and decaf cappuccino.

Customized Trips:
Off The Beaten Path

The Rockies have it all—magnificent vistas, "cold smoke" powder, and a stunning array of cross-country ski areas. The difficulty in planning vacations comes from an excess of riches. Do you prefer to be pampered at a guest ranch, visit an alpine resort with a major cross-country trail system, or ski a region with a half-dozen networks *and* try dog sledding, sleigh rides, and hot air ballooning?

That's just the beginning. What are your true priorities—magnificent scenery, romantic surroundings, exercise, budget, exquisite cuisine, intriguing companions, family atmosphere, polishing technique, wildlife adventures, or avoiding altitudes that sap energy?

Montana-based Off The Beaten Path *customizes* cross-country holidays in the West. In conjunction with winter planner Jonathan Wiesel, they can design anything from week-long trips in Yellowstone, complete with guides, naturalists, and instructors, to visits to backcountry lodges in the magnificent Canadian Rockies. You don't have to be an accomplished skier or hardened Northerner to enjoy these trips. Most winter guests come from exotic climes such as Southern California, Pennsylvania, the Carolinas, Texas, and Florida.

Off The Beaten Path charges a consulting fee, a minor price to pay for the ideal vacation. Off The Beaten Path, 27 E. Main Street, Bozeman, Montana 59715; (800) 445-2995 or (406) 586-1311; fax (406) 587-4147; e-mail travel@offbeatenpath.com; and Web site www.offbeatenpath.com.

Preparing for Your Winter Adventure

Sometimes it seems most of humanity hates winter. The incidence of "couch potatoism" rises swiftly as cold descends on the land; folks shiver, dreaming morosely of sun and sand; the worst afflicted head south.

Admittedly, we're not all genetically predisposed to love snow. But why endorse misery? Why not test whether winter possesses gentle magic? Why not revel in it, *embrace* it? If you choose to try, cross-country skiing provides the surest introduction to the joys of the season.

HAN SOLO AND THE SUNDANCE KID CAN'T BE WRONG

Cross-country (XC) has a complex, contradictory, and often invidious reputation. North Americans used to visualize it as a Scandinavian eccentricity acceptable only when there was no motorized alternative. Indoor vegetables and alpine skiers took, respectively, know-nothing or condescending attitudes. Cross-country was frequently viewed as technically simple to the point of boredom, granola/wool dowdy, and primarily practiced by penurious masochists ("A cross-country skier heads into the woods and returns having changed neither his underwear nor his $5 bill.").

The other side of the cross-country coin was the stereotype of the young "pain is gain" athlete with icicle-laden mustache in sweat-darkened Lycra suit. The image is about as true as the assumption that all joggers are long-distance runners. In reality, the person you're most likely to meet on the trails is an affluent mother in her late 30s out with a small group of friends. At cross-country areas as many as *60 percent* of visitors are female.

Another cliché: "But it's so much work!" It needn't be! Cross-country is a sport that can be done at your own pace. As for the problem of "glowing," aerobics isn't exactly perspiration-free, either. Just think of the ski trail as a mirror-free Outdoor Fitness Room and Natural Tanning Salon.

Downhillers sometimes patronize the sport as unchallenging, utilizing simple equipment. Actually, it takes time and concentration to become an *accomplished* skier, while gear selection is complex because so many options are available. It's also worth noting that nordic skiers have a greater variety of turns to choose from.

Mundane? Well, a few of the people who enjoy cross-country are NBC's Dr. Bob Arnot, Harrison Ford (who has his own track setter), Robert Redford (he went further, creating his own alpine/cross-country resort), statesman Pierre Trudeau, supermodel Kim Alexis, actresses Demi Moore and Cynthia Gibbs,

Pierce Brosnan ("Bond, James Bond"), champion bicyclists Greg LeMond and Davis Phinney, astronaut Roberta Bondar, and tennis stars Ivan Lendl and Chris Evert.

Be reassured: you don't have to be—or have—a celebrated figure to enjoy the sport. But if you recognize the profile of one of your neighbors, be cool, nod equally, and enjoy the fact that this is the most even-handed form of recreation.

THIS MUCH FUN AND STILL LEGAL?

Why cross-country ski? Cardiovascular benefits, yes, but also freedom! Exercise endorphins! Solitude! Conviviality! It's adventure for some, peace of mind for others. There's the technical challenge, grace of movement, and times shared with friends. Many ski for the lyrical quality—the taste of clean air, clear and carrying light, sighing wind, hardwood forests, frozen waterfalls, weathered barns, open prairie, sandstone canyons, alpenglow on snow-mantled peaks, and the miracle of skiing beneath the full moon. More than mere recreation, this is euphoria!

My favorite aspect of cross-country is the diversity of people who love it. It can be either social or solitary, so it appeals to groups, families, couples, and individuals. You'll find cross-trainers: bicyclists, runners, Nordic Trackers, hockey players, and roller bladers. Neither age nor gender matters—women outnumber men, and the majority of skiers are over the age of 30. All it takes is enthusiasm for enjoying the outdoors in winter, at your own speed, with your own choice of companions. Urbanites, rural residents, bird watchers, racers, meanderers, photographers, senior citizens—you name it, they're on the trails!

A skillful skier is a thing of beauty, moving with fluid power, adjusting tempo and technique to terrain, snow depth, and snow type. But one needn't be an adept; the casual day tripper—even a practiced exercise-evader—can get a kick equal to that of a national-caliber athlete from the season's enchantment.

Cross-country skiing is one of the finest aerobic activities available, but you don't have to be a marathoner to enjoy it. The great thing is you can move swiftly or sedately, depending on inclination, energy, and skill. It's also low-impact on joints. I tear up a knee or ankle running every summer. It takes only a couple of weeks of track skiing to get back in shape and decide I don't really need a body trade-in.

Cross-country skiing exercises muscle groups from your feet to your arms, and everything in between. Writer/doctor/racer Peter Dorsen says, "It's one of the greatest calorie-consuming sports there is, partly because both upper and lower body movement are involved."

For those with a hunger for caloric facts, Chris Scott, research associate at the Institute for Aerobics Research in Dallas, has details on comparative sports. He says that a 170-pound man skiing 5 miles per hour on the level uses about 13.2 calories per minute (792 calories per hour). In comparison, a 170-pound man jogging 5.5 miles per hour uses 12 calories per minute (720 calories per hour). All of which is a complex way of saying that cross-country skiing is a superb way to develop a trim body while having fun.

WHAT IS CROSS-COUNTRY SKIING?

Cross-country skiing is as diverse as the terrain it covers—flying over pasture and meadow, meandering through the woods, gliding up gentle slopes and carving down hillsides. Where-to-ski options are marvelously varied, but the choices of *how* to ski are just as gratifying.

The **diagonal stride**, or "classic" technique, is efficient and smooth. Its name comes from the alternate movement of arms and legs—the same movement used in walking but more elongated. Equipment is lightweight, with genuine "skinny skis" and boots that look much like running shoes. Machine-set "tracks" at cross-country areas provide a consistent surface that literally guides skis forward, eliminating most of the balance problems that plague beginners. While learned most easily in tracks, the diagonal stride is used by off-track skiers as well.

In contrast, **skating** is more dynamic, swifter, but more physically demanding. While it's the technique of choice for racers, skating can become an enjoyable part of any skier's technical repertoire. One limitation: it requires a compact surface or you get no glide.

Either style can be employed on uphills, flats, and gentle downhills. Other ascent methods include the herringbone (effective but ungainly), sidestep (practical but boring), and switchbacking.

Backcountry skiing is more rugged and rustic, using wider skis and sturdier boots. Ski tourers carry a day pack with food, clothing, and supplies. By breaking your own trail, you can enjoy the wilderness in a more secluded and contemplative way than at any ski area.

Some people enjoy overnight tours, requiring either an inn-to-inn or hut-to-hut system or even winter camping. It's best to go out on your first trip with a guide. The rewards of solitude are worth the effort, above all the opportunity to learn winter's serenity, from the gentle pace of drifting clouds to the soft movements of birds and animals traveling above and under snowdrifts.

One of the great thrills in cross-country is learning to control yourself skiing **downhill**. (Happily, sitting down is considered quite legitimate. Using a skier below you as a buffer is not as acceptable, though it's a great way to meet people!) The style of turn you employ can vary with mood, skills, and conditions. Experienced alpine skiers often prefer parallel turns, while others are devotees of the spectacular telemark. As they become more expert, people like to mix turns, from the standard snowplow to the dramatic skate.

Your friendly professional instructor can demonstrate and communicate all these techniques—then it's up to you to practice and enjoy them!

NORDIC VOCABULARY

"Alpine skiing" is a term recognized by skiers, media, and a large part of the non-skiing public. Some call it "downhill," but it's known to involve lifts that take you up a mountain so you can happily careen down again, repeating the process until legs give out or slopes close. (True diplomats do not call it "yo-yo skiing.")

While nordic skiing is about 4,000 years older than alpine, it still suffers from an identity crisis. What is skinny skiing? Striding on the tracks or skating; back-country touring; overnight snow camping; riding a lift up and telemarking down free-heeled on metal-edged skis; parallels, wedges, step turns. . . .

Happily, Cross Country Ski Areas Association, an international organization representing ski operators and suppliers, has a standardized nomenclature:

- **Nordic** skiing is the catch-all that includes even jumping and biathlon—everything other than alpine skiing.
- **Cross-country** refers to skiing on machine-groomed surfaces—that is, track for diagonal stride and compacted snow for skating lanes.
- **Ski touring** equates with off-track skiing, from playing in the backyard to treks traversing Wyoming's Tetons. Ski touring can be variously described as "bushwhacking," "mountaineering," or "backcountry," but it always means skiing on ungroomed trails.
- **Grooming** refers to the result of conditioning and compressing snow by machine (snowcat or snowmobile) and attachments to form a solid, consistent base to support skiers. Groomed trails are used by both diagonal striders and skaters.
- **Track-set trails** involve machine-compressing precise grooves into the snow for use by diagonal striders, accompanied by compaction on both sides for pole plant.
- **Skating** is a relatively new technique involving an ice skating–like motion of both arms and legs, thrusting out to the side (as opposed to the traditional forward movement of diagonal stride). To avoid catching an edge, skating requires a smooth dense surface, whether groomed trail or spring corn snow.

So next time you're on skinny boards of any kind, not only can you have fun doing whatever you like most, you can also describe it afterwards to admiring friends, using approved terminology from the Emily Post of nordic skiing!

CROSS-COUNTRY SKI AREAS

Cross-country areas can encompass city parklands, guest ranches, golf courses, B&Bs, historic lodges, alpine ski area affiliates, even real estate developments. There are hundreds of areas to choose from across North America, plus thousands of kilometers of trails groomed by public lands agencies and ski clubs.

There's always the option of strapping on skis your first time and heading out the back door. After an hour you may wonder: "Where's the trail? How do I cross this brook? Ahh, where's the restroom?" (Intimately familiar to parents of small children.) It's a little like choosing to take up golf by playing in the cow pasture next door—convenient but not very satisfying.

Cross-country areas offer the comforts that start you off right. They're *service-oriented*, catering to guests who appreciate amenities such as ski instruction, heated restrooms, food service, and cleared parking lots. Often accommodations and a day lodge are right on the premises. They usually have rental equipment and a retail shop for items you may have lost, forgotten, or never thought you needed.

Groomed trail systems are usually both signed and marked so you know where you're going. Certain trails are lit for night skiing, so you can get an evening workout with friends or family.

Good grooming is a demanding, expensive process. Machinery costs thousands of dollars, and grooming at commercial operations may take place every day. Trail fees also cover costs for trail maintenance, ski patrol, insurance, toilets, parking lots, and snow clearance. It's worth it! Trails groomed by government agencies offer a more unpredictable experience, as public employees usually don't work weekends and holidays, when most people have the time to ski.

FROM SWEDISH BOGS TO LYCRA TOGS: A BRIEF HISTORY

Strange as it may seem, skiing existed prior to chair lifts, stretch pants, fiberglass "boards," plastic boots, and safety bindings. North Americans often forget that nordic skiing is a mere 150 years old on this continent, an import with roots deep in the past of Northern Europe.

If you watched Scandinavians garner multitudes of medals at the Lillehammer and Nagano Olympics, you saw the culmination of 4,000 years of history. Without them there would be no cross-country, no alpine, and no Winter Games (hockey, skating, and so forth are purely parvenus).

Snowshoe-like contraptions made of woven reeds originated in the Siberian steppes around 2,500 B.C., but the first known skis were found in Sweden, dating to around 2,000 B.C. In Norway, a 4,000-year-old drawing of a skier-like figure has been found drawn on a rock wall. To get an idea of how devoted Scandinavians are to the sport, Ullr, god of winter, was described as walking on skis.

Equipment a few millennia ago was rather different from what we see today. Some skis were built from a single ash, pine, or birch board, steamed or soaked to make the tips limber enough to be turned up; others consisted of a frame covered with leather. Skiers often used only one pole, for balance on downhill runs or as a brake. (Eventually they discovered two poles were easier uphill.) Leather bindings attached shoe to ski but let the heel lift free for push forward.

Recreation probably wasn't a primary interest in early days, though we can hope practitioners interspersed some play with transport, hunting, and warfare. The latter's history is a litany of innovations that led to biathlon (ski-and-shoot).

By around A.D. 1300, Swedes and Russians had developed ski troops. Norway's famous Birkebeiner race commemorates the rescue of young Prince Haakon by two loyal soldiers on skis. Much more recently, Finnish ski troops effectively fought numerically superior forces during the 1939–40 Russo–Finnish conflict.

Ski warfare has played a vital role in American skiing as well. The 10th Mountain Division of World War II fame produced key figures in downhill development, such as Vail's founder, Pete Seibert.

Cross-country also had non-military applications, providing a way to move between towns during long winter months, while making hunting swifter and bringing the game home easier. Explorer Fridthjof Nansen made a 500-kilometer trek across southern Greenland in 1888 and then (clever publicist!) wrote about it, for the first time popularizing the sport outside Scandinavia.

Geography probably played a role in the popularity of nordic skiing. Since the far north has so little winter sun, the populace mined every bit of entertainment available, including jumping. Norwegian Sondre Norheim introduced the efficient and elegant telemark turn in the 1860s in his home town of Morgedal in Telemark province. Though the technique fell into disfavor with the advent of alpine skiing's fixed heel, it enjoyed a rejuvenation in Colorado in the 1970s and has been readapted by the Norwegians with great gusto.

There's speculation that skiing made its American debut with Leif Ericsson, who visited "Vineland the Good" around A.D. 1000. Scandinavian immigrants brought the sport to both the Midwest and California during the Gold Rush in the 1840s. Skis were up to 20 feet long, bindings were leather straps, and wax (or "dope") was a marvelous amalgam of substances including tar, turpentine, camphor, and castor oil. Norwegian-born John Thorensen, better known as "Snowshoe" Thompson, was the first skiing mailman, trekking across the Sierras for 20 years on 25-pound boards, carrying a heavy pack. (His widow never received a federal pension, so government wasn't entirely different in those days.) A downhill race some years ago matched modern technology against century-old equipment, and the latter made a very impressive showing—not much on turns but mighty swift heels!

The new century saw growing differentiation between alpine and nordic. Downhill began to evolve along specialized lines, with metal edges and different techniques. Most of these innovations were introduced by Central Europeans, who had to deal with steeper, narrower descents than those in Scandinavia.

Back in the 1970s, virtually the only good cross-country equipment came from Norway, Finland, and Sweden. Never mind the fact that poles were fashioned from Southeast Asian bamboo and hickory often came from American forests; the products had Norwegian names like Epoke, Blå-skia, Asnes, Splitkein, and Bonna. Even today, when Fischer (Austrian) and Rossignol (French) are dominant manufacturers and real innovators, brands like Peltonen and Madshus command respect in North

America. (The wheel has turned full circle—the Madshus factory is owned by American alpine ski manufacturer K2.)

Telemarking isn't the only Scandinavian technique cross-country skiers have adopted. Back around 1981, American Bill Koch started to clean up on the World Cup circuit using skating instead of the traditional diagonal stride. Koch adopted the technique from a Finnish skier, adding his own ingenious variations. Swedes and Norwegians tried to have skating banned from international competition; when this didn't work, they promptly adapted and again dominated the international scene.

Not all ski-related innovations have been Scandinavian, but it's been argued that even sleek one-piece racing suits and track setting also came from that part of the world. So give thanks to Norway when you don your Lifa long johns, put Swix wax on your skis, and place your boots in Rottefella three-pin "nordic norm" bindings for backcountry touring. The slicer used to cut your imported *gjetost* (goat's cheese) for lunch is originally Scandinavian. And at day's end, enjoy a sauna and remember that, too, comes to you courtesy of Norway, Sweden, and Finland.

BARREL STAVES, BAMBOO STICKS, SPAGHETTI SHOES: EQUIPMENT

If you're not yet a cross-country skier, the best recipe for fun right from the start is to combine good equipment, instruction, and groomed trails. First step: make sure skis aren't too heavy or wide, poles aren't too short, and boots don't imitate wet noodles.

Shopping Around

Through the mid-'70s, cross-country skis were wood and required waxing; boots were leather and poles, bamboo; bindings resembled metal rattraps. Changes since then have been nothing short of revolutionary. Tough lightweight synthetics mean better equipment, though color mixes can put you off a good meal. One problem now is selecting from a bewildering number of products at astonishingly different prices.

Not all ski shops are created equal. For better service from more knowledgeable salespeople, visit a specialty retailer rather than one carrying largely alpine equipment.

It's tempting to assume a salesperson is a professional, but it ain't necessarily so. For example, if you go shopping at Christmas, chances are good you'll be dealing with an "on-leave" college student. So inquire: "Do you like to skate or ski classic, backcountry tour, or telemark?" Ask plenty of questions, don't be intimidated by technical jargon, and remember the retailer is there to serve you. If you get a blank look or evasive stammer, smile gently and take your business elsewhere.

There are a couple of ways to save dollars. Retailers usually have sales in the fall, spring, and right after Christmas. You can also do well at ski swaps *if* you know precisely what you want and there's expert advice available.

A number of specialty shops publish extensive catalogues. See the Appendix for a list of leaders.

Try Before You Buy

In a society of immediate gratification, it's very tempting to drive to a ski shop *right now*, buy a bundle of equipment, and head to the snow. But it's a better investment of time and money to test before you purchase. One strategy is to rent the desired skis, boots, bindings, and poles first. (Check to see if you can apply this fee to the purchase price.) Better yet, visit a cross-country ski area, rent their stuff, and see how it goes. You may need to leave a credit card, driver's license, or ID as deposit. Most areas will accept any surety that's small and of significant value.

It's a great sport and you'll probably love it, but don't shell out dollars prematurely and have lonely skis gathering dust in your garage.

Packages

Retailers usually give the best prices on skis, boots, bindings, and pole "packages." Mixing and matching elements costs more but may give you exactly what you want. *Don't be swayed by price alone, and make boots your priority.*

The hallowed $100 cross-country package of the 1970s is hard to find and will be junk. You can get a reasonable combination starting at around $250. Most good ski shops have "demo" (demonstration) skis available for the customer to try out a particular model.

Remember: no single set of equipment will "do it all." Play with different types until you know what you enjoy most, then make the decision.

Short, Long, and In-Between

When Austrian manufacturer Fischer introduced a 147-cm "one-size-fits-all" cross-country ski early in 1993, the company initiated a profound and controversial nordic revolution. These short classic and skating models were new in both concept and appearance. For most beginners who tried them, "micros" (aficionados accustomed to 210-cm clunkers employed less courteous terms) made the sport easier and more fun to learn.

While traditional long boards provide flotation and are inherently speedier than their little cousins, non-experts find them difficult to turn. Shorties proved easy to maneuver, eliminated most falls, made sidestepping and snowplowing feasible, let you skate uphill with short, steady strokes instead of dropping into a boring herringbone, and even allowed kick turns! Above all, they provided control on descents instead of windmilling arms, crossed tips, and mouthfuls of snow.

Unfortunately, shorties were not embraced by most retailers or manufacturers. It's curious that most producers emphasize equipment that's swift rather than frolicsome. Perhaps this is a reflection of the fact that racers have a great deal to do with ski design, while recreationists aren't consulted atall. It may be uncharitable, but I also suspect some long-timers resent the ease with which shorter-ski users master downhills.

While the Fischer Revolution lasted only four years, it led to an ingenious design compromise between innovation and tradition: midlength skis. Mid-length models are both practical and entertaining, providing a nice mix of speed, flotation, and control. And though you may not make a hockey stop in your first hour as with true micros, skis in the 160–180 cm range still add a dimension of turning-play that was missing with long skis, when all attention went to surviving a downhill plunge.

Of Winter and Wardrobe

Objectively speaking, I rate most meteorologists on the same evolutionary rung with politicians and statisticians. They seem intent on raising public blood pressure as well as heating bills, warning listeners to stay indoors because of "windchill." Instead of inciting hysteria, wouldn't it make more sense to recommend *wearing clothing outdoors* (windchill refers to the effect on bare flesh—they seem to assume people run around nude in winter); moving rather than standing; and taking practical precautions such as wearing a hat?

I have no objection to responsible weather evaluations ("The approaching cold front will be accompanied by wind gusts approaching 40 miles per hour, so it would be a good idea to stay warm by cross-country skiing; ski in the woods, avoiding lakes and golf courses."). But I strongly dislike alarmist and erroneous reporting reminiscent of Hearst newspaper headlines supporting the Spanish-American War. In the capitalist tradition, there may be links between hysterical forecasts delivered in grave tones ("Windchills are expected to approximate a nasty day on the dark side of Pluto, except *really chilly*, so plug in your socks, stock up on fuel oil, and turn up the heat.") and vested interests ("And now a word from our sponsors, including rechargeable Hotstockings and your friendly power company. Turn up that thermostat *right now!*").

I've known two highly responsible meteorologists who were nordic skiers. Both understood their reports deeply touch everyone from dedicated practitioners to beginners, who might be affected for a lifetime by scare tactics. On the other hand, I recall watching TV descriptions (no live coverage) of a blizzard and road closures in the Sierra Nevadas when in fact blue skies prevailed for days.

A Word about Ski Conditions

Sometimes cross-country skiers rush to negative judgment about ski conditions, refusing to look beyond noses pressed against window panes.

Area operators are constantly frustrated by downstaters' assumption that if there's no snow in the backyard, there's no skiing within a day's drive. This can be absolutely false. New York, Wisconsin, and Michigan provide cases in point, where "lake effect snow"—moisture stripped off the Great Lakes—can create massive localized storms, which don't necessarily drop most snow at the highest elevations.

If you've been looking forward to skiing but have no white stuff plastered against your door, give a call to a cross-country area. Better yet, check their Web sites or the Cross Country Ski Areas Association's condition reports (www.xcski .org) Most operators are honest about conditions (inaccurate reports create word-of-mouth reputations even faster than good service or a great sale); and if their snow is poor, they'll often refer you to places that that have it in abundance. Remember: good trails only need 6 inches of packed snow for skating and 8 inches for track skiing!

And Thence to Apparel

Cross-country clothing is delightfully versatile. People can use tights and windbreakers for skiing, bicycling, or jogging. Ski shops carry stylish functional materials, but you can supplement specialized garments by raiding the closet for sweaters, long johns, hats, and mittens.

Conventional cold weather togs like bulky parkas are undesirable for cross-country, as they constrict movement and help generate excessive body heat. You may glow, perspire, or even sweat, according to your metabolism and degree of refinement, depending on how fast and hard you ski. The trick is to retain warmth while allowing perspiration to evaporate. This is achieved by layering clothing to adjust heat loss to pace, terrain, temperature, and wind speed.

Wearing several light articles of clothing—for instance, polypropylene or similar underwear and synthetic fleece overpants plus windpants, with a wool or fleece zip sweater and a wind-resistant jacket—allows you to trap warm air in pockets of space. In most conditions, wear just one or two insulating layers, depending on the weather and the kind of skiing you'll be doing. Remove jacket and windpants when you're hot, unzip jacket and sweater if you're only warm. As the day heats up or the breeze dies, wind pants and windshell are removed; as chill sets in, on they go again. And these garments don't restrict movement the way jeans or alpine ski bibs do.

Many synthetic fabrics have the ability to "wick" moisture away from the skin and onto the next layer. In turn, the middle insulating layer should be quick-drying or wicking as well, so moisture ends up as close to the outside as possible.

Moisture and cold air aren't a happy mixture. If underclothes are wet and your skin is clammy, there's an increased chance of hypothermia (a lowering of the body's core temperature, often mistakenly called "exposure"). Cotton acts like a moisture sponge and accelerates chilling, so denim isn't recommended. Gentlemen, those cotton shorts and briefs are best avoided on a cold day.

Aside from buying warm, comfortable, "breathable" boots, the best thing for your feet is layering, too. Try wearing thin polypropylene liners under a pair of wool or wool-blend socks. If your toes are susceptible to cold, resist the temptation to put on too many socks, as you'll only restrict circulation, making feet colder. Instead invest in a pair of light overboots, and occasionally swig something warm, sweet, and non-alcoholic to help cut the chill.

Mittens are best if you're prone to cold hands, as they allow fingers to share body heat. Gloves are better for precise ski pole control. For chilly weather, look for gloves with leather palms, a long gauntlet at the wrist and a light lining; in warmer conditions, critters a lot like handball gloves can be fine. Don't use too heavy a pair or they'll be sweat-soaked in the first kilometer.

A final point: beware the sun. It's amazingly easy to burn your skin, particularly on a hazy day, so wear sunscreen—you'll still get a tan. Sunglasses are vital—snowblindness makes your eyes feel as though they've been sandpapered and can damage corneas.

Keeping Hot- (or Warm-) Headed

Most experienced skiers learn that protecting—or uncovering—one's head is vital to winter comfort. At 40° F, up to half of your body heat can be lost from an unprotected head—and at 5° F, up to *three quarters* of body heat production can be lost this way, especially for distinguished-looking gentlemen with "high foreheads" like mine.

Chilling problems occur more often than overheating. A useful adage to remember is, "If your toes are cold, put on a hat." Its sequel is, "If you're *still* cold, put on another hat!" Layer the hats, with itch-free lightweight polypropylene or tight woven wool next to the skin and a heavier model above. Extra hats or headbands don't take up much room in a fanny or day pack.

CROSS-COUNTRY SKI INSTRUCTION: OUT-THINKING YOUR FEET

Cross-country skiing has a reputation for being easy to learn. Two dozen years ago, an industry catch-phrase was, "If you can walk, you can ski." It's more accurate to say it's simple to *walk* on skis, rather harder to *glide* on them. As with tennis, you can enjoy just hacking around, but expertise improves efficiency and gives you a vast repertoire of entertaining "moves."

Some children and those rare adults gifted with mimicry find cross-country easy to absorb on their own. For the rest of us, it's tempting to "learn" from a friend or spouse, but this is a proven recipe for disaster. Interestingly, high-caliber racers can be poor teachers, perhaps because their level of expectation is conditioned by exercising with other fine athletes. I've found it's fun *and* enlightening to ski with someone better than I am, not in guru/disciple mode, but instead relaxing, talking, and letting my body adapt to the rhythm and pace the other person sets.

Curiously, only modest numbers of cross-country skiers learn from professionals. Part of the problem may be terminology—a lot of us feel reasonably mature, and "lesson" seems to hearken back to authority figure/student relationships. But skiing well increases pleasure, so head to the nearest ski school *right now!*

In general, I'd recommend learning from PSIA (Professional Ski Instructors of America) and CANSI (Canadian Association of Nordic Ski Instructors) professionals. Both organizations educate their people in technique and communications. Certification doesn't guarantee instructors are great skiers—I'm a prime example—but it helps assure they'll be friendly, patient, and effective tutors whose approach is a supportive "Friends, let's savor this together," rather than "Come on, slowpoke, follow me!"

Instruction gives polish and versatility; but real progress requires skiing at least a dozen days annually.

SKIING WITH CHILDREN

Here are a few tips to make outings with children wonderfully memorable. One secret: the more parents enjoy themselves, the more kids see skiing as a treat.

First, gear your outing to a child's age and ability. Take plenty of breaks to allow youngsters time to play in the snow (remember, the object is to have fun!). Truly devoted parents even offer themselves as targets for snowballs. One of my earliest winter memories is throwing snow at (well, near) my father, both of us giggling madly.

For the first few outings, it's advisable to ski in machine-set tracks. This allows kids to make rapid and obvious progress without becoming exhausted. Proximity to plowed parking, shelter, and toilets also helps assure a positive initial experience.

Carry plenty of wholesome snacks. Take along fluids—hot chocolate is usually a big hit—as all of you need to avoid dehydration. You may want to get your youngster a fanny pack or day pack (some kids love to be self-sufficient).

Bring extra socks, mittens, and hats, since children exhibit genius at getting theirs soaked. Wet means cold, and a young body takes longer to recover heat than an adult one.

Be sure children have equipment that fits and is warm—*especially* boots. There are ski packages that allow younger ones to use the insulated, waterproof snow boots they already own. When real ski boots are in order, plan to buy, trade in, or swap a new pair annually.

Head home before everyone is tired. A good ending means a good beginning on the next trip. And don't be a Little League Father. Kids can mimic marvelously well, but not every one chooses to do so—and sometimes they don't have perfect parental role models.

Some cross-country areas have kids' facilities and programs, such as babysitting or day care (check the Special Features Directory). Operators are generally responsive to guest suggestions—so if your favorite place doesn't have something you need, ask for it!

Lastly, don't be envious if your youngster learns faster than you believed possible. Kids are a lot less self-conscious and stiff than adults. They pick up cross-country naturally and often become better skiers than their folks! That's OK, because eventually you'll have sweet revenge watching them go through an identical process with their own young 'uns.

Small Tracks

Children should have not just good equipment, warm clothing, and professional instruction, but also an optimal ski environment. A growing number of areas have small hills for sledding; others build play gardens with painted plywood cutouts to ski around and through. A few even prepare trails especially for kids.

Grooming machinery manufacturers have developed narrow-gauge track setters. Children tire rapidly and fall frequently when forced to ski in adult-width tracks, whereas narrow ones allow youngsters to stay centered over their skis rather than doing the splits.

Special Sleds

Time was, if a parent wanted to ski with a really small youngster, it was a matter of finding a pack that would engulf the child and praying you didn't take a tumble.

Today there are special sleds ("pulks" in Norwegian) designed to be pulled behind a willing adult or *trained* canine, that can keep a child snoozing, warm, and comfortable. Pulks have gotten so good that I actually bought one from Nordic Lynx—quite a tribute, considering I'm not a parent! Most ski areas allow them on trails; many even have them for rent. They're reasonably stable on downhills and even sidehills, so devoted parents don't spend so much time prone, "getting close to nature." My favorite model has an adjustable seat, with lap belt; insulating close-cell foam interior; and heavy-duty nylon cover with a sturdy zipper. Two segmented aluminum poles run from the sled to the puller's padded belt so you can skate or diagonal stride. It also has an optional (but highly recommended) tinted acrylic windshield, rear nylon windbreak, and tinted acrylic top. For pulk sources, see the Special Features Directory.

NO OBSTACLES FOR WOMEN

Examined from a market perspective, cross-country skiing is truly remarkable. It's one of the few sports where women outnumber men, and perhaps the only sports-related *business* in which women play such an important role as managers. This is certainly true of family-owned and -run operations such as Hardwood Hills, Maplelag, Far Hills, Cross Country Ski Headquarters, Izaak Walton Inn, and

Sunday River. But you'll also find women not only as instructors and guides but also ski directors at Beaver Creek, Manning Park, and Kirkwood. The all-woman marketing department at Sleeping Lady are also all certified PSIA instructors; *Cross Country Skier* magazine is run by a husband and wife team; the Cross Country Ski Areas Association's longtime president is a woman.

Christal McDougall, who runs the outstanding *Ski For Yourself!* women's camps and clinics, says, "In order for most women to enjoy an activity, they have to feel that there is a controllable amount of risk involved. Cross-country skiing provides the perfect balance: controllable participation at any level, and the potential for exhilarating speed and thrilling rides down hills. As a woman's confidence and competence grow, so will her threshold for tolerating those scary downhill sections. Every time I teach, I hear women say, 'Wow! I never thought I could get down *that* hill.'"

There are increasing numbers of women destination skiers, both small groups and individuals—not just self-sufficient outdoorsy people but also those looking for beauty, good company, and rejuvenation.

Personal Security

Cross-country skiing involves very few injuries, certainly only a fraction of the incidents that occur in downhill. Few mishaps occur in the social sphere, either. Almost unfailingly, the sport attracts pleasant, interesting people. Sexual harassment is almost unknown, and I've never heard of a case of violent crime at a destination. (You get an idea of the tenor of this life from the fact that many people never bother to lock their doors to a room or cabin.)

Instruction

A woman usually finds it easier to learn without the distractions of family or (well-intentioned but meddling) sweetheart on the spot. It's curious that women seem to absorb good technique faster than many men. I've often thought it's because there's a gender difference in the self-imposed drive to "perform" quickly.

Equally intriguing, female instructors are seldom afflicted with "egoitis" and frequently are more versatile in the types of lesson they'll willingly give. Young guys usually don't find beginner lessons very absorbing. Very occasionally this is expressed through impatience or condescension; usually it's just in their dreamy "This is mildly borrring" look. The majority of ski instructors are males, though not such a large majority as a decade ago. Given the option, whatever your sex, go with a woman instructor.

And may I be a little manipulative? If you find a delightful destination that doesn't have women instructors, suggest to a manager that this is a terrific idea— and would bring you back again. Repeat business speaks with dulcet tones.

CANINE COMPANY

Dogs love to go skiing! My two Newfoundlands weigh a combined 280 pounds. I listen with great respect when they wish to take me out. Here are tips to make skiing with dogs easier.

A constant problem is buildup of snow between the pads of their paws. Some breeds have more of a propensity, and some snow conditions are worse than others. A handy trick is to coat paws with PAM (vegetable oil in a spray container) before you start out. The oil repels the snow and is edible if the dog decides to lick it.

Abrasive types of snow can be rough on pads. The best policy to avoid cuts is to go on gradually longer gallops, letting the pads slowly toughen. Some owners prefer to buy special booties. And remember, older dogs tire quickly in deep snow, so appreciate a packed surface.

It's possible to teach a dog to pull a skiier with a harness (skijor), though you couldn't prove it by my Newfs. For particularly strong or hyper breeds, it's an entertaining option.

Do *not* take dogs on a groomed cross-country trail unless it's designated specifically for the purpose (see Special Features Directory), or unless you're interested in the prospect of a fulminating ski area operator. Even a small dog can punch holes in the tracks. Your beloved pup may also leave calling cards, trip or intimidate people, sit suddenly in the midst of a hill, of even get combative meeting other canines.

That said, take your best friend skiing whenever possible—and don't forget to put treats in your pack. Mush!

Destinations

SKIING SCHOLARSHIP: HOW PLACES FEATURED IN THIS BOOK WERE SELECTED

The first step in researching this book was screening almost 400 cross-country areas across North America. The good part was actually visiting more than 300 of them. If you read about it here, it means I've skied, snowshoed, or walked the trails; visited the restaurants; (almost without fail) tested the beds; and absorbed the views. I saw skiing that ranged from the magnificent to the pedestrian; indulged a taste for history; improved my knowledge of French, geography, geology, and the operation of Jacuzzis; was stalked by a grizzly and met a bison face to face; skied at −40 degrees Fahrenheit to see if it hurt (it did) and at 60 degrees Fahrenheit (about as entertaining as swimming through cool soup). It has been a joyous and enlightening experience. This edition includes completely updated information and several new ski areas (either entirely new, or new to me).

You may inquire as you read the following destination sketches: "Other than indulging yourself, why select these ranches, resorts, inns, B&Bs, and lodges?" Call it an informed/subjective process that revolved around *fun*. Each site has both skiing magnetism and complementary attractions that engender affection. Most offer a wide-ranging winter experience—as near guarantees of a grand vacation as one may find.

And, if there are great destinations missing, well, that's what later editions are for (wiesel@imt.net).

THE PEOPLE YOU MEET

The folks who run ski areas usually do it for love as much as income, and their affection for their land and way of life imprints every aspect of the business. What were cross-country operators in former lives? A few were racers and coaches, but the great majority came from other walks of life. The crazy-quilt pattern of their careers suggests the fascinating spectrum of ski experiences and clientele. How do you categorize psychologists, yoga teachers, wheat and dairy farmers, attorneys (attorneys!), a wine merchant, a tennis pro, an anthropologist, an antique clock repairman, a graphic designer, a chemical engineer, a demolition expert, a Naval intelligence officer, and the Swiss Sailing Team's Olympic Coach? The only common denominator is their hospitality—visit for a week and become friends, come again and you're part of the extended family.

I've been involved with sports and the outdoors virtually all my life. For reasons that remain mysterious, cross-country skiing attracts the most interesting, genuine, and genial people I've ever encountered—both those who run areas and the good folk who visit with them.

LODGING

There are almost always motels available near a ski area. But if you like a sip of luxury—or just enjoy dreaming of accommodations that lay chocolate truffles on your pillow instead of that familiar mint—I've presented a few suggestions.

It's tempting to generalize about these destinations, but every one has its own character. Rooms at some are clean, bright, and simple; others are members of Relais & Chateaux, an international byword for elegance. There can even be diversity within a single property; in these cases, I've recommended a specific type of room or cabin.

Destination descriptions note when they're particularly well suited to families. If you're interested in trail convenience, check for "ski-in/ski-out" situations. If you dislike tobacco, look for smoking restrictions. As for dining, it's usually on the side of copious, consistently tasty, and in many cases exquisitely prepared.

Rates in this book are for an adult for one night, in 1999 U.S. dollars, usually based on double occupancy. Please note that rates are subject to change.

$ = $0–$50
$$ = $50–$100
$$$ = $100–$150
$$$$ = $150–$200
$$$$$ = above $200

WHICH DESTINATION IS RIGHT FOR YOU?

Not all cross-country areas are equal or alike. They vary in size, setting, accessibility, amenities, length of season, cost, and fun quotient.

Even sites which at first glimpse look like attractive destinations can swiftly pall if there's nothing to do but ski. On the other hand, a fair number of individual areas and regions can be immensely fulfilling for a week or more, with a great variety of adventures available. Many places fall somewhere in between—fine skiing, multiple diversions, worth a long midweek visit.

Whether your goal is beauty, romance, intriguing companions, or endless exercise, the ideal vacation awaits.

The Selection Process

Rather than just heading for the nearest, most famous, or largest trail system, I'd like to propose a sweeping framework for planning a cross-country ski sabbatical. The methodology is suitable for both "never-evers" and experienced lovers of winter. To help select the appropriate circumstances, destinations are divided into "pure" cross-country operations; those with alpine skiing; and "regions" with several trail systems in conveniently close proximity.

The three primary elements are **ambiance, time available**, and **budget**. Are you looking for a family atmosphere, a second-honeymoon spot, or a place where you're comfortable as a single woman and/or a senior citizen? Is a January week (can be cold, but snow may be great) less desirable than a long weekend in February (may be crowded)? Should you plan on spending $50 a day, or $150?

Other considerations may include anything from the practical (are you affected by altitude?) to personal preferences (mountain or forest scenery, plain or luxurious accommodations, fine or simple dining, an intimate experience or one shared with several dozen people, computer port and fax and photocopier on premises or no phones in rooms. . .).

Range of activities definitely merits consideration. A lot of vacationers are nordic enthusiasts; others enjoy the sport but want a little daily relief. Would you like to hone technique? If so, some areas include instruction in a lodging/meal package; others merely make it available; a few don't have it at all. You might also be intrigued by guided tours, dog sledding, sleigh rides, snowshoeing, overnighting in a yurt, ballooning, ice climbing, even snowmobiling!

To provide an example of the screening process, let's assume you're an adventurous type in New York City who wants to spend five days at a classy establishment with outstanding food and excellent skiing, all for a reasonable price—so look to Québec's inns midweek (fly to Montréal and ski the same afternoon). With more flexibility in time and spending, definitely consider the guest ranches of the Rockies.

The Special Features Directory (see page 207) can guide you to ski-in/ski-out B&Bs, horseback riding, even spas; just check the list, cross-reference as needed, and choose your spot. I've been thoroughly subjective in recommending certain destinations as Romantic Getaways (very conventionally defined as: "Would I propose if we can head there right after the wedding? Rather!"). Sometimes this is based on seclusion, but mostly on the "taste" of a place.

Best Vacation Buys

Let's say you're skiing on a budget but looking for a special place. One option is "low season," including most of January, when consumers are recovering from holiday credit card shock.

Another possibility is a midweek vacation. Lodges often drop prices Monday to Friday (or by another interpretation, raise them weekends and holidays). Added value for some: no crowds.

For Americans, a third choice is Canada. The U.S. dollar continues to be far stronger than its Canadian counterpart. Add the fact that prices are geared toward the weak Canadian economy and you may get fantastic package deals for less than $70 per night. For the best of all price worlds, consider a trip to Canada during a

January midweek and check to see if you can get an AARP (aging has its benefits!) or AAA discount.

Christmas sees highest prices, fewest openings, and longest required stays. Still, it's a trade-off, particularly for families or gregarious types—you'll find the greatest range of festivities and the most people, and above all the most kids.

Trail Keys

In the cross-country world, distances are measured in kilometers (1 km = 0.62 miles). You'll notice that saying brightly, "I skied 10 kilometers this afternoon!" marvelously improves the appetite—much more impressive than a lifeless, "I went 6.2 miles." For a novice, 15 kilometers can provide a fine weekend's workout; for the expert, it only titillates taste buds. (Check the Special Features Directory if you desire a major trail system.)

If you're an energetic skier, you may wish to call a prospective destination to see how much skiing they really have. Operators measure the size of their trail systems in different ways. I've visited "50-kilometer" areas that have perhaps 30 "linear" (non-repeat) kilometers, and others where the true distance is underestimated.

The customary yardsticks for trail difficulty designations are distance and downhills (gradient, length, width, visibility, runout). Only Québec has standardized ratings. Other areas define difficulty relative to other routes in the network. If you're concerned about getting in over your head, consult the map and chat with staff to get pointers (gentle, short, great scenery...).

You'll notice I frequently mention "snowcat grooming." These big vehicles generally but not always create a better product faster than a snowmobile, especially for large trail systems.

Hint: Two-way trails potentially provide more skiing for a given number of kilometers than do one-way routes, but they may provide less of a sense of solitude. Double tracks allow more conviviality than single track because people can ski side by side, but single track creates a heightened feeling of wilderness.

Regional Skiing

This book presents cross-country ski destinations in the United States in alphabetical order by state, then in alphabetical order by Canadian province. Yet the states and provinces can also be grouped into four geographic regions, each offering its own distinct experience for the cross-country skier.

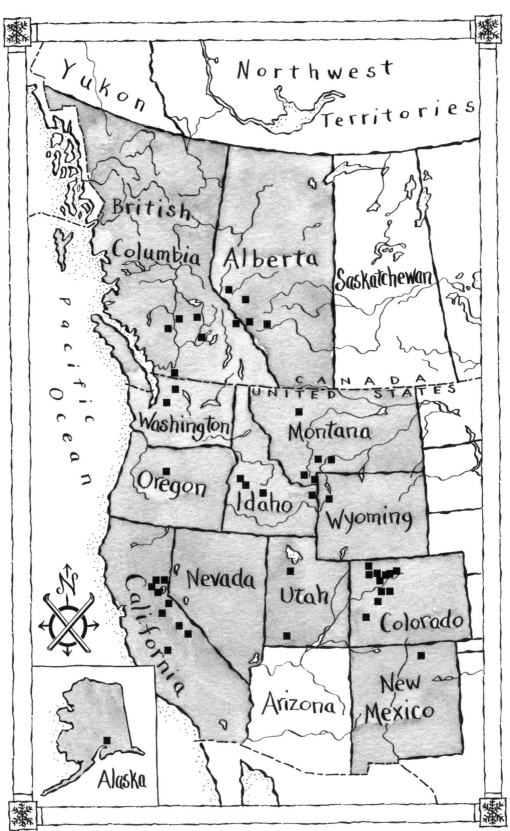

■ = Ski Destination

WESTERN U.S. AND CANADA:

ALASKA, CALIFORNIA, COLORADO, IDAHO, MONTANA, NEW MEXICO, OREGON, UTAH, WASHINGTON, WYOMING, ALBERTA, AND BRITISH COLUMBIA

It's not all mountain, but more than 40 peaks claw to 14,000 feet; not every day sees "champagne powder," but a winter's fall may exceed 500 inches—an endless land of light, from the Grand Canyon almost to Denali . . .

The scope and sweep of the West are astounding. The Sierras run almost the length of California; the Cascades tumble down from British Columbia into Oregon; the Rockies stretch from Arizona to Alberta—and there are highlands between. Three huge spines of mountain in two countries, with dozens of smaller but distinctive ranges, some of different geology—the San Juans, Tetons, Monashees, Mogollons, Whites, Wallowas, Smokies, Sawatch, Big Holes, Big Horns, Absarokas, and Lillooets—inhabit the West. Then there are the splendid national and provincial parks—Yoho, Banff, Bryce Canyon, Yellowstone, Wells Gray, Jasper, Yosemite, Grand Canyon, Glacier, Sequoia—each one unique. Anchorage itself has several ranges within sight of town—the Chugach, the Kenais, even Mount McKinley.

For skiers, the draws are scenic splendor, tremendous snowfall, and mountain serenity. Somehow the size of the land has carried over to human aspirations. On the average, a Western cross-country area masses at least twice the trails of its Eastern counterparts. There's a desire to set precedent, too—there are, of course, ski regions, inns, lodges, alpine resorts, and even grand hotels, but there are guest ranches as well. And there's a sense of history, too, though neither memory nor structures date back into the 1700s.

This high majesty carries a price. It's wise to ski the backcountry with guides, to carry chains in your car to cope with heavy wet snow ("Sierra Cement") along the West Coast, and to allow your body time to adjust to altitude. But these precautions are a small cost when measured against Colorado's endless groves of aspen, Alberta's Icefields Highway, the northern lights at play, evening alpenglow, or standing on skis outside your door, watching house lights miles away blink on in a remote Washington valley.

■ = Ski Destination

MIDWESTERN U.S. AND CANADA:
MICHIGAN, WISCONSIN, MINNESOTA, AND ONTARIO

Before humanity came the glaciers, and their imprint remains in hills and river valleys . . .

The Midwest is cross-country skiing's heartland—more devotees per square kilometer than anywhere else in North America—but it doesn't have the mountain magnetism of the Rockies. How can Ontario or Wisconsin compete with Colorado peaks and "cold smoke" Montana powder, New England's village charm and skiing history, West Coast size and sizzle?

In answer: don't try to compare apples, anchovies, and aardvarks. The region has its own winter allure. Not only are the cross-country trails customarily the best around (that is, skiable by people without Olympic credentials), but non-ski activities abound as well, some quite unexpected—wineries, cheese factories, and museums; ice fishing; snowmobiling; learning to speak Minnesoootan. Landscapes are softer here, and there's no need to spend a precious day or two acclimating to altitude. In many places snow is more dependable than in the Northeast. And excellent highways create easy access from metropolitan areas.

Still, from Ontario down into the northern tier states, they don't get no respect. If anything, it's believed to be "the land of the Birkebeiner" (the Birkebeiner is America's greatest cross-country race)—frozen-mustache-and-spray-on-plastic-suit territory, with bitter cold and worse winds. Yet Midwesterners thrive in this environment, and surely not all are of Finnish extraction.

There are ski lodges, regions, and resorts to enjoy, large and small—a few famous, many hardly recognized outside of a 100-mile radius. And the skiing! Ice advanced, scoured, depressed, and departed, leaving behind all manner of eskers, kettles, drumlins, and moraines. They translate into wonderful fun, flowing trails that rise and dip without the precipitous drops of major mountain chains.

Last is the service factor. Not every destination has a retail outlet or state-of-the-art skate rentals, but grooming is as caring as anywhere, and Midwestern hospitality can't be beaten.

■ = Ski Destination

THE NORTHEAST UNITED STATES:
MAINE, MASSACHUSETTS, NEW HAMPSHIRE, NEW YORK, AND VERMONT

Before the car replaced the train, there were lodges, country inns, and regal hotels— first for summer guests, later for the joys of winter sport; all of this is not gone . . .

The era of majestic resorts in the mountains of the Northeast is largely past, though a few magnificent places remain. But for winter travelers, inns and country lodges abide, many handsome and historical. They've been complemented by the evolution of alpine ski areas as well as bed and breakfast establishments— perhaps not as visually intriguing but often at least as comfortable. (And oh, the dining!) Many downhill resorts now run their own cross-country areas—some modest in size, some significant and sophisticated.

The weather seems to have changed as well, with shorter, warmer winters. But more northerly locations often offer skiing from late November to late March; more southerly areas sometimes add snowmaking; and there are surprising "snowbelts" in between.

This is a region without the vast sweep of the Rockies, Sierras, or Cascades, but it is a land of cultural and geological diversity, fascinating history, and, at times, very serious mountains and weather, indeed. Virtually every significant cross-country area is within easy driving distance of major metropolitan areas; many are within an hour of major airports (Albany, Hartford, Portland, Burlington); and there are a surprising number just minutes from rail service.

The Northeast is not huge, but it's divided by a multitude of mountain ranges—the Whites, the Greens, Catskills, Adirondacks. What seems close "as the crow flies" can consume an hour on winding roads following river valleys. So take a week, or two, to ski different places in New York's highlands, Vermont's Northeast Kingdom, and the endless forests of northern Maine. There is nothing like it in the Americas.

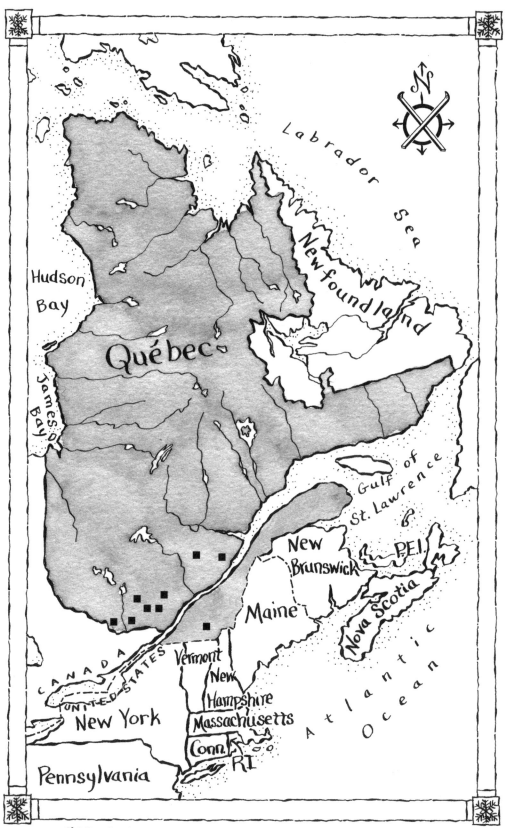

■ = Ski Destination

QUÉBEC

Scent of hardwood smoke, crunch and taste of fresh croissants, lilt of a tongue perhaps more pure than spoken now in France . . .

Which Canadian province borders four states, is little more than an hour's flight from Detroit, reveals a delightfully mixed heritage, revels in fine cuisine, is chock full of marvelous cross-country ski destinations, yet remains a winter mystery to most Americans and Canadians?

If your immediate response isn't "Québec," you probably suffer from a hate affair with geography ("It's where?" "Do they have mountains?" "Do they have snow?" "Do they speak *English*?"). And if you haven't skied there, it's a grievous error. The cross-country inns and lodges rival the best found elsewhere in North America in terrain and grooming, surpass almost all in culinary accomplishments and accommodations, and carry it off with Gallic flair but French-Canadian hospitality. Québec does have mountains—gently rounded rather than sky-towering— and snow—20 feet or more in some places most winters.

The Québecois have an ingrained sense of fun, and very European priorities— most noticeably, dining is savored at leisure rather than counted as the day's caloric intake. Someone at every destination is bilingual. One thing you may not find is non-smoking accommodations; however, innkeepers air out rooms so thoroughly that this is seldom a problem.

As you travel through towns and hamlets, the influence of the Catholic Church—a force in this land since Europeans arrived centuries ago—reveals itself in place names (for example, Saint-Jean-de-Matha, Sainte-Anne-de-Beaupré).

Québec offers not only skiing but also an introduction to the charms of another culture.

Resorts, Lodges, and Groomed Trails

United States

Anchorage Region
Alaska

Welcome to 1,955-square-mile Anchorage, a wondrous mix of frontier and sophistication, home of the Iditarod and Fur Rendezvous, neighbor to 20,320' Mount McKinley. It's Alaska's most populous city, where 40% of residents XC ski, thanks to the Nordic Skiing Association of Anchorage and Municipality of Anchorage. Some 150 kms of connected groomed trails—bridges and underpasses instead of road crossings!—are equally accessible from downtown or birch-and-spruce-forested parks. Part of the network runs just above the ice floes of Cook Inlet. November and December nights are long, but the city has 40 kms of illuminated trails. Come February, sunlight stretches into late afternoon.

Contact Address: Anchorage Convention & Visitors Bureau, 524 W. 4th Avenue, Anchorage, AK 99501-2212
Tel/fax: (800) 478-1255 or (907) 276-4118; fax: (907) 278-5559
e-mail: acvb@alaska.net
Internet: www.alaska.net/~acvb
Location: South-central Alaska
Airport: Anchorage International (trails visible while landing)
Train: North end of city; special ski trains
Medical: Several in the city
Special Accommodations: Copper Whale Inn is a minute from Tony Knowles Coastal Trail. Fourteen rooms, all but two with private baths. Eighty-mile views west over Cook Inlet. Cheerful host Tony Carter is a grand resource on city and state. Non-smoking environment. No minimum stay. 440 L Street, Anchorage, AK 99501; (907) 258-7999, fax (907) 258-6213
Guest capacity: 33 at Copper Whale, substantial and varied around town
Conference capacity: Extensive downtown
Rates: $–$$ (includes breakfast)
Credit cards: Visa, MasterCard, American Express, Diners Club, Discover
Season: November into April, annual snowfall 69" (snow comes and stays)
XC Skiing: 150 kms total, maintained in part by Anchorage Parks snowmobiles, 115 kms by Nordic Club snowcats. Some classic-only routes, more classic/skate, and a number to also walk/run/bike/skijor. Rentals at shops including REI. Voluntary donation. Altitude range -4' to 800'. Highlights include:

- *Kincaid Park:* XC kingpin, 60 kms maintained by snowcat (of which 17 kms have lights), chalet. Site of major races; biathlon range. Single track plus skating; 10 kms classic-only. Essentially one-way. Mize Loop is glorious! Instruction by reservation; moose appear spontaneously.
- *Russian Jack Springs Park:* 7.5 gentle kms, all classic and unidirectional; groomed weekly by snowmobile; 2.5 kms lighted; chalet.
- *Coastal Trail/Chester Creek:* 23 almost-flat kms from Russian Jack to Kincaid, much running along Cook Inlet. Snowmobile-groomed, single track plus skate lane, two-way, multiple-use.
- *Hillside Park:* 20 kms, 7 kms with lights, skating plus single track, novice-to-advanced, snowcat-groomed; chalet.

Maps: There's a splendid foldout containing a general locator plus specific site descriptions.
Activities and Entertainment: Great Alaska Shootout basketball, alpine (local slopes and Alyeska), snowshoeing, wildlife tracking, horseback riding, canine activities, sleigh rides, ice activities, Aurora Borealis, ski tours, snowmobiling; cultural attractions include magnificent Museum of History and Art.
Dining Recommendations: Seafood is consistently superb. Lively Glacier BrewHouse has fine salmon, king crab, and and wood-grilled meats, and its own ales, lager, and stout. Crème brulée is gigantic.
Special Nordic Distinction: Alaska Ski For Women is the best-attended women's XC event in North America, although it's scheduled against the Super Bowl.
Summary: Anchorage provides a delightful winter destination for couples, friends, and families (there's a lot for kids, such as Charlie's Alaska Trains store.)

See color photos, page 83
See color photos, page 83

Bear Valley Cross Country
Bear Valley, California

More than a century ago, Bear Valley was home to a considerable grizzly population. Times change, the grizzlies are gone, and the valley is known for bicycling and paddling in summer, XC and alpine in winter. Evidently Paul Petersen, founding partner of Bear Valley Cross Country, has nostalgic moments—they show up in trail names such as Pooh, and Grin and Bear It. Paul has taken 3,000 acres of vast meadow and dense forest to craft a winter playground. He chose to develop routes designed specifically for skiing instead of using the path of least resistance (roads). Trails swing up to ridge tops (views south to Yosemite) and open up powder bowls. One of the most pleasing trails is Walden Meadow—difficult access through high rock walls but a beautiful wind-protected oasis for picnics in a mature aspen grove. Bear Valley is a good early-season bet because skiing begins in meadow with a northern exposure (part used to be a landing strip), so Paul needs only 6 inches of snow to groom 10 trails. Recent innovations include more ski and snowshoe trails, new grooming equipment, and trail and directional signage programs.

Address: P.O. Box 5120, Bear Valley, CA 95223
Tel/fax: (209) 753-2834; fax: (209) 753-2669
e-mail: bvcc@sonnet.com
Internet: www.bearvalleyxc.com
Location: East-central California
Airport: Stockton, 90 miles
Train: Stockton, 90 miles
Memberships and Awards: Cross Country Ski Areas Association, Rossignol Demo Center, 1998 Waste Reduction Awards Program winner
Medical: Arnold Family Medical Clinic, 25 miles
Accommodations: Bear Valley Lodge is a minute's walk from the trails. It offers a choice of rooms, studios, or suites, all with private bath, on three floors. Cathedral lounge with five-story stone fireplace and enclosed mall, with village shops and restaurants. Massage

by appointment. No minimum stay. P.O. Box 5440, Bear Valley, CA 95223; (209) 753-2327.
Guest Capacity: 102
Conference Capacity: 125
Rates: $$ (midweek package includes use of trails)
Credit Cards: Visa, MasterCard, American Express
Season: Thanksgiving–mid-April; annual snowfall 450"
XC Skiing: Paul snowcat-grooms 70 kms on 36 trails, one- and two-way. 40% Easier, 40% More Difficult, 20% Most Difficult. Groomed downhill practice area; dog trail. Four buildings to warm up in along the trails, including a café and the Tamarack Pines Inn. One road crossing. Excellent ski school (all disciplines); guide service. Large, wide-ranging rental department. Daily trail fee. Altitude range 7,000'–7,700'.
Maps: Brochure includes an excellent map with route descriptions.
Activities and Entertainment: On-site: snowshoeing, sauna, snow play, small indoor "walking village" (art gallery, coffeehouse, restaurants), snowmobiling. Nearby: alpine skiing, touring among the Calaveras Big Trees redwoods, Old Timers Museum in Murphy.
Children's Programs: Two narrow-groomed special trails (bear cut-outs, of course), Skiing Bears Ski School, equipment, pulks, sledding.
Dining: The Creekside Dining Room in Bear Valley Lodge features a variety of main courses, including steaks, chicken, and pasta. Also try Bear Valley Pizza Company and Red Dog Lodge restaurant.
Special Nordic Distinction: Paul has trained staff to *communicate*, not just ski well. Add great learning terrain at the trailhead and excellent kids' activities, and you have an outstanding area for families.
Summary: Bear Valley combines fine skiing, beautiful views (catch the Dardanelles massif at sunset!), and moderate altitude. It's also remote enough to avoid hordes of visitors, particularly midweek.

Kirkwood Ski & Summer Resort
Kirkwood, California

Kirkwood Resort has a large XC operation affiliated with a moderate sized (but fast growing) alpine area. With luck, the nordic element will retain its character. At one time they were unmarried neighbors. The center was founded in 1972 by former U.S. Biathlon Team member Glenn Jobe, who sold it to Kirkwood while he was working at Tahoe Donner, up north by Truckee. Debbi Waldear, not long ago a leading American racer, has done a bang-up job running the area for years. It's a region rich in frontier history: the Mormon Emigrant Trail ran by here, and Snowshoe Thompson probably strode and skied through on one of his mail routes. The XC ski center building is separated from the resort, though there are trail and shuttle connections. Three distinct trail systems are served by two trailheads, both of which have easy skiing nearby. It's classic High Sierra country—forests of big pines, open bowls, and masses of exposed granite faces. Local variants are lava plugs and striking pinnacles above the high alpine valley. Head up for views to the east and as far west as the Coastal Range, best seen from the Schneider trail system. Check with Debbi about Kirkwood's environmental awareness programs and tree carvings from the 1800s.

Address: P.O. Box 1, Kirkwood, CA 95646
Tel/fax: (209) 258-6000, XC center (209) 258-7248; fax: (209) 258-8899
Internet: www.skikirkwood.com
Location: Slightly south of Lake Tahoe
Airport: Reno/Tahoe International, 75 miles
Train: None nearby
Memberships and Awards: Cross Country Ski Areas Association, *Snow Country* magazine's Top 10 XC Areas in the Far West, Rossignol Demo Center
Medical: Clinic at resort
Accommodations: Caples Lake Resort is a near neighbor. Nine snug cabins with kitchens and modern bathrooms each can house three to six people; alternatively, there are simple rooms with shared bath in the lodge. The lodge also contains restaurant and lounge. Sauna. No smoking in buildings. Two- to three-night minimum on holidays. P.O. Box 88, Kirkwood, CA 95646; (209) 258-8888.
Guest Capacity: 60 at Caples Lake Resort
Conference Capacity: 320 at Kirkwood
Rates: $–$$$ (an amazing package includes breakfast, dinner, bag lunch, equipment, instruction, and trail use)
Credit Cards: Visa, MasterCard
Season: Late November–early May; annual snowfall 400"
XC Skiing: Kirkwood grooms 80 kms by snowcat (which is absolutely necessary in the Sierras!)—20 trails spread over 4,200 acres. All is double track with skating lane, 16' wide. Almost all trails are one-way. 20% Easier, 60% More Difficult, 20% Most Difficult. Meadows across the road from the center provide a fine beginner area as well as groomed dog trail; lessons are taught just behind the center. Three warming shelters. Fine ski school covering all disciplines as well as guide service. Excellent rentals. Daily trail fee. Altitude range 7,800'–9,000'.
Maps: Built into the XC brochure, the map is graphic but not ornate.
Activities and Entertainment: On-site: snowshoe trails. At resort: alpine skiing, sleigh rides.
Children's Programs: Day care at resort, "Kiddie Kilometer," instruction, equipment, pulks.
Dining: Caples Lake's dinner menu includes particularly good pasta. Chocolate Decadence comes highly recommended. Pleasant wine list. For a good hot lunch, drop by the Kirkwood Inn, next to the center.
Special Nordic Distinction: Kirkwood has trails near condos and trails up in the high wilds. Explore them all but remember that altitude!
Summary: While not an undiscovered jewel, Kirkwood delivers uncrowded trails and personal service.

Montecito-Sequoia Nordic Resort and Winter Sports Center
Kings Canyon National Park, California

A drive to Montecito-Sequoia involves remarkable transitions in vegetation and topography. Head east through Fresno's palms and vineyards, pass through oak and chaparral as you rise, and end among the Sierras' vast evergreens and deep snow. Traffic congestion is not an issue on the way to the resort (there's auto escort service for registered lodge guests following storms). Montecito-Sequoia began as a girls' camp, introduced skiing in 1976, and became a family center a decade later. Today it offers a comfortable, active, and affordable winter vacation. Owner Virginia Barnes has created diverse programs that extend into the midweek—not simply the familiar ski instruction and tours, but also park ranger presentations, visits to stands of giant redwoods, slide shows, and evening entertainment. At Christmas, there's simply no way to participate in every festivity. The main lodge competes for popularity with an outdoor hot tub, from which you can look east toward 12,160-foot Mt. Eisen. Trails wind through white and red fir; sugar, lodgepole, and Jeffrey pine; incense cedar; and manzanita. There are several bowls for telemarking. Climb to Baldy Peak for the best views of the Western Divide.

Address: 8000 Generals Highway, Box 858, Kings Canyon National Park, CA 93633
Tel/fax: (800) 843-8677 or (559) 565-3388; fax: (559) 565-3223
e-mail: msreservations@montecitosequoia.com
Internet: www.montecitosequoia.com
Location: South-central California
Airport: Fresno Air Terminal, 60 miles
Train: Fresno, 60 miles
Memberships and Awards: Cross Country Ski Areas Association
Medical: Sierra Kings Hospital, 40 miles
Accommodations: Options include rustic cabins and four lodge buildings, of which the most pleasant is probably Sugar Pine (simple, comfortable rooms with private bath). No TV or phones in rooms. Ski-in/ski-out. Two-night minimum.

Guest Capacity: 208
Conference Capacity: 125
Rates: $$ (can include meals, instruction, guided tours, use of trails)
Credit Cards: Visa, MasterCard, American Express, Discover
Season: Early December–mid-April; annual snowfall 204"
XC Skiing: Montecito-Sequoia snowcat-grooms 25 kms on eight trails, all double track with skate lane. (A lighted trail may be evolving.) Most routes are two-way; Otter Slide is a definite one-way downhill. 25% Easier, 60% More Difficult, 15% Most Difficult. Some routes are wide and comfortable, others are substantially narrower and hillier. One warming shelter. Instruction in all techniques; guide service. Remarkable rental selection. Daily trail fee. Altitude range 7,000'–7,811'.
Maps: On one side of the XC brochure is an introduction to services; on the other, an artistic rendering that's not to scale but helps explain terrain.
Activities and Entertainment: On-site: snowshoeing, ice skating, snow play, recreation room, outdoor hot tub, occasional wine tasting. Snowmobiling guests can motor right up to the lodge. Nearby: naturalist programs at Grant Grove in Sequoia National Park.
Children's Programs: Babysitting, indoor and outdoor supervised activities, from crafts to snow sculpting; special trail, instruction, equipment, pulks, sledding, tubing, snowboarding.
Dining: Two entrées nightly include a vegetarian dish and another such as veal osso bucco, served buffet style. There's emphasis on nutritional balance, low fat, and low sugar. Licensed bar. Snacks and hot drinks available 24 hours a day.
Special Nordic Distinction: One of the most active programs in the business, including "Winter Adventures" for seniors.
Summary: Montecito-Sequoia provides the ultimate convivial, low-key, inexpensive vacation for groups and families.

See color photos, page 84

North Lake Tahoe Region
California/Nevada

Two misleading ways of measuring skiing quality are, "We're the biggest!" and "There's something for everyone!" The first statement is reminiscent of alpine skiing's equating quantity with quality; the second usually means no single element is truly outstanding. The North Lake Tahoe XC region is an exception to these rules, combining gigantic size with superb variety—over 650 kilometers of trail on 200 groomed routes. Whether you're a couple, group, family, or singleton, you can laze around on the tracks, leave the kids at a day care center, sightsee, or ski till you drop. Trail fees tend to be pricey, but you can save with an Interchangeable Trail Pass.

Address: North Lake Tahoe Resort Association, P.O. Box 5459, Tahoe City, CA 96145
Tel/fax: (800) 824-6348; fax: (530) 581-1686
Internet: www.tahoefun.org
Location: Far eastern California/far western Nevada
Airport: Reno-Tahoe International, within an hour
Train: Truckee or Reno, within an hour
Medical: Tahoe Forest Hospital in Truckee, various clinics
Accommodations: Resort at Squaw Creek has a small XC operation with 18 groomed kms, rentals, instruction. Aquatic center, spa, restaurants, shopping arcade, ice skating. More than 400 luxurious guest rooms and suites. P.O. Box 3333, Olympic Valley, CA 96146; (530) 583-6300.
Guest Capacity: Tremendous diversity in region but a little shy on B&Bs
Conference Capacity: Numerous facilities
Rates: $$$–$$$$ at Resort at Squaw Creek (includes use of trails)
Season: Early December–mid-April; annual snowfall up to 400"
XC Skiing: In addition to Royal Gorge, Tahoe Donner, and Northstar-at-Tahoe (all described elsewhere in this book), there are three major areas. Altitude range 6,300'–9,100'.
• *Diamond Peak* continues to negotiate with

landowners to create a new base area and expand the 35 kms of trail. Magnificent lake views. Instruction and rentals. Trails progress nicely from easier circuits to blues and blacks, with an intriguing stop at "Knock Your Socks Off Rock." (Don't climb up, with skis or without—it's a lo-o-ong way down.) Dog trails. Daily trail fee. (775) 832-1177.
• *Lakeview* is only ½-mile from Tahoe, with 65 kms of mostly forested trails. Snow-laden conifers screen even close-in trails from nearby houses. The renovated day lodge is attractive and comfortable. Daily trail fee. (530) 583-9353.
• *Spooner Lake* is set on the Nevada side of Tahoe, with 91 kms of trail. It's a longish haul up to Snow Pass, along Snow Valley, and around to High Notch View, including an elevation gain of 2,200', but you can see both the lake below and desert country of the Washoe Valley. Instruction and rentals. Daily trail fee. (775) 749-5349.
Maps: Contact individual areas.
Activities and Entertainment: Try downhilling, snowboarding, bungee jumping, lake cruises, fishing, ballooning, tubing, snowmobiling; ice skate; take a sleigh ride; savor a different culinary style each night; marry; divorce; visit Nevada's flesh pots (that can be taken literally, but there's also gambling, floor shows, and antique cars).
Dining: Le Petit Pier has a deserved reputation for French-style cuisine. It merits repeated visits to sample appetizers such as warm foie gras de Périgord and entrées including noisette of lamb en croute.
Special Nordic Distinction: Big is one thing, but there are also dizzying choices—track, skate, telemark—all with views.
Summary: Anticipate the finest in new equipment; expect grooming quality as good as anywhere in the world; bring tire chains and a snow snorkel.

Northstar-at-Tahoe
Truckee, California

The name is a slight misnomer, since Northstar is a 10-minute drive from the lake—actually about halfway between Tahoe and Truckee. Everything else about the resort rings true. It's a media favorite (featured by *Skiing, Snow Country,* and *Travel & Leisure* magazines) in part because it has designed downhill facilities and programs for families. Just as it doesn't particularly try to draw alpine experts, trails at the Cross-Country and Telemark Ski Center seem designed for visitors with rational energy levels. As at Beaver Creek, skiing is reached by lift (actually by a gondola, which allows easy entry and exit and keeps you warm and dry on the way up and down). A subdivision recently absorbed several of the trails. As it turns out, replacement routes have better snow and views (Lake Tahoe to the south, summits including Castle Peak to the west). Avoid alpine afternoon crush hours, but try skiing down Village Run, which is usually well groomed, has a compassionate gradient, and can help you end the day on a euphoric note.

Address: P.O. Box 129, Truckee, CA 96160
Tel/fax: (800) GO NORTH (reservations), XC center (530) 562-2475; fax: (530) 562-2214
e-mail: northstar@boothcreek.com
Internet: www.skinorthstar.com
Location: Lake Tahoe, just on the California side of Nevada
Airport: Reno-Tahoe International, 40 miles
Train: Truckee, 6 miles (free shuttle)
Memberships and Awards: Cross Country Ski Areas Association, *Snow Country* magazine's Top 10 XC Areas in the Far West
Medical: Tahoe Forest Hospital, 7 miles
Accommodations: Though there are lodge rooms or lofts with color TVs, VCRs, and phones, most of Northstar's lodging is condominiums. Free shuttle conveys you to the lift in minutes. Non-smoking rooms available. One-night minimum except during holidays.
Guest Capacity: 5,500

Conference Capacity: 250
Rates: $$–$$$
Credit Cards: Visa, MasterCard, American Express, Discover
Season: Thanksgiving–mid-April; annual snowfall 300"
XC Skiing: Northstar's 65 kms of trail are snowcat-groomed for double track and skate lane. 25% Easier, 60% More Difficult, 15% Most Difficult. Three trailside shelters. Skate, classic, and telemark instruction; excellent rentals. Full-moon barbecue and ski tours, Gourmet Tour in March. Daily trail fee includes limited use of lifts. Altitude range 6,600'–7,800'.
Maps: A recent version is included with the alpine map; it offers little detail.
Activities and Entertainment: At resort: alpine, snowshoeing, horseback riding, sleigh rides, teen center, Swim & Racquet Club (outdoor heated lap pool, workout room, saunas, outdoor whirlpools); limited shopping in the village. Nearby: Truckee; Nevada casinos 8 miles away; the bright lights and varied entertainment of Reno are less than an hour away; and there's always a tour of the Ponderosa Ranch.
Children's Programs: Day care, First Tracks, equipment, pulks.
Dining: There are several restaurants at the resort (Village Food Company has a good deli), but it's fun to drive 10 minutes to Truckee to sample OB's Pub and Restaurant, which has a varied menu and lively crowd in a building more than a century old.
Special Nordic Distinction: "Pure" XC skiers either don't know of Northstar or disdain to visit a downhill resort. This adds up to very few skiers (especially weekdays) on a very large trail system. The telemarking program is the best in the North Lake Tahoe area.
Summary: Family-friendly, with easy access to hundreds more kms within 20 minutes' drive.

Royal Gorge Cross Country Ski Resort
Soda Springs, California

Royal Gorge is both huge and cutting edge. If the trails were laid end to end, it would be equivalent to skiing from San Francisco to the Sierra crest, with sightseeing detours thrown in. This is the largest private trail network in the *world*, with the largest snowcat grooming fleet. Add two hotels (one reached over-snow), two ski schools, four cafés, nearly a dozen warming huts, and California sun and snow. And if on-site skiing isn't adequate, the Tahoe locale has the greatest concentration of groomed trails in North America.

Address: P.O. Box 1100, Soda Springs, CA 95728
Tel/fax: (800) 500-3871 or (530) 426-3871 in Northern California; fax: (530) 426-9221
e-mail: info@royalgorge.com
Internet: www.royalgorge.com
Location: Northeastern California, 25 minutes from North Lake Tahoe
Airport: Reno-Tahoe International, 45 miles
Train: Truckee, 9 miles
Memberships and Awards: Cross Country Ski Areas Association, *Snow Country* magazine's Top XC Area in North America
Medical: Tahoe Donner Memorial Hospital, 9 miles
Accommodations: The Wilderness Lodge has rustic private rooms with shared unisex bathrooms, separate shower house with hot tub and sauna, and an international staff (many Australians). It's more suited to adults than small children (Royal Gorge's Rainbow Lodge, just off Interstate 80, is a better bet), though there are special family weekends in December and April. New private cabins at Wilderness Lodge. Smoke-free environment. Two-night minimum. Ski-in/ski-out.
Guest Capacity: 67+ at Wilderness Lodge
Conference Capacity: None
Rates: $$–$$$ (includes transportation by sleigh pulled by snowcat, lodging, meals, teatime, instruction with video, trail fee)
Credit Cards: Visa, MasterCard, American Express

Season: Thanksgiving–mid-April at least; annual snowfall 408". Several kms of snow-making on key trails.
XC Skiing: You can ski for weeks on 88 trails (328 kms), double-tracked with skate lane, mostly two-way: 32% Easier, 50% More Difficult, 18% Most Difficult. Routes wind through pine and fir forest, follow ridges, and meander across meadows and around lakes. Excellent instruction in all styles. For day visitors, Summit Station can be crowded weekends and holidays, so try the Van Norden system, which also doesn't require an uphill return to the trailhead. Outstanding landmarks are Devil's Peak, to the west, and Castle Peak, to the north. Tows save uphill energy and provide the ideal setting for refining downhill control. Fabulous spring corn snow, which is the best time to visit the Mariah Point overlook, a 4,400' drop to the American River. One-way 22-km trail to Rainbow Lodge, weekends and holidays. Enormous rental fleet. Dog trails. Snowshoers welcome. Daily trail fee. Altitude range 5,800'–7,500'.
Maps: Extraordinary graphic representation showing trails and setting.
Activities and Entertainment: On-site: limited nightlife at Wilderness Lodge (hot tub, sauna), more lively at Rainbow Lodge (32 private rooms, bar/lounge). Nearby: Four alpine ski areas within 10-minute drive, and Western SkiSport Museum.
Children's Programs: For day skiers, kids under 12 ski free. Lunch, skiing, rentals, and instruction in Pee-Wee Snow School; Family Center at Summit Station; pulks.
Dining: Wilderness Lodge serves breakfast and lunch buffet style, afternoon teatime and hors d'oeuvres, and dinner with wine. House cuisine is French country (single entrée).
Special Nordic Distinction: You name it! Founder John Slouber has pioneered everything from surface tows to micro skis.
Summary: The scale of things can be initially overwhelming, but simply ski a few kms and congestion disappears. This place is unique!

See color photos, pages 85–87

Tahoe Donner
Truckee, California

The Northern Sierras are rife with XC ski areas, and Tahoe Donner is one of the largest. Founded by former biathlon team member Glenn Jobe (who also begat Kirkwood), the center has been operated by the Tahoe Donner Homeowner Association since 1996. In a rare role reversal, nordic enjoys more popularity than the affiliated but separate downhill operation. Three distinct track systems spread over 4,800 acres: Home Range, Euer Valley (lower), and Sunrise Bowl (largely above tree line). Many trails have fine views of dominating Castle Peak to the west. Routes up toward Donner Ridge are more open and sometimes wind-exposed. The Euer Valley system (named after a Swiss-born settler) is easy to reach. This site is wooded and sheltered and includes a Cookhouse, open weekends and holidays. Trail names are often both evocative and clever (Badlands and Boot Hill are definitely black diamonds). Tahoe Donner is also an equestrian center in the summer, but don't worry, there's no horsy effluvia.

Address: 11509 Northwoods Boulevard, Truckee, CA 96161-6000
Tel/fax: (530) 587-9484; fax: (530) 587-9409
e-mail: xcski@tahoedonner.com
Internet: www.tahoedonner.com
Location: Northeastern California
Airport: Reno, 35 miles
Train: Truckee, 5 miles
Memberships and Awards: Cross Country Ski Areas Association
Medical: Tahoe Forest Hospital, 8 miles
Accommodations: The 10064 House at 10064 South East River Road is a B&B run by long-time ski company representative Kent Bocks and wife Monica. Located minutes from Tahoe Donner on the eastern edge of trendy ex–railroad town Truckee. There are three lovely rooms; the master bedroom has an antique soaking tub. Non-smoking atmosphere. No minimum stay. Beer and wine license. P.O. Box 1863, Truckee, CA 96160; (530) 582-1923; request directions.

Guest Capacity: 6 at 10064 House
Conference Capacity: 170 at Tahoe Donner
Rates: $–$$ (including very complete breakfast; special midweek multi-night rates)
Credit Cards: Cash or personal checks
Season: Thanksgiving–Easter; annual snowfall 350"
XC Skiing: The area snowcat-grooms 94 km on 37 trails, double track plus skating. All green trails are one-way, others both directions. 35% Easier, 40% More Difficult, 22% Most Difficult, 1 expert-only route. 2.5 km lit (the only such in California). Excellent ski school, fine rental fleet, including snowshoes. Daily trail fee. Altitude range 6,250'—6,750'.
Maps: A single brochure describes all Tahoe Donner's winter recreation. The XC material includes a presentable and accurate but somewhat small map.
Activities and Entertainment: Within Tahoe Donner: alpine, fitness center, major snow play area. Every January, engineering students from University of Nevada at Reno attempt to build the world's largest snowman. Nearby: a vast amount of alpine and XC, Donner Memorial State Park (Gary Larson has a hilarious cartoon spoofing the monument), snowmobiling, Lake Tahoe (driving tour, shopping, gambling, all sorts of night life).
Children's Programs: Special trails narrow-groomed, Tiny Tracks snow school, equipment, pulks, snowplay 1 mile away.
Dining: Among Truckee's fine restaurants is Cottonwood. The building itself is intriguing; the food even more so (grilled chipolte chile marinated breast of chicken. . .). Their little brochure says it succinctly: "eclectic menu. . . adventurous wine list." Saturday night jazz.
Special Nordic Distinction: The area is extensive enough to please both beginners and experienced racers.
Summary: Always a friendly place, Tahoe Donner reflects the geniality and sense of humor of XC manager Andrew Hall.

See color photos, page 88

Tamarack Lodge Resort
Mammoth Lakes, California

Central California might not seem a nordic hot spot, but there's an exception near the town of Mammoth Lakes, which sits in a glacier-scoured bowl. The Eastern Sierras gain in majesty as you drive through town and reach Tamarack Lodge, a little higher than the village. Tamarack is one of the most popular XC areas in the Sierras, despite its remote location. Built in 1924 as a hunting and fishing lodge on Twin Lakes in a heavily forested area, it was recently acquired by Mammoth Mountain Ski Area. (There's a regular shuttle 'twixt Lodge and Mountain.) The ski service building (a trailer that's moved in summer) is the center for information, rentals, instruction, and tours. Most easy trails take off from here (for example, Cabins and Dome), but the real visual treat is to follow groomed snow-covered roads toward Lake Mary, Lake Mamie, Lake George, and above all (geographically and aesthetically), Horseshoe Lake. You can breezily ski across the latter, looking up to the magnificent Mammoth Crest. On a lower plane, Mammoth Lakes is quite attractive, still growing but with considerable attention to appearance—even McDonald's has Tyrolean decor.

Address: Twin Lakes Road, P.O. Box 69, Mammoth Lakes, CA 93546
Tel/fax: (800) 237-6879 or (760) 934-2442; fax: (760) 934-2281
Internet: www.tamaracklodge.com
Location: East-central California
Airport: Reno, 150 miles
Train: None nearby
Memberships and Awards: Cross Country Ski Areas Association, Rossignol Demo Center
Medical: Mammoth Hospital, 4 miles
Accommodations: There's a choice between lodge rooms (private or shared bath) and 25 cabins. A number of the latter have been recently renovated and have very pretty and comfortable interiors, fully equipped kitchens, wall heaters, and some wood-burning stoves. Ski-in/ski-out. No smoking in buildings. Minimum stay varies.

Guest Capacity: 134
Conference Capacity: 60
Rates: $–$$ (multi-day package can include breakfast, rentals, instruction, and use of trails)
Credit Cards: Visa, MasterCard, American Express
Season: Mid-November–mid-April; annual snowfall 250"
XC Skiing: Tamarack snowcat-grooms 45 kms on almost two dozen trails—single track with skating lane on side trails, double track with skating on arterials, almost all two-way. 45% Easier, 35% More Difficult, 20% Most Difficult—mostly gentle routes on the way to the Upper Lakes Basin. Instruction covers classic and skating techniques; customized guided tours (give a thought to backcountry tours on spring corn snow). Designated snowshoe-only trails. Good rentals. Daily trail fee. Altitude range 8,600'–9,008'.
Maps: They've changed with the years, but usually there's a four-color version that nicely portrays vegetation and topographic features.
Activities and Entertainment: On-site: snowshoeing, snow play. Nearby: alpine (Mammoth Mountain), dog sledding, sleigh rides, ice-skating, bobsledding, hot air ballooning, ghost town Bodie (not always accessible), Mono Lake, factory outlets, snowmobiling.
Children's Programs: Special trail, narrow tracks, instruction, equipment, pulks.
Dining: Tamarack's Lakefront Restaurant presents a half dozen dinner entrées, including pan-seared pistachio crusted elk loin. Good wine list. Visit Paul Schat's Bakery in town for great bonbons.
Special Nordic Distinction: The area is unusually family-oriented. It's also a particularly alluring destination for skiers splitting their time between XC and alpine. And if you feel greatly moved while enjoying the High Sierra, it may just be an earthquake.
Summary: For Southern Californians, Tamarack is attractive and affordable. Driving distance is significant, so a long stay is sensible.

Yosemite National Park
Yosemite, California

Founded as a national park in 1890, Yosemite spreads over 1,170 square miles. In full winter it's glorious. Only 25 percent of the year's tourist flood enters during the snowy months, which by itself would distinguish the season. Promotional material has attributed to the park "the most stupendous views in the *world*"—ski to Glacier Overlook and you may not be inclined to argue the point, watching the wondrous light and cloud shadow racing across sheer rock walls. There's nothing in North America that surpasses the views of Half Dome's incredible granite face 4,882 feet above the valley floor or the 12,000- to 13,000-foot mountains on the eastern horizon. Elsewhere in the park are 2,425-foot Yosemite Falls and the still magic of redwood groves to ski, snowshoe, or walk through. Snow in the valley can be sporadic but is quite dependable around Badger Pass (about 40 minutes' drive), site of California's oldest alpine area and take-off point for the XC trails.

Address: Yosemite Cross-Country Ski Center, Yosemite National Park, CA 95389
Tel/fax: for XC (209) 372-8444; fax: (209) 372-8673
Internet: www.yosemitepark.com
Location: East-central California (best access is Highway 140; carry chains)
Airport: Fresno Air Terminal, 105 miles
Train: Merced, 75 miles (bus connections)
Memberships and Awards: Cross Country Ski Areas Association, PSIA
Medical: Yosemite Medical Clinic, in valley
Accommodations: The Ahwahnee is Yosemite's classic lodging choice, sited below the cliffs of Royal Arch Cascade. Built in 1927 and now a National Historic Landmark, each room in this splendid edifice has a Native American design and private bath. Afternoon tea served in The Great Room. No smoking in buildings. Less expensive rooms are available at Yosemite Lodge and Curry Village. 5410 East Home Avenue, Fresno, CA 93727; (209) 252-4848.

Guest Capacity: 150 at the Ahwahnee
Conference Capacity: 150
Rates: $$–$$$ (includes instruction)
Credit Cards: Visa, MasterCard, Diners Club, Discover, Carte Blanche, American Express
Season: Late November–early April at trailhead; annual snowfall 125"
XC Skiing: Yosemite's 45 snowcat-groomed kms consist of two trails; both are two-way, with double track and skating lane. The first heads up from Badger Pass to Glacier Point, "point to point" rather than in a loop. The other is a point-to-point spur off that route. 25% Easier, 50% More Difficult, 25% Most Difficult. The 33-km round-trip distance on Glacier Point Road is more intimidating than the terrain; the entire tour is usually fine for strong intermediates. Overnight guided tours to the new stone-and-log Glacier Point Winter Lodge. Instruction and guide service. Rentals. Park entrance fee. Altitude range 7,200'–8,200'.
Maps: The superb new trail guide covers groomed trails and popular backcountry routes, supplemented by detailed text.
Activities and Entertainment: On-site: snowshoeing, alpine skiing, snow play. In valley: ice skating, waterfall watching, ranger-led snowshoe tours, walking, Ansel Adams Gallery, sumptuous Bracebridge Dinner at Christmas (available by lottery), Chefs' Holiday, Vintners' Holiday, Yosemite Museum.
Children's Programs: Day care, equipment.
Dining: The Ahwahnee's 130'-long dining room affords great views. Prime rib and salmon are long-time favorites. Desserts baked on the premises.
Special Nordic Distinction: Groomed trails may prove too limited for avid track skiers. However, there's opportunity to mix in day and overnight backcountry tours on marked trails.
Summary: Yosemite is geologically fabulous and fascinating. Views and vegetation are riveting. No wonder John Muir and Ansel Adams each sought in different ways to capture its magnificence.

Aspen/Snowmass Region
Aspen, Colorado

When songstress/humorist Christine Lavin wrote "Nobody's Fat in Aspen," perhaps she was referring to a fitness cult reinforced by free XC skiing to the east and west of town. Modeled on European networks, "Aspen's Fifth Mountain" operates under the aegis of the Aspen/Snowmass Nordic Council. Just as this resort is unique for its vibrant cultural life (which receives less attention than après-ski doings, autograph hounding, and shopping), nordic skiing is differentiated by its diversity. Creating a valley-wide network linking small existing systems was the brainchild of Olympic skier Craig Ward (now a real estate broker).

Along the tracks you'll find rentals and instruction at the Snowmass Club Cross Country Center and Aspen Cross Country Center. More adventurous visitors can head for day tours in the highlands, or overnight at a 10th Mountain Hut Association or Alfred A. Braun Hut System "shelter" (some are impressively comfortable and sophisticated).

Address: Aspen/Snowmass Nordic Council, P.O. Box 10815, Aspen, CO 81612
Tel/fax: (970) 925-2145
Location: West-central Colorado
Airport: Aspen, 1 mile from town
Train: Glenwood Springs, 42 miles
Medical: Aspen Valley Hospital, 2 miles from town
Accommodations: There's a local bed base of nearly 9,000, but if you'd like to go absolutely first class, stay at Sardy House. Built in 1892, there are 14 rooms and six suites decorated in the Victorian tradition, each with Jacuzzi. Pool, sauna, spa. Three- or four-night minimum stay for holidays weekends. 128 E. Main Street, Aspen, CO 81611; (800) 321-3457 or (970) 920-2525.
Guest Capacity: 40 at Sardy House
Conference Capacity: 40
Rates: $$$–$$$$ (includes a big breakfast)
Credit Cards: Visa, MasterCard, American Express, Discover

Season: Mid-November–early April; annual snowfall 100"
XC Skiing: Visitors can enjoy 60 kms of snow-cat-groomed trails, mostly skating lane plus double track. 50% Easier, 25% More Difficult, 25% Most Difficult. Dog trail. Road and alpine trail crossings. There's a scattering of ski schools with daily instruction in classic and skating, plus backcountry tours and a slathering of good places to rent equipment, such as Aspen Cross Country Center and Ute Mountaineer. Guide service available. Altitude range 7,900'–9,000'.
Maps: Overall it's an excellent product, though there's an uneasy rider: "Please be aware that some sections of trails have different difficulty ratings than others."
Activities and Entertainment: "Aspen" and "ennui" are not on speaking terms. Select among four major alpine areas, Elvis and Jerry shrines on Ajax, fly fishing, snowshoeing, dog sledding and free kennel tours, ice skating, ballooning, paragliding, hiking, historic walking tours, sleigh rides, and more XC skiing at Ashcroft. Indoors, there's music, museums, arts, crafts, dancing, environmental discussions, a cabaret, chocolatiers, yoga.
Children's Programs: Day care (numerous locations), equipment, pulks.
Dining: Aspen is a gastronome's fond dream. Sardy House has excellent cuisine, but for something more exotic, try Vinh Vinh (Vietnamese). Unless you're accustomed to lively foods, it's best to be conservative when stating your preference in spiciness level.
Special Nordic Distinction: Owl Creek Trail connects the Snowmass network to loops near town; it also has many of the best views. Not all trails are linked, but a free shuttle system makes almost everything accessible.
Summary: The trails testify to the local teamwork of visionary managers, generous landowners, and financial support from the town of Aspen, Snowmass Village, Pitkin County, and skier donations.

Beaver Creek Cross Country Ski Center
Beaver Creek, Colorado

Vail Resorts has devoted considerable time and vision to developing nordic trails and programs at Beaver Creek. Since property in the valley was so valuable, planners cleverly decided to use the Strawberry Park lift (also known as Chair 12) to reach higher Forest Service land. The XC center and instruction area remain at the base. Trails at McCoy Park opened in 1984, named after a homestead/logging site of the early 1900s. Rise 1,300 feet the easy way, then gaze around. Trails pass through meadow, interspersed with willow and groves of aspen and evergreens. There's surprising wildlife (fox, porcupine, squirrel, hare, coyote), and tremendous views—Gore Range to the north, Sawatch Range to the south, Eagle River Valley to the west, Jackson's Peak to the East, but it's at the price of skiing 2 miles above sea level.

Address: P.O. Box 7, Vail, CO 81658
Tel/fax: (970) 476-5601, XC (970) 845-5313; fax: (970) 845-5316
Location: Central Colorado
Airport: Eagle County, 25 miles
Train: None nearby
Memberships and Awards: Cross Country Ski Areas Association, Colorado Cross Country Ski Association, Atlas Snowshoe Center
Medical: Beaver Creek Medical Center, at base of mountain
Accommodations: The Poste Montane is an easy walk from Chair 12. It has a European look (something that neighboring Vail tries to achieve, with limited success) and American comfort. Deluxe rooms have fireplaces; one- and two-bedroom suites are also available. Hot tub and sauna in building. Enjoy! East/West Resorts, P.O. Box 5480, Avon, CO 81620; (800) 497-9238.
Guest Capacity: 88 at The Poste Montane
Conference Capacity: Extensive locally.
Rates: $$$–$$$$
Credit Cards: Visa, MasterCard, American Express

Season: Thanksgiving–early April; annual snowfall 331"
XC Skiing: Beaver Creek uses a humongous snowcat to groom 32 kms of double track and skate lane, spread over 12 trails. 20% Easier, 60% More Difficult; 20% is rated Most Difficult and routed one-way (Sluicebox and Wildside). Two warming shelters. Excellent ski school run by longtime XC Director Jean Naumann includes telemarking; daily guide service, both on trails and in the backcountry; and a special nature tour, available by reservation. Lots of ski and snowshoe tours. Good rental selection. All-day trail fee covers two rides up and down Chair 12, so you can pop down for lunch. Altitude range 9,840' (at lift unloading zone)–10,255' (Discovery Overlook). Another XC center 10 miles away at Vail.
Maps: Impressively accurate and vivid, showing the land's shape and forestation.
Activities and Entertainment: On-site snowshoeing. Almost next door or down the road at Vail are alpine skiing galore, ice skating, dog sledding, sleigh rides, hot air ballooning, fly fishing, ski biking, upper-end shopping, Colorado Ski Museum, Vilar Center for the Arts, snowmobiling.
Children's Programs: Day care, instruction, equipment, snow play.
Dining: Mirabelle is known to be expensive, but it may also be the finest French restaurant in the Rockies. Housed in a century-old farmhouse, chef de cuisine Daniel Joly presents an admirable range of both dishes and wines. No credit cards.
Special Nordic Distinction: Don't hurry yourself those first few hours! If you're concerned about energy (and breathing), consider a free shuttle to the Vail Golf Course for a warm-up day.
Summary: Some lovely, lilting trails complemented by instruction and guide service. The tracks access vistas as fine as any in Colorado.

Cordillera
Edwards, Colorado

If you ever believed XC skiing is designed strictly for stoics, Cordillera will shatter the preconception—gracefully rather than rudely, but definitively. In conjunction with a full-scale spa, skiing dominates winter recreation here. The resort is primarily an exclusive, private home development spread over 6,500 acres that opened in 1988, but this in no way detracts from natural beauty, services, or facilities—and certainly not from the winter trails. The golf pro shop converts to a remarkably pleasant Nordic Center, while the 8,300-square-foot timber-framed golf clubhouse houses the Timber Hearth Grille, with full dinner and limited lunch. Cordillera does a first-class job grooming, and overnight guests are given equipment and services as part of their stay. Owner/founder Felix Posen is an avid XC skier; perhaps this has helped shape the private tenor of existence here that contrasts markedly with nearby Vail.

Address: P.O. Box 988, Edwards, CO 81632
Tel/fax: (800) 877-3529; fax: (970) 926-5101, XC (970) 926-5100
e-mail: cord@vail.com
Internet: www.cordillera-vail.net
Location: Northwestern Colorado
Airport: Eagle County, 14 miles
Train: Glenwood Springs, 30 miles
Memberships and Awards: Cross Country Ski Areas Association, *Condé Nast* Gold List, AAA Four Diamond, Mobil Four Star
Medical: Beaver Creek Medical Center, 8 miles
Accommodations: 56 rooms at the lodge border on opulent, with hand-troweled plaster walls, high ceilings, and tiled bathrooms; most have fireplaces and decks. Indoor smoking in lodge living room only. Ski-in/ski-out on lodge trail system. Seven-night minimum Christmas holidays.
Guest Capacity: 187 (recent expansion)
Conference Capacity: 150
Rates: $$$–$$$$$ (includes instruction, guiding, equipment, use of trails)

Credit Cards: Visa, MasterCard, American Express, Diners Club, Discover
Season: December 1–April 1; annual snowfall 150"
XC Skiing: Cordillera has two separate networks, totaling 12 kms on 10 trails, with a mix of single track with skating and double track with skating, groomed by snowcat. 65% Easier, 35% More Difficult. Road crossing. Shuttle for the 6-mile drive from spa to clubhouse. Instruction in classic and skating; guide service. Road crossing. Up-to-date rentals. Daily trail fee. Altitude range 8,200'–8,600'.
Maps: It's a pleasant and amusingly illustrated product. One side describes trails on the ranch, the other, those by the lodge.
Activities and Entertainment: On-site: snowshoeing (moonlit tours), sleigh rides, dog sledding, outdoor and indoor hot tubs, spa (whirlpool, sauna, massage, hydrotherapy, body wrap, lymphatic drainage, Shiatsu), wellness program. Nearby: alpine (Beaver Creek, Arrowhead, Vail; complimentary shuttle), snowmobiling, hot air ballooning, 10th Mountain Trail Association hut system, hockey, figure skating.
Children's Programs: Day care can be arranged, equipment.
Dining: Restaurant Picasso is extravagant. Not only are there original Picasso lithographs on the walls, but gastronomy is as high as the altitude, prepared with a Gallic flair and attention to salt and fats. The Timber Hearth Grille has similar quality; entrées include roasted medallions of pork tenderloin.
Special Nordic Distinction: Golf at Cordillera must be interesting because the skiing is exciting—lots of up and down, lots of vertical, though trails are wide enough to prevent panic. There are distracting views of the Gore and Sawatch Ranges. On the ranch trails you can ski by ponds and a historic cabin.
Summary: Day skiers are indeed welcome, but it's even more fun to be pampered as an overnight guest.

C Lazy U Ranch
Granby, Colorado

Some winter guest ranches are blessed with magnificent vistas; others create their own legacy. C Lazy U has natural endowments (it's situated in the Willow Creek Valley, looking toward the Continental Divide). The first noteworthy element is the riding program, in a 10,000-square-foot arena and on trails—perhaps the most popular program at the ranch. The second characteristic: C Lazy U is to day care as Mark McGwire is to baseball. They have one of the country's outstanding children's programs, with separate activities for different age groups. To top it all, manager John Fisher invented KnickerKnickerland, where adults must be accompanied by a child. Yes, there's skiing, too, predominantly intermediate terrain through sage, meadow, aspen, and pine. Staff particularly enjoy leading you up to Baldy Mountain, with 50-mile views. Architecture is eclectic, centered around the hand-hewn lodgepole pine lodge. Originally a sheep and dairy cattle operation, the ranch opened for guests in 1925. To bring things full circle, the Murray family (themselves long-time guests) purchased the property in 1988 and are reintroducing Herefords.

Address: P.O. Box 379, Granby, CO 80446
Tel/fax: (970) 887-3344; fax: (970) 887-3917
e-mail: ranch@clazyu.com
Internet: www.clazyu.com
Location: Northwestern Colorado
Airport: Denver International, 115 miles
Train: Granby, 7 miles
Memberships and Awards: Cross Country Ski Areas Association, Mobil Five Star and AAA Five Diamond (don't be intimidated—this place is *friendly*)
Medical: Granby Medical Clinic, 7 miles
Accommodations: Though there are pleasant rooms in the lodge, the 36 one- to three-room cabins are still more attractive, all with private bath, some with fireplaces and Jacuzzis; no phone or TV. Ski-in/ski-out. Smoking allowed only in bar. Two-night minimum.
Guest Capacity: 80

Conference Capacity: 65
Rates: $$$–$$$$ (includes meals, complimentary shuttle to alpine slopes, instruction, guiding, equipment, use of trails)
Credit Cards: Personal checks or cash only
Season: Mid-December–early April; annual snowfall 180"
XC Skiing: The ranch sets a single track plus skating lane on all 30 kms, grooming with a small snowcat. People tend to ski everything both ways. 10% Easier, 80% More Difficult, 10% Most Difficult. Lake Lookout via Wilson Trail is a dandy. Road crossing. Daily instruction covers the whole gamut of techniques. Rentals are primarily three-pin, as guides enjoy leading backcountry tours. Altitude range 8,100'–8,500'.
Maps: Lack of contour lines leaves the topography slightly mysterious, but trail names such as Meadow Loop help.
Activities and Entertainment: On-site: snowshoeing, ¾-mile sledding hill, sleigh rides behind massive Levi and Strauss, dog sledding, ice skating and broomball, racquetball court, exercise equipment, hot tub, sauna, snow play, horseback riding, trap shooting, and, for the ultra-civilized, billiards. Nearby: alpine (SilverCreek, Winter Park), more XC (Snow Mountain Ranch, Devil's Thumb).
Children's Programs: The ranch offers virtually everything except a college degree.
Dining: Specialties include rack of lamb and beef medallions, but there are customarily lighter entrées as well. Meals are served family style. Handsome wood-faced living room and bar.
Special Nordic Distinction: Guests can purchase designer Western clothing at Luis' Old Place (a converted barn that once housed Sicilian donkeys); however, it's not advisable to ski in them.
Summary: The phrase "rustic elegance" crops up frequently in ranch descriptions—but that's just the raw material. C Lazy U's amazingly helpful, cheerful staff make it all work, although the great views don't hurt at all.

C Lazy U Ranch, Colorado

Rod Walker

Rod Walker

Devil's Thumb Ranch
Tabernash, Colorado

In the early '80s Devil's Thumb was the dominant XC area in the Rockies—most trails, most visited, and most talked about in racing circles. (Famous Black 10 is still there.) Then, after four years' closure, the co-owners didn't quite synchronize winter activities. Today, lodging, meal service, and skiing are concentrated in the hands of Englishman Barry Gordon. Results are gratifying—best grooming ever on the huge trail system, good food, and fine staff. Seclusion and beauty haven't changed at all—the ranch is still 3 miles from a highway, while a line of 13,000-foot peaks along the Continental Divide rises almost a mile above the ranch. The drive from Denver is magnificent (believe the signs along Berthoud Pass warning of avalanche danger!), while Devil's Thumb—subject of fascinating legends among both Utes and white settlers—stabs the eastern skyline.

Address: P.O. Box 750, Tabernash, CO 80478
Tel/fax: (800) 933-4339 (U.S. only) or (970) 726-5632, XC center (970) 726-8231; fax: (970) 726-9038
e-mail: devthumb@rkymtnhi.com
Internet: www.rkymtnhi.com/devthumb
Location: North-central Colorado
Airport: Denver International, 90 miles
Train: Fraser, 6 miles (free shuttle)
Memberships and Awards: Cross Country Ski Areas Association, Colorado Cross Country Ski Areas Association, voted "Colorado's Favorite XC Center" by *Rocky Mountain Sports* readers, Fischer Key Nordic Center
Medical: Granby Medical Clinic, 11 miles
Accommodations: Guests can choose lodge rooms or cabins—never sumptuous but all pleasant; neither TV nor phones in rooms. Fox Cabin seems designed for couples, combining seclusion and views; double bed, pine furniture, wood-burning fireplace, shower, and antique tub. Smoke-free environment. Ski-in/ski-out. Three-night minimum holidays, two-night on weekends.
Guest Capacity: 75
Conference Capacity: 50

Rates: $–$$$$ (package can include breakfast, dinner, trail fee discount)
Credit Cards: Visa, MasterCard
Season: Thanksgiving–early April; annual snowfall 275"
XC Skiing: Devil's Thumb snowcat-grooms around 100 kms, a mix of single and double track, primarily with skating. Most of the two dozen trails are two-way, running through meadows and coniferous forest. 45% Easier, 40% More Difficult, 15% Most Difficult. Moose, deer, and elk enjoy the grooming, too. Full moon tours. Special outings conducted by the National Ski Center for the Disabled. Groomed dog trail. Excellent rental and retail departments and a fine ski school. Daily trail fee. Altitude range 8,600'–8,900'.
Maps: New in brochure; colorful, artistic, and helpful.
Activities and Entertainment: On-site: sleigh rides, snowshoeing, sauna, hot tub; live music weekends at the Saloon. Nearby: alpine (free shuttle to Winter Park), tubing in Fraser, *reindeer*-drawn sleigh rides, dog sledding, snowmobiling, and the Cozens Ranch Museum—a famous stage stop from 1876 through 1904.
Children's Programs: Instruction, rentals, pulks; babysitting can be arranged.
Dining: The Ranch House Restaurant and Saloon was built as a homestead; now it specializes in vegetarian entrées and Southwestern cuisine. Full license. Smoking in bar only.
Special Nordic Distinction: Excellent skiing, but lowlanders should keep an eye on the altitude; plan on treating yourself to a substantial stay so you'll have energy to enjoy longer peripheral trails. Eastern and Midwestern skiers can revel in bounteous Colorado powder.
Summary: The glory days are back; they'd be even better if the cappuccino machine were re-installed at the XC center!

High Meadows Ranch
Steamboat Springs, Colorado

The Steamboat region already has two famous winter ranches, Vista Verde and The Home Ranch. High Meadows is both newer (opened in 1990) and different in everything from size to type of activities. It's 25 miles southeast of town and is definitely low-key, though a long way from austere. The ranch is equally ideal for honeymooners absorbed in each other and for downhill skiers who want to escape society after a long day on the slopes. Dennis and Jan Stamp, founders, owners, and operators, are both Midwesterners with a wry sense of humor; he formerly ran a family seed company in Iowa. High Meadows presents an intriguing contrast between seclusion and comfort level. Forty minutes from Steamboat, it's situated in the lovely and quiet Morrison Creek Valley, with aspen groves, pine, and spruce forest rising to ridges and peaks to the west and east. The region is characterized by sweeping fields (sagebrush is buried by snow early on) popular with elk, deer, and coyote. The Stamps intend to maintain that peaceful character; the only change in recent days is a cabin ½-mile from other buildings, connected by trails—no gift shoppe, nothing commercial.

Address: P.O. Box 771216, Steamboat Springs, CO 80477
Tel/fax: (800) 457-4453 or (970) 736-8416; fax: (970) 736-8416
e-mail: highmeadows@sprynet
Internet: www.hmranch.com
Location: Northwestern Colorado (four-wheel-drive vehicle advisable)
Airport: Hayden, 40 miles
Train: None nearby
Memberships and Awards: Cross Country Ski Areas Association
Medical: Routt Memorial Hospital, 25 miles
Accommodations: Accommodations are in Elk and Columbine Lodges, each a moment's walk from an outdoor hot tub. Both are log-built, snug, handsomely decorated and furnished, with private bath for each bedroom, wood-burning stove, and complete kitchens.

New log lodge has five bedrooms, two baths. And if your idea of vacation doesn't include whipping up three meals daily, then count on Jan for tasty vittles. No smoking in buildings. Ski-in/ski-out. Two-night minimum.
Guest Capacity: 18
Conference Capacity: 15
Rates: $$$ (includes meals, instruction, guided tours, use of trails)
Credit Cards: Visa, MasterCard
Season: Mid-December–mid-April; annual snowfall 300"
XC Skiing: Denny snowcat-maintains at least 12 kms of two-way double track and narrow skate lane; he also practices "responsive grooming," adding another 8 kms on request. There's a mix of meadow and tree-lined trails. For "outsiders," daily trail fee with lunch costs $25. Instruction for beginners. Ski and showshoe rentals now on-site. Altitude range 8,000'–8,150'.
Maps: Small and informal, basically indicating trail layout related to buildings, fences, and roads.
Activities and Entertainment: On-site: snowshoeing, hot tub. Nearby: ice fishing at Stagecoach Reservoir, the sinful attractions of thriving Steamboat Springs (alpine, hot air ballooning, hot springs, snowmobiling, bobsledding at Howelsen Park, bungee jumping).
Children's Programs: Child care can be arranged; snow play.
Dining: The Stamps are very health-conscious, thus concentrate on "Western Gourmet" low-cholesterol meals (elk, turkey bacon, mesquite-grilled trout). Jan also bakes delicious breads. B.Y.O.B.
Special Nordic Distinction: Though the ranch is set at 8,000', skiing is remarkably gentle, so a first-day visitor won't experience the huff-and-puff climbing endured at so many XC areas in the Rockies.
Summary: Small, personable, easy to love, hard to leave, High Meadows provides a marvelous sanctuary for harried urbanites.

The Home Ranch
Clark, Colorado

Colorado has a near-monopoly on winter guest ranches, and The Home Ranch is as posh as any, enjoying membership in the select Relais & Chateaux. Built specifically for guest ranching, it has achieved an international reputation since opening in 1979 but is not in the least stuffy. Partner/manager Ken Jones is a Montana singing cowboy with a great sense of fun (the collection of fossil Naugahyde is hilarious, including graphic "finds" by guests). Located a half-hour from Steamboat Springs on 1,500 acres in the upper end of the secluded Elk River Valley, there are fine views of the Mount Zirkel Wilderness and Hahn's Peak. Hay meadows mix with hillsides forested in aspen, spruce, and fir, home to elk, deer, and fox. On moonlit nights, stand for a moment on your cabin porch and listen for a coyote serenade.

Address: P.O. Box 822, Clark, CO 80428
Tel/fax: (970) 879-1780; fax: (970) 879-1795
e-mail: hrclark@cmn.net
Internet: www.homeranch.com
Location: Northwestern Colorado
Airport: Hayden, 40 miles
Train: None nearby
Memberships and Awards: Cross Country Ski Areas Association, Colorado Cross Country Ski Association, Relais & Chateaux, Mobil Four Star
Medical: Steamboat Medical Center, 18 miles
Accommodations: Visitors have the choice of staying in the lodge (nice proximity to pool, sauna, dining) or handsome cabins furnished with Western antiques and art works, as well as private hot tubs. No phones, TVs, or radios in rooms. Everything is immaculately maintained. Smoke-free environment. Ski-in/ski-out. Three-night minimum.
Guest Capacity: 40
Conference Capacity: 17
Rates: $$$–$$$$$ (includes meals, airport and alpine skiing transfers, downhill skiing at Steamboat Springs, XC equipment, instruction, guided tours, use of trails)

Credit Cards: Visa, MasterCard, American Express
Season: Mid-December–late March; annual snowfall 200"
XC Skiing: 40 kms of double and single track with skating, groomed by snowcat, spread over 35 trails; the longest is around 8 kms. 40% Easier, 40% More Difficult, 20% Most Difficult; but unlike neighbor Vista Verde, the vertical change jumps right at you, moving from meadow into rolling hills. There are also some delightful ungroomed powder runs within the network. Programs cover the whole nordic range, including vehicle-accessed backcountry tours. Slim Boards Ski Shop has classic and new telemark gear available. Daily trail fee. Altitude range 7,200'–7,500'.
Maps: An impressionistic overview; look closely at difficulty designations, as hills aren't indicated by contour lines.
Activities and Entertainment: On-site: snowshoeing, sleigh rides to feed livestock, huge new tubing hill, indoor riding arena, indoor lap pool, sauna, recreation room; Cowboy Ken and his Ranch Hand Band perform weekly. Nearby: alpine (Steamboat Springs), hot air ballooning, snowmobiling, dog sledding, massage.
Children's Programs: Child counselors offer group activities daily; equipment, instruction.
Dining: Many guests consider meals the high point of every day. Chef Clyde Nelson creates delicacies such as roast rack of Colorado lamb with pecan crust (dinner is actually more elaborate in winter than summer), but buffet-style breakfasts and lunches are equally tasty. B.Y.O.B.
Special Nordic Distinction: There are two telemarking areas. Definitely inquire how trails received their names (for example, Jelly Bean Memorial and St. Louis Blues). Guests can ski to the Clark General Store in "town," an eclectic treat.
Summary: The Home Ranch presents a classic chance to escape city pressures (no cellular phones allowed)—and with Ken's example, sharpen your sense of humor.

Latigo Ranch
Kremmling, Colorado

Latigo is rapidly gaining a reputation as one of the great winter ranches in the Rockies. It's a family-run business in all the best senses, owned and operated by Jim and Kathie Yost, and Lisa and Randy George. They remain amazingly serene despite their roles as hosts, chefs, instructors, guides, reservationists, raconteurs, and parking clearance experts (a busy snow month sees 60 inches of fresh powder!). The ranch is remote from population centers (Kremmling is hardly a byword for Colorado winter entertainment), but the hospitality, skiing, and storytelling are all great. Founded in 1928 as a cattle, sheep, and dude ranch, dedicated full-time to guests since 1987, there is no hint of asceticism here. Anticipate a warm atmosphere and lively conversation, since Latigo seems a magnet for guests with diverse backgrounds. Almost straddling the Continental Divide, views east are nothing less than superb—70 miles of mountain and valley snowscape.

Address: P.O. Box 237, Kremmling, CO 80459
Tel/fax: (800) 227-9655 or (970) 724-9008
e-mail: latigo@compuserve.com
Internet: www.latigotrails.com
Location: North-central Colorado
Airport: Hayden, 65 miles; Denver International, 150 miles
Train: Granby, 50 miles
Memberships and Awards: Cross Country Ski Areas Association, Colorado Cross Country Ski Association, Dude Ranchers' Association, *Best Places to Stay in Colorado*
Medical: Kremmling Hospital, 16 miles
Accommodations: Latigo has seven comfortable log cabins with wood stoves or fireplaces, nestled into pines above the lodge. No TVs in rooms. Ski-in/ski-out. No minimum stay.
Guest Capacity: 24
Conference Capacity: 30
Rates: $$ (includes all meals, instruction, guiding, and trail fee)
Credit Cards: Visa, MasterCard

Season: Saturday before Christmas–end March; annual snowfall 200"; the last several winters have been unusually warm and snowy.
XC Skiing: Jim is the principal snowcat driver, maintaining 65 kms of skate lane plus double track with the new Bombardier 400 snowcat. Pine, spruce, and aspen are interspersed with vast meadows. 25% Easier, 50% More Difficult, 25% Most Difficult. Cutting off-track, you can ski down to the Red Earth Creek Waterfall. For a good adrenaline tour, try the 15-km Hinman Reservoir trail but don't forget to arrange a shuttle home (a long way uphill). When you've acclimated to the heights, head up to Jumper Flats and tear downhill on The Luge, finishing at sunset, watching the play of colors over Indian Peaks Wilderness. There is a 2-acre groomed downhill practice area. New ski rentals at ranch. Daily trail fee. Altitude range 8,600'–9,400'.
Maps: The new map is superb. It's colorful, contoured, precise; and now you can find exactly where 1.2 mile long "!Aargh!" runs.
Activities and Entertainment: On-site: snowshoeing, sledding, and tubing; dog sledding can be arranged; hot tub in the Social Center.
Children's Programs: Packed sledding hill; games in the Social Center.
Dining: Food is excellent, with a different dinner entrée each evening (swordfish, prime rib, baked chicken, for example). Desserts include everything from peach pie to chocolate mousse. For breakfast, Randy enjoys making pancakes imprinted with the ranch brand and served with genuine maple syrup. B.Y.O.B.
Special Nordic Distinction: Magnificent snow and intelligently laid-out trails allow guests to start on easier routes immediately. Ask Jim about his anthropological research in the Amazon.
Summary: A wonderful place where you're virtually assured of seclusion and fresh snow. The night stars are hard, clear, and near.

See color photos, page 89

San Juan Guest Ranch
Ridgway, Colorado

The San Juans—abrupt young peaks sometimes reaching more than 14,000 feet—are arguably the most spectacular major mountain range in the American Rockies. This was Ute hunting ground little more than a century ago. Distinctive red stone flaunts itself on the 6-mile drive from San Juan Guest Ranch to the old mining town of Ouray (nine blocks long, six blocks wide). The ranch was founded as a boys' camp in 1970 by the MacTiernan family (both sons are dedicated skiers), and they started grooming in 1981. It's a small, comfortable place on 3,500 acres, nestled among cottonwoods in an unspoiled valley; a stream flows through it, and the Uncompahgre River runs nearby. It functions at full tilt in summer, but come snow season, the MacTiernans operate it as an unusual B&B. The ranch house is a fine place to lounge and enjoy morning coffee. Winter days tend toward the mild and sunny. There's a major elk herd on the way to Telluride.

Address: 2882 Country Road 28, Ridgway, CO 81432
Tel/fax: (800) 331-3015 or (970) 626-5360; fax: (970) 626-5015
Location: Southwestern Colorado
Airport: Montrose, 32 miles
Train: None nearby
Memberships and Awards: Cross Country Ski Areas Association, Colorado Cross Country Ski Association
Medical: Ouray Medical Clinic, 4 miles
Accommodations: Nine separate choices in the guest lodge, ranging from single rooms to a small apartment, each with private bath. All but singles have refrigerator. Mostly nonsmoking rooms. Ski-in/ski-out. No minimum stay.
Guest Capacity: 30
Conference Capacity: 25
Rates: $$ (package includes breakfast, half-price ticket at Telluride, use of trails)
Credit Cards: Visa, MasterCard
Season: Mid-December–late March; annual snowfall 110" (lots of small storms rather than huge dumps)
XC Skiing: The amount of trail Scott grooms by snowmobile varies according to guests' needs. Customary minimum is 12 kms, double track and (usually) a skate lane, but this can be expanded to 26 kms. 50% Easier, 40% More Difficult, 10% Most Difficult. Instruction available upon request (Scott also used to teach alpine skiing at Aspen). Ouray Mountain Sports is a good source for rental equipment. Daily trail fee. Altitude range 7,300'–10,000'.
Maps: None currently.
Activities and Entertainment: On-site: snowshoeing, ice skating, ice fishing, sleigh rides with Percherons Rex and Rosie, hot tub. Nearby: alpine skiing (Telluride or at Ouray's free rope tow), Ouray County Museum, ice climbing at the Uncompahgre Gorge Ice Park, sledding on Vinegar Hill in Ouray, dog sled races, snowmobiling, famous non-sulfurous Ouray Hot Springs Pool.
Children's Programs: Special tracks groomed upon request; ranch animals, snow play.
Dining: The ranch customarily operates as a B&B, but groups can arrange dinners, with such specialties as fresh smoked trout. B.Y.O.B. The Bon Ton Restaurant at the century-old St. Elmo Hotel in Ouray is a lot of fun, with Italian cuisine, good wines, and a jovial owner.
Special Nordic Distinction: There's a remarkable contrast between lower and higher trails. The meadows are great for beginners and skaters; higher routes involve a gain of 2,500'. Scott can transport guests up by four-wheel drive or snowmobile, but you need to ski down with care.
Summary: Small, hardly known, caring, very responsive to individual needs, with a grand backdrop of looming mountains. The MacTiernans particularly enjoy families as guests.

Snow Mountain Ranch
Tabernash, Colorado

It's very easy to assume that a YMCA facility has to cater to so many interests that skiing quality suffers. Not so in Colorado, nor at Frost Valley in New York! Former Nordic director Nancy Young and her husband, Jim (once coach of both the Swiss Olympic Sailing Team and the U.S. Biathlon Team), exercised unusual vision in developing a vast trail system that's the most popular in the state. Snow Mountain Ranch is large in every sense (4,900 acres, more than 1,000 pillows). It could have been a haven for just elite skiers, cyclists, and runners, but instead it's a recreational skier's paradise as well as a famous race center because the trail network is laid out so the two don't conflict—no irritated competitors, no intimidated tourers. The result is loads of *fun*—the friendly, gregarious person you meet may be on the way to the National Championships. (Another thoughtful touch: Kidney Center dialysis for people who need the treatment but also need winter.) Most trails pass through lodgepole pine forest, but they incorporate "view breaks." As for people who also downhill, modest-sized SilverCreek and huge Winter Park are minutes away. If you're a hyperenergetic nordic purist, first exhaust the possibilities at Snow Mountain, then drive over to Devil's Thumb Ranch for another 100 kilometers.

Address: P.O. Box 169, Winter Park, CO 80482
Tel/fax: (970) 887-2152; fax: (303) 449-6781
Internet: www.snowmtnordic.com
Location: Northwestern Colorado
Airport: Denver International, 104 miles
Train: Fraser, 11 miles
Memberships and Awards: Cross Country Ski Areas Association, Colorado Cross Country Ski Association
Medical: Timberline Clinic, 4 miles
Accommodations: Pleasant cabins provide one option; the new and attractive Indian Peaks Lodge (79 hotel-style rooms), another.

Ski-in/ski-out. Mostly non-smoking rooms. No minimum stay.
Guest Capacity: 1,600
Conference Capacity: 1,600
Rates: $–$$
Credit Cards: Personal checks and cash only
Season: Early November–mid-April; annual snowfall 200", yet most days are sunny
XC Skiing: 100 kms groomed with snowcats, two-thirds double track with skating, one-third single track and skating; most two-way. 30% Easier, 40% More Difficult, 30% Most Difficult. 3-km lighted trail. Peter's Trail (packed dog trail named after the former XC managers' husky/coyote mix). Biathlon range. Instruction in all disciplines; guide service available. Good rental selection at the pleasant Nordic Center. Daily trail fee. Altitude range 8,200'–10,600', but 80% of trails are at 8,200'–9,600'.
Maps: It's a good product, especially for trail names, though contour indications would be useful.
Activities and Entertainment: On-site: snowshoeing, ice skating, sleigh rides, indoor roller rink, sauna, gym, swimming pool. Nearby: alpine skiing, snowmobiling, snow play.
Children's Programs: Day care, narrow track-set "candy cane" trail, bumps and jumps, instruction, equipment, pulks; kids can ski with great role models.
Dining: Schlessman Commons serves nutritious meals and, on weekends, special baked goods. Nordic Center cafeteria has chili, pasta.
Special Nordic Distinction: In addition to the early and long season (remember that altitude?), how many areas have ski-in/ski-out dining areas? These lighted trails are a rarity in the Rockies. Home of the Snow Mountain Stampede in March, part of the American Ski Marathon series.
Summary: Guests receive *great* value in skiing, lodging, and staff.

Vista Verde Ranch
Steamboat Springs, Colorado

This is a place that seamlessly melds elegance and entertainment. Founded 75 years ago as a working cattle ranch, remodeled as a guest ranch 50 years later, purchased in 1991 and improved still more by Midwesterners John and Suzanne Munn, Vista Verde appeals to anyone with good taste and time—frenetic business types who learn to live without cell phones, tentative skiers who find the trails are compassionate to beginners, downhillers headed for Steamboat Springs' trails and glades, and young honeymooners reveling in quiet and privacy. Skiing is the catalyst that brings most visitors, and virtually everyone spends time on tracks and tours. But there's an unprecedented range of non-skiing fun as well, from dog sledding through the Routt National Forest to climbing frozen waterfalls. The ranch itself is extensive, beautiful, and secluded (45 minutes from town).

Address: P.O. Box 465, Steamboat Springs, CO 80477
Tel/fax: (800) 526-7433 or (970) 879-3858; fax: (970) 879-1413
e-mail: vistaverde@compuserve.com
Internet: www.vistaverde.com
Location: Northwestern Colorado
Airport: Hayden, 40 miles (complimentary shuttle)
Train: None nearby
Memberships and Awards: Cross Country Ski Areas Association, Colorado Cross Country Ski Association, Dude Ranchers' Association, Mobil Four Star, *Snow Country* magazine's Top 10 XC Areas in the Rockies
Medical: Routt Hospital, 25 miles
Accommodations: Handsome rooms in the lodge are complemented by eight exceedingly comfortable log cabins, screened by aspen and pine, most with hot tubs. Ski-in/ski-out. Smoke-free environment. Three-night minimum.
Guest Capacity: 36
Conference Capacity: 40
Rates: $$$ (includes meals, riding, instruction, guided tours, use of trails)

Credit Cards: Personal checks or cash only
Season: Mid-December–mid-March; annual snowfall 300"
XC Skiing: Vista Verde has one of the most beginner-friendly networks in the Rockies. It features 30 kms on 15 snowcat-groomed trails; 75% Easier, 25% More Difficult. Most are double-tracked with skating, but there are also single tracks threading through the forest. Peek at the Peaks gives glimpses of the Continental Divide. Instructor/guides are outstanding, as is the telemarking program. Two warming shelters. Rentals include track, skating, and telemark gear. Daily trail fee. Altitude range 7,700'–7,900'.
Maps: Entertaining (includes information on animal tracks) but practical.
Activities and Entertainment: On-site: snowshoeing, sledding resembling a luge run, horseback riding, sleigh rides, hot tubs, sauna, and exercise room. Postprandial entertainment includes an oldies-but-goodies performance by local duo Legal Tender (alter egos for a printer and an attorney). Nearby: alpine (complimentary shuttle), dog sledding, snowcat skiing, snowmobiling, shopping in Steamboat Springs, even fly-fishing!
Children's Programs: Vista Verde aims to please families: child care by arrangement, rentals, instruction, sledding, treasure hunts, and a quinzee to play in.
Dining: John Munn's description, "a touch of gourmet," is excessively modest. Sensational dinners include a choice of entrées such as wild game, followed by one of the chef's succulent desserts. Wine and beer license.
Special Nordic Distinction: Most visitors from sea level can ski right away on these gentle trails. For a new thrill, try skijoring behind a galloping horse. There's a wonderful wide-packed hill for play and practice (you can arrange to be pulled up by snowmobile).
Summary: Great facilities, superb staff, wonderfully reliable snow, *and* a sense of humor. Vista Verde earns that much-overused adjective "world class."

See color photos, page 90

Vista Verde Ranch, Colorado

©Vista Verde

©Vista Verde

McCall Region
Idaho

There's more to Idaho than Sun Valley. The small town of McCall (100 miles north of Boise) is surrounded by Payette National Forest. It's 12 miles from New Meadows, which is exactly on the 45th parallel. (Travel due east and you'll eventually encounter Yellowstone's Boiling River Hot Springs.) This is "Idaho's Heartland," a land of shallow soils and glacial moraines. Founded in the 1890s, it's historically a timber, mining, and ranching community, though tourism is on the increase. There's a long skiing heritage—Finns once composed two-fifths of the region's population. Cross-country attractions are familiar to some racers (former U.S. Biathlon Champion Lyle Nelson comes from McCall); but the town is almost unknown to recreational skiers. Operating since 1937, the Little Ski Hill is the local area, with downhill and XC.

Address: McCall Chamber of Commerce, Box D, McCall, ID 83638
Tel/fax: (208) 634-7631; fax (208) 634-7752
e-mail: mccallcc@cyberhighway.net
Internet: www.mccall-idchamber.org
Location: West-central Idaho
Airport: Boise, 120 miles
Train: None nearby
Medical: McCall Memorial Hospital, in town
Accommodations: 1920 House Bed & Breakfast is a restored historic home, convenient to both trail systems. Three rooms, each with a different Southwestern flavor; breakfasts are wonderfully sumptuous. Non-smoking environment. Two-night minimum weekends. P.O. Box 1716, McCall, ID 83638; (208) 634-4661.
Guest Capacity: 6 at 1920 House B&B
Conference Capacity: Available locally.
Rates: $$ (includes breakfast, mulled cider, afternoon snacks)
Credit Cards: Personal checks and cash only
Season: Late November–late March; annual snowfall 151"
XC Skiing:
• *Little Ski Hill*, north of town, snowcat-grooms 25 kms of single track and skate lane. There are some great workouts. You'll find both a dog trail and biathlon range. Instruction weekends; good telemarking opportunities on alpine slopes. Altitude range 5,000'–5,600'. Daily trail fee. (208) 634-5691.
• *Ponderosa State Park*, on the south end of McCall, has 20 kms of snowcat-groomed trail amid towering pines, mostly both classic and skating, with 2 kms lighted. Site of the 1998 XC Junior Nationals. About half the trails are quite easy. Best views are from basaltic cliffs overlooking Payette Lake, accessed by 4-km Thread the Needle, the most advanced trail. Heated restroom. Altitude range 5,060'–5,350'. $2 vehicle entrance fee. (208) 634-2164.
• *McCall Cross Country & Snowshoe Trails*: Five mostly flat open routes, for man and dog.
Maps: Both major sites have useful topo-type maps; Ponderosa's also has route descriptions.
Activities and Entertainment: Locally: alpine (family-oriented Mt. Brundage), snowshoeing, sleigh rides, ice skating, snowmobiling, hot springs. February Winter Carnival includes laser light show, intricate snow sculptures, and the Beard and Hairy Leg contest. Tours of the Smokejumper Base, galleries. There's also a vivid arts scene, including theater, music society, and chamber orchestra.
Children's Programs: Limited.
Dining: Bear Creek Lodge, near Little Ski Hill, presents a contemporary Northwestern menu. Sample: crab quiche florentine as appetizer, quail with pomegranate as entrée. For lunch, head to the Harvest Moon—sandwiches are delicious and copious to overflowing.
Special Nordic Distinction: Home Town Sports is a fine source of both information and equipment.
Summary: McCall has a welcoming atmosphere, fine and consistent snow, and excellent skiing. Its obscurity won't last.

Sun Valley Nordic
Sun Valley, Idaho

Most Sun Valley winter visitors come intent on alpine skiing, enjoying Bald Mountain with its history, views, high-tech lifts, and award-winning architecture. Celebrated as America's first destination resort, skiing opened in December 1936. Since then, slopes and rinks have been visited by the likes of Gary Cooper, Clark Gable, Marilyn Monroe, and Katarina Witt. The Nordic Center has its own history and influence. Director Hans Muehlegger was formerly an alpine instructor—very outgoing, he sets the tone for all the staff. (His predecessor was known for skiing ability, Scandinavian sweaters, striking good looks, and a short fuse.) Hans pioneered special trails and narrow tracks for children, creating an environment where kids absorb good technique while playing. The route to Trail Creek Cabin passes the Hemingway Memorial (Ernie's daughter Margaux was a XC devotee). Most visitors are also downhilling, but many of the skaters and striders are local folks. The region has an avid XC population, including svelte grandmothers who are particularly taken with skating.

Address: Sun Valley Company, Sun Valley, ID 83353
Tel/fax: (800) SUN-VALY or (208) 622-2250, XC info (208) 622-2251; fax: (208) 622-3700
Internet: www.sunvalley.com
Location: South-central Idaho
Airport: Friedman Memorial, 12 miles (complimentary shuttle)
Train: Shoshone, 50 miles
Memberships and Awards: Cross Country Ski Areas Association
Medical: Wood River Medical Center, ¼-mile
Accommodations: While there are plenty of other places to stay at the resort, the Sun Valley Lodge is a classic. Built in 1936, it has enduring elegance and tells the resort's story in photographs of distinguished visitors on the walls. All 148 rooms have been recently remodeled. Pool, sauna, massage, beauty salon, game room, restaurants. Customarily one-night minimum.

Guest Capacity: 300 at Sun Valley Lodge
Conference Capacity: 800-plus
Rates: $$–$$$$
Credit Cards: Visa, MasterCard, American Express
Season: Thanksgiving–early April; annual snowfall 180"
XC Skiing: Sun Valley uses a big 'cat to maintain 40 kms of trail, mostly double-tracked with skate lane. 30% Easier, 40% More Difficult, 30% Most Difficult, with the three toughest trails well separated from the others. Nearest stuff is easy two-way on the golf course. (Even Diamondback isn't terribly intimidating because it's wide and open—no surprises around a wooded corner.) One road crossing, one dog trail, new snowshoe trails, one warming shelter. High quality instruction in classic, skating, and telemarking; top-flight ski and snowshoe rentals. Daily trail fee. Altitude range 5,940'–6,420'.
Maps: The nice, compact XC brochure has a great photo spread—in fact, an aerial shot of the trail system is more effective than the smallish map.
Activities and Entertainment: Within walking distance: sleigh rides, ice skating, heated pools, sauna, hot tub, bowling, shopping, movie theater. Nearby: alpine skiing at Dollar Mountain and Bald Mountain, snowmobiling, and much more nordic activity.
Children's Programs: Day care, narrow-groomed special trails (wonderful creations in the terrain garden), instruction, equipment.
Dining: Breakfast at The Kneadery promises stained glass windows, fresh-squeezed orange juice, and sprightly staff.
Special Nordic Distinction: KART provides free valley-wide transportation, so you can stay in Ketchum, reach the trails in minutes, and never have to worry about parking. Next on Hans' agenda is a new XC building that can double as the golf course clubhouse.
Summary: The Nordic Center is removed enough from the resort to be more than an amenity, close enough for walking.

Sun Valley Region
Idaho

"A cross-country skier's paradise," says the promotional brochure. This is country Ernest Hemingway loved, and it's fun to speculate whether he would have been a nordic habitué. Beyond the 180-plus kilometers of regularly groomed track and skate trails that spread from Bellevue up towards Galena Summit, the framework lies within the Boulder, Smoky, and Sawtooth mountain ranges. The rest of the story embraces backcountry trips and hut-to-hut tours, with views from on high to the Pioneer and White Cloud Ranges. Most trails are available courtesy of government agencies (it doesn't hurt that administrators tend to be skiers). Though Sun Valley was home to the world's first chairlift, XC has a major presence in the region. And don't forget the largest concentration of dog trails in North America!

Address: Sun Valley/Ketchum Chamber of Commerce, P.O. Box 2420, Sun Valley, ID 83353

Tel/fax: (800) 634-3347 or (208) 726-3423; fax: (208) 726-4533

e-mail: sumktge@micron.net

Internet: www.visitsunvalley.com

Location: South-central Idaho

Airport: Friedman Memorial, 10 miles from Ketchum

Train: Shoshone, 50 miles from Ketchum

Medical: Wood River Medical Center, Sun Valley

Accommodations: Built in 1985, the River Street Inn is a quiet, convenient, and elegant B&B. Nine suites have walk-in shower, Japanese soaking tub, and small refrigerator. Overlooks Trail Creek. Non-smoking environment. Two-night minimum weekends. P.O. Box 182, Sun Valley, ID 83353; (888) 746-3611.

Guest Capacity: 7,000 in region, 16 at the River Street Inn

Conference Capacity: Extensive in region

Rates: $$–$$$ (full breakfast)

Season: Thanksgiving–Easter; annual snowfall up to 200"

XC Skiing: Sun Valley Nordic has its own destination stature, but the locale has much, much more. There are Forest Service trails (not noted below), maintained on a less regular basis. Altitude range 6,000'–8,500'.

- *Billy's Bridge:* 8 kms, classic and skating. Daily trail fee.
- *Boulder Mountain Trail:* 27.5 kms, classic and skating. Daily trail fee.
- *Galena Lodge:* the region's XC kingpin, with 50 kms, classic and skating. Instruction, tours, food, rentals, overnight yurts. Daily trail fee. (208) 726-4010.
- *Lake Creek:* 15.5 kms, classic and skating (with some real whoop-de-doo downhills). Daily trail fee.
- *North Fork:* 4 kms, classic and skating. Daily trail fee.
- *Prairie Creek:* 7.5 kms, classic and skating. Daily trail fee.
- *Wood River Trails:* 30 kms, classic and skating, from Ketchum south beyond Hailey. Daily trail fee.

Maps: Compact and useful, one map introduces the entire region, with insets describing individual areas. Lots of snowshoeing added.

Activities and Entertainment: Whoo!—alpine, heli-skiing, ice skating, sleigh rides, dog sledding, hot springs, snowmobiling, fly-fishing, ballooning, power shopping, galleries, lots of good coffee, theater, new Ski Museum, historic photos in Ketchum Community Library, and an outstanding collection of political buttons in the Blaine County Museum.

Dining: Big Wood Breads, in Ketchum's industrial district, has great breads and pastries.

Special Nordic Distinction: If snow is sparse in the valley, head up to Galena—terrific skiing, convivial staff. The Elephant's Perch is one of the great XC specialty shops in the U.S. Sun Valley Trekking and Sawtooth Mountain Guides have huts and guided trips. Boulder Mountain Tour draws both serious racers and sane people, all of whom enjoy the mostly downhill course and entertaining atmosphere.

Summary: "Nordic mecca" or "cross-country paradise"—it's just a matter of semantics.

Wapiti Meadow Ranch
Cascade, Idaho

"Wapiti" is the Shoshone name for elk, and it aptly suggests the type of neighbors the ranch sees come winter; others include deer, moose, otter, bobcat, wolf, and mountain lion. Wapiti Meadow—a homestead long before it became a dude ranch—is a bastion of civilization on the western edge of the 2.3-million-acre River of No Return Wilderness. You're 4.5 hours by four-wheel-drive vehicle from Boise, somewhat less than that from the nearest ski shop. There are a few houses further up Johnson Creek, along the headwaters of the Salmon River, but most of this part of Idaho remains magnificently wild, with snow patches in the high country into August. Still, humans have lived in the area for 6,000 years, and owner Diana Swift and manager Barry Bryant gently ease lingering fears of savage nature (though your first encounter with the cougar mounted above the piano can be startling). Raised in the East, Diana purchased the 160-acre property and received her first guests in 1987; Barry is fourth generation in the valley. With the log and stone lodge as backdrop, they combine the best of Virginia grace and Western charm.

Address: H.C. 72, Cascade, ID 83611
Tel/fax: (208) 633-3217; fax: (208) 633-3219
Location: West-central Idaho
Airport: Boise, 150 miles (better yet, 45 minutes by plane to Johnson Creek airstrip)
Train: None nearby
Memberships and Awards: Cross Country Ski Areas Association, Dude Ranchers' Association
Medical: McCall Memorial Hospital, 108 miles
Accommodations: There are four pleasant, handsomely furnished guest cabins, each with baseboard heat, wood-burning stove, kitchenette, and living room. No smoking in buildings. Ski-in/ski-out. No minimum stay, but due to remote location, three to five days is sensible.
Guest Capacity: 20
Conference Capacity: 18
Rates: $$$ (includes meals, snowshoeing, trails; round trip by ski plane also available, two-person minimum)
Credit Cards: Personal check or cash only
Season: Mid-December–early March; annual snowfall 165"
XC Skiing: Wapiti presents 30 kms of trail. Several very mild single-tracked two-way routes are groomed by snowmobile in open meadow up and down the valley. Skate trails are maintained by snowcat and sometimes shared with snowmobiles; they can have real elevation gain. Chat with Barry about snowmobile access to and from great ski tours such as Thunder Mountain, Riordan Creek, and Ditch Creek (especially inviting grade and switchbacks). Instruction by prior arrangement. Altitude range 5,000'–7,000'.
Maps: Skiers use a hand-drawn map that has been adapted for summer hiking trails.
Activities and Entertainment: On-site: outdoor hot tub, dedicated relaxation and romance, stargazing. Try snowshoeing up to the heavily timbered hidden ridgetops above the ranch (ski descents can be rather tricky). Skiers enjoy weekdays most, as there may be snowmobilers on weekends.
Children's Programs: The winter experience isn't suited to small children.
Dining: A cookbook author and editor, Diana terms the cuisine here "hearty gourmet," but emphasis should be on the latter word. Atmosphere is informal, yet guests dine off fine china. Single dinner entrée ranges from prime rib to spinach pasta primavera, with generous portions. Beer and wine are available.
Special Nordic Distinction: Weekdays, about as near as you can come to absolute privacy on tracked trails.
Summary: The ranch is a luxurious enclave in the midst of beautiful rugged country, ideal for both the energized and the aesthete.

Teton Ridge Ranch
Tetonia, Idaho

Most writers—even ski journalists—ultimately succumb to the temptation to embellish their prose. Pretty evolves into "sensational," unusual becomes "unique." But some destinations *deserve* superlatives, and, despite its license plate, Idaho has more than just "Famous Potatoes." Teton Ridge, the smallest of winter guest ranches in the Rockies in terms of accommondations, pampers guests with Western hospitality, elegance, and extraordinary snow. Part of the largest intact ecosystem in the Lower 48, the property is simply beautiful. It's also huge (4,000 rolling acres), remote (5 miles from the nearest paved road), and private (just look at the math: 25 kilometers divided by five guest rooms). Weather is benevolent on the "sunny west side of the Tetons," largely immune to the temperature inversions of Jackson Hole, a dozen miles east. And from the upper-floor living room of the 10,000-square-foot log lodge, one's eye is drawn to a stunning profile of the Grand Teton, soaring to almost 14,000 feet.

Address: 200 Valley View Road, Tetonia, ID 83452
Tel/fax: (208) 456-2650; fax: (208) 456-2218
e-mail: atilt@aol.com
Location: Southeastern Idaho
Airport: Jackson Hole, 40 miles; Idaho Falls, 70 miles
Train: None nearby
Memberships and Awards: Cross Country Ski Areas Association
Medical: Teton Valley Hospital, 8 miles
Accommodations: The lodge has five suites, each with Jacuzzi, steam shower, wood stove, and mountain views. Small separate two-bedroom lodge. Ski-in/ski-out. Two-night minimum.
Guest Capacity: 14
Conference Capacity: 14
Rates: $$$ (includes all meals, instruction, guided tours with a skier-naturalist)
Credit Cards: Personal checks or cash only
Season: Mid-December–end March; annual snowfall 300"

XC Skiing: The new snowcat grooms 25 kms of single track plus skating on 11 trails. 60% Easier, 40% More Difficult. This is "ego skiing" for the neophyte or the expert—modest uphills and descents winding through fields and evergreen forest, with mountain outlooks toward both the Tetons and the Big Holes. One trail series swings east through pine, fir, and meadow. Routes heading south and west wind gently downward (there's an occasional plunge), following miniature valleys crested by groves of young aspen. Some long downhills, such as Porcupine Ridge, have good runouts to help restrain your adrenaline count. Bring your own equipment, or rent top gear at Skinny Skis in Jackson or Yostmark in Driggs. Altitude range 6,400'–7,000'.
Maps: Updated and improved every couple of years, it's accurate but doesn't show the flow of the land.
Activities and Entertainment: On-site: snowshoeing, sleigh rides, dog sledding, sporting clays. Nearby: alpine skiing at Grand Targhee (bring a *telescoping* powder snorkel!), telemarking on Teton Pass, plus all the wiles of Jackson Hole. Two hours' drive north, you can visit Yellowstone National Park by snowmobile or snowcoach.
Children's Programs: Families may find there's not enough to entertain smaller kids.
Dining: Meals are always good and can verge on the sublime. Single dinner entrée, such as rack of lamb. Other than wine, B.Y.O.B.
Special Nordic Distinction: This is the only network that moves between two states, starting in Idaho, winding into Wyoming, then slicing back to meet up with Uncle Sam, the longest regularly groomed trail on the property. The ranch can also arrange an overnight in one of the wilderness yurts operated by Rendezvous Ski Tours.
Summary: Teton Ridge is ideal for couples or small groups who enjoy privacy, pristine setting, a taste of luxury, and stellar skiing. Moose and coyote enjoy it, too.

See color photos, page 91

Teton Ridge Ranch, Idaho

Karin Prescott

Jonathan Wiesel

Bethel Inn & Country Club
Bethel, Maine

Every XC area has its own history and character. Bethel Inn seems to be the only establishment dedicated to a neurologist by grateful (and affluent) patients. Based on this knowledge and the names of neighboring hamlets (China, Poland, Denmark, Naples, Sweden, Mexico, South Paris, Norway, Peru), one might assume that the inn and the town it's named after are exceedingly cosmopolitan, but in fact they are 22 miles from the nearest McDonald's. Bethel is one of New England's prettiest and least spoilt towns, with parts listed in the National Historic Register; even population numbers haven't changed much in the past 200 years. Dairy farming and logging are still economic mainstays (Bethel is a major producer of broom handles). Bethel Inn opened in 1913, flourished for many years, then fell on hard times in the 1960s, passing through the hands of several owners. Repurchased in 1979, the new proprietor refurbished and upgraded to the current impressive stature. It sits on 200 acres of wood and meadow; the golf course is used in winter as ski trails and a teaching area. Trails near the inn provide the best views of the Mahoosuc Range and New Hampshire's White Mountains.

Address: P.O. Box 49, Bethel, ME 04217
Tel/fax: (207) 824-2175; fax: (207) 824-2233
e-mail: info@bethelinn.com
Internet: www.bethelinn.com; video concentrates on conferencing
Location: Southwestern Maine
Airport: Portland International Jetport, 75 miles
Train: None nearby.
Memberships and Awards: Cross Country Ski Areas Association, Maine Nordic Council
Medical: Bethel Area Health Center, ¼-mile
Accommodations: Guests can choose between townhouses skirting the golf course or rooms at or near the inn. All rooms have private bath, cable TV, and phones; luxury suites are equipped with fireplaces and Jacuzzis. Some ski-in/ski-out. Some rooms are non-smoking. Three-night minimum holidays.
Guest Capacity: 450
Conference Capacity: 300
Rates: $$–$$$ (includes breakfast, dinner, use of trails and health club)
Credit Cards: Visa, MasterCard, American Express, Diners Club, Discover
Season: December 20–April 1; annual snowfall 110"
XC Skiing: Bethel snowcat-grooms 30 kms (the 'cat was proudly acquired in 1996), largely two-way double track with skate lane, spread over nine trails on the rolling golf course and in mixed coniferous and hardwood forest. 42% Easier, 42% More Difficult, 16% Most Difficult. Amusing and apropos trail names, such as Hedgehog Highway and Corkscrew. One shelter. Instruction in classic, skating, and telemarking. Groomed downhill practice hill. Daily trail fee. Rentals, including telemark gear. Altitude range 500'–1,100'.
Maps: The XC brochure/map gives limited feel for terrain change. Signage can be confusing, as it doesn't always accord with the map.
Activities and Entertainment: On-site: ice skating, sleigh rides, snow play, snowshoeing; outdoor pool; sauna, whirlpools, and fitness room in health club. Nearby: alpine skiing (Sunday River), dog sledding, crafts shops, excellent bookstore; Maine Line Products, home of the unforgettable Moose Drop Earring line.
Children's Programs: Narrow tracks, instruction, equipment, pulks, babysitting.
Dining: The evening meal offers a variety of entrées; specialties include prime rib and sautéed filet of salmon. One dining room is non-smoking. The candlelit evening meal is accompanied by live piano music.
Special Nordic Distinction: Regardless of what the map indicates, this is a prime beginner area.
Summary: Cordial and convenient.

The Birches Resort
Rockwood, Maine

Northwestern Maine is a sparsely settled, heavily forested land bordered by Québec. For decades the economy has depended on logging for pulp paper, though "sporting camps" have been popular since at least the 1860s. More recently, rafters have learned of whitewater on the Kennebec, and snowmobilers have taken to trails and old roads. But there's a skiing alternative up by the little town of Rockwood. The Birches is located on the west shore of 40-mile-long Moosehead Lake (the largest body of water in the state), in the midst of Maine's "North Woods." It's 11,000 acres of forest and lake—remote, secluded, no condos, no glitter, just warm, cozy cabins. The resort is owned by brothers John and Bill Willard, second-generation operators from a family who bought the 1930s fishing lodge in 1969. Originally it was a small property, but the boys purchased the vast bulk of the land from a paper company in 1993. The Willards introduced skiing in 1974 and have evolved a sizable trail system, which they can expand as demand grows. John *loves* skiing and doesn't mind spending those hours grooming to prepare first-quality trails.

Address: P.O. Box 41-N, Rockwood, ME 04478
Tel/fax: (800) 825-9453 or (207) 534-2242; fax: (207) 534-8835
e-mail: wwld@aol.com
Internet: www.birches.com
Location: Northwestern Maine
Airport: Bangor, 100 miles (two private airports nearby)
Train: None nearby
Memberships and Awards: Cross Country Ski Areas Association, Maine Nordic Ski Council
Medical: Charles A. Dean Memorial Hospital, 20 miles
Accommodations: The lodge's four upstairs rooms operate as a B&B, but there's another choice among the 15 cabins alongside the lake. The latter are hand-hewn, have one to three bedrooms, living rooms with wood-burning stoves or fireplaces, and showers; some have kitchens. The Willards' father was musically inclined, naming cabins after Henry Mancini hits. Ski-in/ski-out. No minimum stay.
Guest Capacity: 100
Conference Capacity: 100
Rates: $$ for cabins (includes breakfast and dinner, use of trails)
Credit Cards: Visa, MasterCard, American Express, Discover
Season: December 15–April 1; annual snowfall 100"
XC Skiing: The Birches' trails are particularly well suited to folks with limited experience, though there are a few twisty, narrow up-down routes that advanced skiers will enjoy. Staff snowcat-grooms 40 kms of two-way single track and skate lane, rated 60% Easier, 20% More Difficult, 20% Most Difficult. It's a kick to ski across Moosehead and hike up Mt. Kineo. Groomed dog trail. Instruction in classic and skate, by reservation. Rentals. Daily trail fee. Altitude range 1,050'–1,450'.
Map: Incorporated into the brochure, it's clear and simple, listing trail lengths and difficulty ratings, though no contours are indicated.
Activities and Entertainment: On-site: snowshoeing, snowmobiling to keep the cash flowing (limited to peripheral routes), ice fishing, hot tub, sauna, regularly scheduled musical entertainment. Nearby: alpine skiing at Squaw Mountain.
Children's Programs: Instruction, equipment.
Dining: The lodge has a good restaurant and pleasant lounge, pervaded by an agreeable wood smoke scent. Emphasis on healthy foods such as stir-fry and seafood. Tasty Belgian waffles. Wine list of around two dozen labels. Smoking permitted only in cabins.
Special Nordic Distinction: Three wilderness yurts, one on neighboring Brassua Lake and the other near more advanced trails, are equipped with bunks and wood stoves.
Summary: Venture into this land to find few people and less wind. Even the moose are reputed to be amiable.

Smiling Hill Farm
Westbrook, Maine

To some it may seem perverse to think of ingesting ice cream in winter, but to the cognoscenti it's just a healthy way to equalize external and internal temperatures. Regardless of the logic of that behavior, visitors to Portland should swing by Smiling Hill Farm in Westbrook, an agricultural/recreational oasis in an urban setting. Six miles from the downtown Federal Building (you can almost scent the sea), it's a 130-year-old dairy farm, logging operation, and lumber mill, and (as of 1995), an XC ski center like no other. The 535-acre property has been in the Knight family since the 1700s, and it remains a working farm with Holstein dairy cows. Some paths are hundreds of years old, some recently built for winter. When the snow falls, the Knights break out their German-made snowcat to open the trails. But there's more than skiing. Smiling Hill literally swings, chimes, and yaks—there are swings in several places; wind chimes at intersections; and llamas, goats, alpacas, and yaks to supplement indigenous wildlife. Views are limited by tree cover and lack of a dominating hill. If there's a free moment, chat with Warren Knight about Colonel Thomas Westbrook's ghost (a grave story, indeed).

Address: 781 County Road, Westbrook, ME 04092
Tel/fax: (207) 775-4818; fax (207) 839-3799
e-mail: smilinghillfarm@csi.com
Internet: www.mallofmaine.com/smiling.htm
Location: Southern Maine
Airport: Portland International Jetport, 4 miles
Train: Portland, 7 miles
Memberships and Awards: Cross Country Ski Areas Association, Maine Nordic Ski Council
Medical: Maine Medical Center, 6 miles
Accommodations: Though there are 2,000 beds within a 20-mile radius of the farm, PineCrest is a particularly pleasant five-room B&B, ten minutes from Smiling Hill. It's a nineteenth-century colonial home, light and airy. Rooms are named after towns where the owners (the Carlozzis) lived. No smoking. No minimum stay. 91 South Street, Gorham, ME 04038; (207) 839-5843.
Guest Capacity: 10 at PineCrest
Conference Capacity: None
Rates: $–$$ (includes breakfast)
Credit Cards: Visa, MasterCard
Season: Late December–early April; annual snowfall 67"
XC Skiing: The Farm grooms 35 kms; two-way, primarily double track with skating, some single track with skating, some skate lane alone. (They use a horse-drawn eighteenth-century oak snow roller to compact sleigh trails.) 75% Easier, 15% More Difficult, 10% Most Difficult. More flat or gentle than hilly, though there are surprises, such as Hawk Hill and Holstein Hill. Instruction in classic and skating, primarily weekends and holidays. Full rental shop. Daily trail fee. Altitude range 45'–170'.
Maps: True to form, it's illustrated, amusing, and useful.
Activities and Entertainment: On-site: snowshoe trails, pony rides, sleigh rides with Percherons Bob and Dan or one-horse open sleigh, maple sugar operation, dairy barn tours, homemade yogurt and ice cream (over 150 flavors—area motto: "Come Ski The Cow!"). Nearby: L.L. Bean in Freeport; all the attractions of a major city (Portland Art Museum and, next door, Children's Museum of Maine).
Children's Programs: Special trails, instruction, pulks, equipment, animals to admire.
Dining: For dinner, various fare within easy walking distance of PineCrest; coffee house, too. Smiling Hill Farm Snack Bar specializes in overstuffed sandwiches, chowders, and chili.
Special Nordic Distinction: You can arrange a birthday party, including use of Nate's Place (log cabin) and a horse-drawn sleigh or wagon ride. Don't forget to wear your Holstein hat.
Summary: Deep-forest feeling minutes from Maine's largest city.

Sugarloaf Ski Touring Center
Carrabassett Valley, Maine

There are private XC areas, alpine resort affiliates, trail networks that form a coherent region—but surely Sugarloaf is the only destination that's owned by a town, operated by a non-profit corporation, and managed by an alpine area. This is not only a major trail system, it also has one of the more sophisticated (solar-heated) base facilities, including the Klister Kitchen and an outdoor skating rink next door. Sugarloaf Mountain (second-highest peak in Maine) is visually dominant, but the center stands some distance from the alpine village, though connected by trail and shuttle. Much of the land is leased from the Penobscot Nation. Names are drawn from the Penobscot language; several are extremely apropos (Wachoo/Mountain) while others seem obscure (Jezhawuk/Mosquito). Trails are still evolving from fresh logging roads; one-third of the network needs only 6 inches of snow to open.

Address: R.R. 1, Box 5000, Carrabassett Valley, ME 04947
Tel/fax: (800) THE-LOAF for lodging, (800) THE-AREA or (207) 237-2000 for general information, (207) 237-6830 for XC information; fax: (207) 237-6943
e-mail: nordic@sugarloaf.com
Internet: www.sugarloaf.com
Location: West-central Maine
Airport: Portland International Jetport, 110 miles
Train: Bethel, 60 miles
Memberships and Awards: Cross Country Ski Areas Association, Maine Nordic Ski Council
Medical: Sugarloaf Clinic, 3 miles
Accommodations: The Herbert (20 minutes from the XC center) is handsome, historic, and informal (pets allowed). Built in 1918, the hotel was a wreck (237 burst water pipes) when purchased in 1982. Delightfully restored, rooms are simple but comfortable, with private baths and rubber ducks; most with Jacuzzis; no TV or phones. P.O. Box 67, Kingfield, ME 04947; (800) THE-HERB or (207) 265-2000.

Guest Capacity: 80 at The Herbert
Conference Capacity: 80
Rates: $–$$ (can include breakfast and dinner)
Credit Cards: Visa, MasterCard, American Express, Diners Club, Discover
Season: Mid-December–early April; annual snowfall 200"; 3 kms snowmaking
XC Skiing: Sugarloaf snowcat-grooms 90 kms: 40% Easier, 45% More Difficult, 15% Most Difficult, mostly two-way. At times it's better to depend on intersection signage than trail names. Seeboosis sees the most use, connecting the center and alpine base area. Long, gentle Woodabogan follows an abandoned, narrow-gauge railroad bed and the Carrabassett River. A considerable number of road crossings. Full instruction program. Good rental shop. Daily trail fee. Altitude range 1,300'–1,800'.
Maps: The brochure has excellent text; the map is complex and slightly incomplete but with a useful inset of the lodge area.
Activities and Entertainment: At center and resort: snowshoeing, ice skating, sleigh rides, sports/fitness center, microbrewery. Nearby: dog sledding, snowmobiling, Stanley Museum (of Stanley Steamer fame), Western Maine Children's Museum, Chester Greenwood Day (annual event in Farmington to honor the inventor of earmuffs).
Children's Programs: Day care, instruction, equipment.
Dining: The Herbert's Public Room is one of the best places to dine in western Maine, with a Gilded Era setting. "Heart-healthy" entrées as well as dishes such as tournedos cabernet; 100-plus wines.
Special Nordic Distinction: Maine's largest XC network has considerable diversity in both skiing and surroundings—wooded lowlands and a golf course 'twixt condos and alpine slopes.
Summary: It would be pleasant to see more alpine resorts developing *partners* like Sugarloaf Ski Touring, rather than token amenities.

Sunday River Cross Country Ski Center
Bethel, Maine

When you meet a ski area owner whose business card reads "Aspiring Eccentric," it's only natural to anticipate the unusual. Sunday River fulfills expectations most delightfully. Situated in the Mahoosuc Range near the New Hampshire border, the ski center is next door to the Sunday River Inn. Strongly family-oriented, it's run by innkeepers Steve and Peggy Wight. (Steve has the family monopoly on whimsy; Peggy, the forbearing smile.) Scenery, terrain, and forest cover are varied. Every aspect of skiing is highly professional, but enter the inn and it's like coming home.

Address: R.R. 3, P.O. Box 1688, Newry, ME 04261
Tel/fax: (207) 824-2410; fax: (207) 824-3181
e-mail: srinn@nxi.com
Internet: www.sundayriverinn.com
Location: Southwestern Maine
Airport: Portland International Jetport, 75 miles
Train: None nearby
Memberships and Awards: Cross Country Ski Areas Association, Maine Nordic Ski Council, L.L. Bean Premier Pass, *Snow Country* magazine's Top 10 XC Areas in Northeast
Medical: Bethel Area Health Center, 6 miles
Accommodations: Sunday River offers a number of lodging choices, including a four-bedroom, two-bath chalet. The inn has several upstairs rooms, most with central bathroom/shower facilities; there are even bring-your-own-sleeping-bag dorms. The beamed and paneled living room, with its larger stone fireplace, serves as an informal social center. Smoke-free environment. Ski-in/ski-out. Two-night minimum on weekends.
Guest Capacity: 75
Conference Capacity: 35
Rates: $ (includes breakfast, dinner, trail fee)
Credit Cards: Visa, MasterCard, American Express
Season: December 1–April 1; annual snowfall 120"
XC Skiing: The center has 40 kms groomed by snowcat on 23 two-way trails, mostly double-tracked with skate lane, 2 kms lighted. 40% Easier, 40% More Difficult, 20% Most Difficult. Groomed dog trail, downhill practice area, two warming shelters. Daily instruction—classic, skate; guide service, with tailored trips. There's an unusual variety of programs for kids, women, and seniors, plus Maine handicapped skiers program. Wide variety of modern rentals. Daily trail fee. Altitude range 650'–1,200'—David's Drop is aptly named, losing 400'.
Maps: Entertaining trail map, separate "Adventure Map" for the young at heart.
Activities and Entertainment: On-site: ice skating, snowshoeing, snow play, sleigh rides, historic tours; outdoor hot tub, sauna. Nearby: Sunday River Brew Pub, downhill skiing at Sunday River Ski Resort. Talk with Peggy and Steve about their Weather Sticks, which are more reliable than meteorologists and give more lead time than a Weather Rock.
Children's Programs: Tots & Parents Ski (preschool children), special trail, pulks, snow play.
Dining: Meals served buffet style; fresh breads and pies; dinner specialty New England baked chicken. Light lunch is available at the center. B.Y.O.B. For variety, the Sudbury Inn in Bethel serves fine full-course dinners at a reasonable price.
Special Nordic Distinction: An excellent learning area. Sunday River breaks the traditional "nature and granola" system of naming trails; names are drawn from logging or reflect the character and history of the land.
Summary: Sunday River is one of the most hospitable XC areas in North America—nicely flowing and innovative trails (swing, wind chimes, Cornelius the Totem Pole), the latest gear, and, above all, friendly staff. If daughter Sara is home, she makes killer brownies. Altogether, a celebration of life!

Bucksteep Manor
Washington, Massachusetts

Long famous for classical concerts in summer such as the Tanglewood Festival, the Berkshires have also been loved by literary figures such as Hawthorne, Wharton, and Melville, as well as artists including Norman Rockwell. A century ago, these mountains were the playground of wealthy industrialists, who built spacious summer retreats. Bucksteep Manor is of this era, though it was largely the creation of an Englishman, not an American. Formed from the merger of two estates—one formerly owned by the Episcopal Church, thus the stone chapel at the entrance way—today it's a 400-acre year-round resort run by the Sacco family.

Address: 885 Washington Mountain Road, Washington, MA 01223
Tel/fax: (413) 623-5535 or (800) 645-BUCK; fax (413) 623-5231
Internet: www.berkshireweb.com/bucksteep
Location: West-central Massachusetts (be sure to request a local road map)
Airport: Bradley International, 60 miles
Train: Pittsfield, 10 miles
Memberships and Awards: Cross Country Ski Areas Association
Medical: Berkshire Medical Center, 10 miles
Accommodations: Bucksteep is comfortable rather than elegant. The Manor, a pleasant building with dark-to-somber wood paneling, contains 8 of the 22 rooms; shared baths. Corner chambers have most light. Ski-in/ski-out. Two-night minimum weekends.
Guest Capacity: 80
Conference Capacity: 80
Rates: $ (includes use of trails)
Credit Cards: Visa, MasterCard, American Express, Discover
Season: Mid-December–mid-March; annual snowfall 80"
XC Skiing: Grooming on the 25-km network by a small snowcat and snowmobiles. Most of the 15 wooded routes are two-way, single track with skating lane. 40% Easier, 30% More Difficult, 30% Most Difficult. There's an excellent teaching area—with gazebo—near the ski shop (a converted barn), which is the focal point for trail dispersion. Trail names are amusing, indicating family members, friends, and dogs (Creo and Mu). Best views are north toward Middlefield from Ridge Run. Instruction in both classic and skate styles. Guide service for group tours into nearby October Mountain State Forest. Equipment rentals. Daily trail fee. Altitude range 1,500'–1,800'.
Maps: A hand-drawn photocopy handout with no contour lines; however, signage largely makes up for it.
Activities and Entertainment: On-site: sleigh rides, snowshoeing, ice skating, outdoor hot tub; live entertainment weekends in the barn, which was once a rock 'n' roll nightclub. Nearby: the National Music Center, commemorating folk and pop music, plus all the attractions noted in the Cranwell listing. The once-sleepy town of Lee (downtown is listed in the National Register of Historic Places) figures in some of Norman Rockwell's most famous paintings. You can still buy the cheapest cup of coffee in Massachusetts at Joe's Diner.
Children's Programs: Babysitting offered by arrangement, instruction, equipment.
Dining: Meals at Bucksteep (served in the Manor's restaurant, which is open to all for lunch) are unpretentious and copious. Dinner has a single entrée. No smoking until after 8:00 p.m. Full beverage license.
Special Nordic Distinction: Wintertime, but the skiing is gentle. There's one serious downhill (Mad Dog Loop), but that's about it despite 300' total elevation change. Beginners enjoy well-named Over Easy, which is both serene and very accessible from the ski shop.
Summary: Bucksteep feels very off-the-beaten-path (the Appalachian Trail runs just north and west of the resort) but is only 15 minutes from the towns of Pittsfield and Lee, as well as the Massachusetts Turnpike. It's not simply inexpensive but also thoroughly low-key friendly.

Cranwell Resort & Golf Club
Lenox, Massachusetts

Some resorts are created for a single purpose; Cranwell has already lived through an amazing variety of incarnations. Once a farm owned by Henry Ward Beecher, it has been successively a privately held and very imposing brick mansion in the Tudor style, built in the "Gilded Age"; a hunt club; and a Jesuit-run boys' prep school. Set high on a hill, with 60-mile views of the southern Berkshires, it's now a luxurious destination where cross-country skiing has been taken very seriously. Trails wind throughout the property, swinging near to almost all the dispersed accommodations. One of the more interesting architectural features is an unused cement opera hall.

Address: 55 Lee Road, Lenox, MA 02140
Tel/fax: (800) 272-6935 or (413) 637-1364; fax: (413) 637-0571
e-mail: info@cranwell.com
Internet: www.cranwell.com
Location: West-central Massachusetts
Airport: Albany, 45 miles
Train: Pittsfield, 10 miles
Memberships and Awards: Cross Country Ski Areas Association
Medical: Berkshire Medical Center, 5 miles
Accommodations: Ninety-five deluxe rooms are situated in several restored buildings on this 1894 estate. All have private baths and are individually decorated, with modern conveniences such as in-room coffee makers, hair dryers, and ironing boards. Ski-in/ski-out. No minimum stay.
Guest Capacity: 200
Conference Capacity: 200
Rates: $–$$ (includes continental breakfast and use of trails)
Credit Cards: Visa, MasterCard, American Express, Diners Club, Carte Blanche
Season: Mid-December–mid-March (perhaps a little optimistic); annual snowfall 100"; 2 kms of snowmaking
XC Skiing: The resort uses a major snowcat to groom 15 kms of two-way tracked trail plus skate lanes, set on 380 acres. 45% Easier, 45% More Difficult, 10% Most Difficult. Almost all of the 11 trails are less than 1 km long, with the Cranwell perimeter loop as the major exception (4.5 kms); a number are named after earlier owners of the property. This is fine beginner-to-intermediate terrain, and it gives the lie to assumptions that golf course skiing has to be wind-exposed. At least half the skiing passes through or alongside woods (and, incidentally, beside several gazebos). Snowmaking takes place near the mansion, and, though this is open land, the tradeoffs are good downhill practice and wonderful views. Daily instruction available. Modern rental fleet. Daily trail fee. Altitude range 1,100'–1,220'.
Maps: Nicely illustrated, on reverse of XC brochure.
Activities and Entertainment: On-site: indoor golf, fitness center, snowshoeing, tubing. Recreational and cultural choices nearby are legion: alpine, tubing, tobogganing, ice skating, sleigh rides, snowmobiling, horseback riding at Undermountain Farm; great antiquing regionally, chamber music concerts in Lenox, the Norman Rockwell Museum in Stockbridge. For something completely different, try glass blowing at the Berkshire Center for Contemporary Glass in West Stockbridge, or trace your family's history at the National Archives and Records Information Center in Pittsfield.
Children's Programs: Instruction, rentals, snow play.
Dining: The Wyndhurst Restaurant has a fine and wide-ranging menu, including delicious roast of baby lamb, plus a good wine list. Choose the light-filled Sun Room for breakfast. No smoking in restaurants.
Special Nordic Distinction: For a small network, terrain is surprisingly varied. Add snowmaking, and the resort has perhaps more consistent skiing than anywhere else in southern New England.
Summary: Cranwell is not just a convenient getaway for visitors from Boston, Hartford, and New York City, it is a historic, romantic, and remarkably affordable destination for any skier.

Boyne Nordican
Boyne Falls, Michigan

Boyne Nordican reflects the passion for skiing of long-time director Lou Awodey, a PSIA nordic examiner (one who trains the instructors) who maintains a sense of humor. The center has a separate building and individual character. Enter and you'll catch the aroma of cappuccino; head out the door and into the woods; or just sit, chat, relax. A particular treat is to take a rest break at Vojin's Hut or the Hunde-Hütte. Sixty percent of visitors are women, about the same percent as Nordican's staff. XC skiers enjoy visiting nearby Boyne City for everything from bookstore-browsing to good local beer.

Address: P.O. Box 19, Boyne Falls, MI 49713
Tel/fax: (800) GO-BOYNE or (616) 549-6088 ext. 6088; fax: (616) 549-6094
e-mail: lawodey@unnet.com
Internet: www.skinordic.org/boyne
Location: Northwestern Lower Peninsula
Airport: Traverse City, 60 miles
Train: None nearby
Memberships and Awards: Cross Country Ski Areas Association, Great Lakes Nordic Ski Council, *Snow Country* magazine's Top 10 North American Trail Systems at Downhill Resorts
Medical: Northern Michigan Hospital, 15 miles
Accommodations: Wolverine-Dilworth Inn in nearby Boyne City is a refurbished, Victorian downtown hotel built during the region's lumbering era, with 26 rooms and suites (kitchenettes), bar, and several dining options. Registered historic landmark. Two-night minimum weekends. 300 Water Street, Boyne City, MI 49712; (616) 582-7388.
Guest Capacity: 68
Conference Capacity: 68
Rates: $–$$
Credit cards: Visa, MasterCard, American Express, Discover
Season: Early December–mid-March; annual snowfall 120"; 3 kms snowmaking
XC Skiing: Boyne has 35 kms of tracks with skate lanes, 3 kms lit; one-third flat, one-third rolling, one-third "world-class hilly," spread over eight trails. Skating lanes run everywhere, most with single track. If you thought Midwest golf courses were boring, prepare for revelation. Begin with Pancake, test yourself on Twister, and graduate to the 15-km Grand Tour. Top-flight grooming. And true to Lou's puckish humor, you'll ski by "Heritage Park," an informal but historic collection of ski tows and snowmaking equipment from the past 50 years. Excellent rental, retail, and demo equipment. Daily trail fee. Altitude range 600'–1,050'.
Maps: Simple handout, with an introduction to Boyne Nordican on the reverse.
Activities and Entertainment: On-site: snowshoeing and rentals, outdoor ice skating. Nearby: sledding and skating at Avalanche Preserve in Boyne City, and a walking tour of historic Boyne City (70 years after opening, Herb's Super Service gas station is now a real estate office). XC skiers enjoy Boyne River Brewing Company (smoke-free; nice unfiltered, low-carbonation ales).
Children's Programs: Special instruction, day care at alpine area, pulks.
Dining: Try Stafford's One Water Street in Boyne City, 10 minutes from the resort, on the shore of Lake Charlevoix. It has a Victorian decor (though built in 1985); dinners feature a "Michigan Heartland Menu," but also salmon, venison, bison.
Special Nordic Distinction: XC has real stature at Boyne Mountain; expect this to evolve even more. There are special workshops, telemarking, demonstrations, and nature tours. Ask Lou about skiing in Australia and playing in a jazz combo. He's also the only Boyne Mountain staff person with a beard.
Summary: Whether you're a downhiller intrigued by telemarking or a track purist, this is a fine place to vacation midweek. The cordiality needs no improvement.

Crystal Mountain Resort
Thompsonville, Michigan

Fifteen-hundred-acre Crystal Mountain has a secluded setting (one stoplight in the county) and rarefied reputation. Architecturally attractive and physically cohesive, it has been selected by L.L. Bean to join their XC *and* alpine Premier Pass programs. Family-owned Crystal welcomes children as few places do. Possibly geology influences the pervasive playful quality among the resort's activities and staff—it's built on a huge glacial-deposited sand hill. If your interests extend to visual and experiential art, snowshoe through the Michigan Legacy Art Park, whose features are also placed along Flying Squirrel and Hawk Ridge XC trails.

Address: M-115, Thompsonville, MI 49683
Tel/fax: (800) 968-7686 or (616) 378-2000; fax: (616) 378-4592
e-mail: info@crystalmtn.com
Internet: www.crystalmtn.com
Location: Northwestern Lower Peninsula
Airport: Traverse City, 32 miles
Train: None nearby
Memberships and Awards: Cross Country Ski Areas Association, Great Lakes Nordic Ski Council, Fischer Revolution Cross Country Ski Center, L.L. Bean Premier Pass Program, *Snow Country* magazine's Top 10 XC Ski Resorts in Midwest
Medical: Paul Oliver Memorial Hospital, 15 miles
Accommodations: Choose from 217 studios, suites, condos, and vacation homes. The Pinehurst Condos are very attractive (studio or two-bedroom configurations, full kitchen, fireplace, Jacuzzi baths), two minutes from the center, and right on beginning trail Otter Loop (ski-in/ski-out), which is lit until 10 nightly. Non-smoking rooms available. Two-night minimum weekends and holidays.
Guest Capacity: 1,200
Conference Capacity: 300
Rates: $–$$ (package includes use of trails)
Credit Cards: Visa, MasterCard, American Express, Discover

Season: Early December–early April; annual snowfall 180"
XC Skiing: 35 kms (12 trails) spread over hundreds of acres, with 6 kms lighted. Virtually everything is single-tracked with a skate lane; most is one-way. 33% Easier, 33% More Difficult, 33% Most Difficult. Grooming is consistently excellent, though the snowcat driver isn't a skier! Almost without exception, easier trails are on golf courses (customary at Michigan alpine ski affiliates), with the more advanced paths climbing through hardwood forest. Best views: the Betsie (corruption of French *Bec aux Sais*) River Valley from Aspen. Full instruction range. Daily trail fee includes lift access to Badger Pass, which feeds the more advanced trails. Altitude range 820'–1,200'.
Maps: Very useful, graphically relating XC to the rest of the resort.
Activities and Entertainment: On-site: alpine skiing, snowshoeing (separate trails), sleigh rides, ice skating, indoor pool, fitness center, and whirlpool. The urban delights of Traverse City are 40 minutes away (music, theater, factory outlet shopping).
Children's Programs: Child care at Piglet's Place is first rate. Private instruction, rentals, babysitting, special narrow track, pulks.
Dining: Wildflower Restaurant in Crystal's main lodge is small, pleasant, and moderately priced. Beef, seafood, and pasta are good; nice selection of mostly domestic wines.
Special Nordic Distinction: Most media attention goes to Screaming Eagle, a 3.9-km expert route with Michigan's first Double Black Diamond rating, but almost all trails close to the center are flat-to-gentle. Recent additions include a classic-only trail (Stride Right) and low-snow grooming.
Summary: Competes with Silver Star, B.C., as the most friendly alpine-based resort around—warm and genuine.

Crystal Mountain Resort, Michigan

Cross Country Ski Headquarters
Roscommon, Michigan

Bob and Lynne Frye have created one of the most engaging cross-country areas around; founded in 1973, it's also one of the oldest. Trails are very user-friendly, staff are entertaining and informed. This is a great place to play with new equipment for free before you buy; they are among the top retailers anywhere for gear and clothing. In fact, Cross Country Ski Headquarters is simply a great place to play. It's particularly well suited for inexperienced skiers, popular with women, and strongly committed to introducing local children (and their parents) to the sport. Check their newspaper, *Drifting Times*, for events, sales, equipment reviews, and the Fryes' "style."

Address: 9435 N. Cut Road, Roscommon, MI 48653-9366
Tel/fax: (800) 832-2663 or (517) 821-6661; fax: (517) 821-5868
e-mail: skibones@aol.com
Internet: www.cross-country-ski.com
Location: North-central Lower Peninsula
Airport: Midland–Bay City–Saginaw, 72 miles
Train: None nearby
Memberships and Awards: Cross Country Ski Areas Association, Great Lakes Nordic Ski Council
Medical: Grayling Mercy Hospital, 14 miles
Accommodations: Springbrook Inn is 20 minutes away. Eight pleasant rooms with separate design themes; the Western Room has Jacuzzi, waterbed, fireplace. Tanning booth. No minimum stay. P.O. Box 390, Prudenville, MI 48651; (517) 366-6347 or (800) 424-0218.
Guest Capacity: 16 at Springbrook Inn
Conference Capacity: None
Rates: $$ (includes breakfast)
Credit Cards: Visa and MasterCard
Season: Thanksgiving–March 30; annual snowfall 122"
XC Skiing: 18 kms are snowcat-groomed on eight trails, mixing double and single track, all with a skate lane. Largely one-way; longest trail 8 kms, 4-km lantern-lit trail open Friday and Saturday nights. 60% Easier (gentle terrain courtesy of the last Ice Age), 30% More Difficult, 10% Most Difficult, but hills have good runouts. Ski to Trapper's Cabin for cocoa. Trails predominantly flow through modest-sized forest. Views are limited due to lack of major hills. Connector to The Odder's Den—sip tea and enjoy handcrafted wood and clay products. Skiers have to cross a county road to reach most trails—watch the traffic! Daily trail fee, but it's the lowest among significant Midwestern areas. Altitude range 1,100'–1,160'.
Maps: Simple photocopied handout, with contour lines indicating hills.
Activities and Entertainment: On-site: snowshoeing rentals and trail. You can rent everything needed for ice fishing next door at the Sports Barn. Nearby: alpine skiing 8 miles away; great sledding and good views just up the road at Pioneer Hill, which lies along a continental divide. Shoot pool down the street at Ely's Roadhouse (tobacco products heavily favored); enjoy concerts at Kirtland College.
Children's Programs: Short, tracked trail (Dragon Back), including hills, behind the center. Equipment, instruction, pulks; baby-changing stations in both men's and women's bathrooms.
Dining: Excellent and copious breakfasts, good dinners and private atmosphere at Springbrook (open to public Friday and Saturday nights), with liquor license. Closer to the center is Ron's Restaurant, with good home-made soups and fresh breads (no liquor license). XC Ski Headquarters serves soups and sandwiches.
Special Nordic Distinction: Particularly comfortable for women; special skate clinic taught by women. Free clinics Saturday afternoon. This the home of Ski Bones, a unique, edible-looking ski clamp. Coming soon: snowmaking!
Summary: You'll enjoy the skiing *and* the people. It's an insuperable challenge to leave without at least one small useful purchase.

Garland
Lewiston, Michigan

Garland has long been one of the leading golf resorts in the Midwest, 72 holes and growing. Now it's making the moves to become the leading cross-country resort in the Midwest. All the fundamentals are here: magnificent grounds spread over 3,500 acres, vast log lodge, and first-class facilities. The major real estate element offers very varied lodging. Winter staff are experienced, and the resort has some of the most creative programs anywhere. This is not the place if you're looking for hills, but it's a delight for beginners, lovers, and sybarites.

Address: HCR 1, Box 364M, Lewiston, MI 49756
Tel/fax: (800) 968-0042 or (517) 786-2211; fax: (517) 786-2254
Internet: www.garlandusa.com
Location: North-central Lower Peninsula
Airport: Traverse City, 90 miles
Train: None nearby
Memberships and Awards: Cross Country Ski Areas Association, Great Lakes Nordic Ski Council, AAA Four Diamond
Medical: Montmorency Medical Clinic, 8 miles
Accommodations: Though you can rent a log chalet, upstairs rooms at the lodge facing onto the fairways are highly desirable—step outside onto a private balcony, taste the wind, and retreat into your own Jacuzzi. Non-smoking rooms available. Ski-in/ski-out. Weekends two-night minimum.
Guest Capacity: 500
Conference Capacity: 400
Rates: $$$–$$$$
Credit Cards: Visa, MasterCard, American Express, Diners Club, Discover
Season: End November–mid-March; annual snowfall 150"
XC Skiing: There is no tough skiing here, so estimate 80% Easiest and 20% More Difficult. 40 kms of snowcat-maintained trail, groomed for skating and single track. Though XC operations began in 1987, Garland didn't fully commit to winter operations until 1996; then they jumped in, expanding and refining, building trails instead of using golf cart paths, adding more lighting (2-plus kms), staffing, programs, and rentals, and building a sledding/downhill practice hill. They recently added a snow play area for skiers, with small hills, turns, and challenges. One trail serpentines through dense spruce forest, utterly unlike the stately rows of planted trees around the golf courses. Daily trail fee. Altitude range 1,180'–1,230'.
Maps: A handy pocket-size description, including distances and difficulty ratings but no contour lines.
Activities and Entertainment: Garland is a self-contained resort. On-site there is snowshoeing, a snow play hill, massage (XC director Larry Kinney is also a masseur), catch/filet/fry-'em-on-the-spot ice fishing, skating, sleigh rides, snowmobiling, indoor and outdoor Jacuzzis. If you're lucky, you may see a pair of bald eagles. Nearby: alpine skiing 30 minutes away, around Gaylord.
Children's Programs: Equipment, pulks, snow play area; babysitting by reservation; special ski instruction.
Dining: Garland equals any place for gastronomic creativity. Not only is Herman's Restaurant in the lodge excellent (wild game specialty, a nice list of French and California wines), but Zhivago Nights are among the Midwest's most famous XC "events." A pair of Belgian draft horses carry guests on a 40-minute ride to an old hunting lodge for a five-course feast. Assemble a party of 16, and Garland will devise a private banquet, complete with minstrel.
Special Nordic Distinction: The seriously noncompetitive Gourmet Glide now passes through an elk and whitetail deer game preserve; five trailside buffets (four indoors) along 10 km, each with different tastes and treats.
Summary: Garland combines magnitude with good taste. The resort makes no claim to being a wilderness experience, but it is a one-of-a-kind romantic getaway.

Gaylord Region
Michigan

Gaylord has the largest concentration of both lighted and groomed trails in Michigan, all within about a 30-minute radius, and most of them resort-based. The town is readily accessible from the south, just off Interstate 75 and little more than an hour's drive from the airport in Traverse City. The last glacial epoch left high ridges and long views. Gaylord hosts entertaining events, such as the annual February Winterfest. California visitors will feel comfortably self-indulgent because this is dedicated Jacuzzi country.

Address: Gaylord Area Convention and Tourism Bureau, P.O. Box 3069, Gaylord, MI 49735
Tel/fax: (800) 345-8621 (nationwide and Canada) or (517) 732-4000, fax: (517) 732-7990
Internet: www.gaylord.mich.com
Location: Northwestern Lower Peninsula
Airport: Traverse City, 60 miles
Train: None nearby
Medical: Otsego Memorial Hospital in Gaylord
Accommodations: Marsh Ridge Golf and Nordic Ski Resort offers wide variety. Great for a group: four-bedroom Scandinavian Lodge has a handsome interior, full kitchen, living room with gas fireplace, two bathrooms, views (sadly, the only building without a hot tub). Elsewhere on property: restaurant, open-air swimming pool, six-person whirlpool, exercise and tanning facilities. Non-smoking rooms available. Two-night minimum weekends. P.O. Box 1367, Gaylord, MI 49734 (800) 743-7529 (U.S. and Canada).
Guest Capacity: Several thousand beds in region's motels, cottages, B&Bs, resorts
Conference Capacity: 1,000 at Treetops Sylvan
Rates: $ (based on five or more at Scandinavian Lodge)
Credit Cards: Visa, MasterCard, American Express, Diners Club, Discover
Season: Mid-December–early March, possibly longer at some areas; annual snowfall 180"

XC Skiing: There are four cross-country areas locally:
- *Marsh Ridge Resort:* 20 kms, 4 kms lit; mix of diagonal-only and classic/skate trails. Primarily golf course, but there's a lively lilt from ridge to lowland. Rentals, instruction. Daily fee. (800) 743-PLAY.
- *Michaywé Resort (at alpine area):* 14 kms almost entirely diagonal stride; easy, pretty trail along the Au Sable River; rentals. Donation. (800) 322-6636.
- *Treetops Sylvan Resort (at alpine area):* 20 kms, 5 kms lit, predominantly classic. A lot of fun, especially for intermediates. Rentals, instruction, great trail names, nice nordic building. Daily fee. (800) 444-6711.
- *Wilderness Valley:* 56 kms (about half skate/classic mix), instruction, rentals. By far the largest network, with a lovely remote feeling and some tough trails. Daily fee. (616) 585-7090.

Maps: New handy-size map/guide covers all local trails.
Activities and Entertainment: In addition to the customary range of recreation, you can swim, ice skate, or watch high-school hockey at the Otsego County Sportsplex, shop downtown in Swiss Village–motif Gaylord, walk through Coca-Cola history at the Bottle Cap Museum, take part in a Murder Mystery weekend at Marsh Ridge (gather 40 friends and reserve the event), and enjoy the event-filled Winterfest.
Dining: The Big Buck Brewery & Steakhouse in town dishes up meals and humor together. They produce a deep-textured, tangy, dark root beer.
Special Nordic Distinction: An unusual trail mix of the civilized (resorts) and the wild (on far-flung routes), all very accessible to one another.
Summary: The region is in a snowbelt and includes an extraordinary topographic mix. It's an invitation to entertainment.

LakeView Hills Country Resort
Lewiston, Michigan

LakeView Hills is a tiny resort in major transition. Founder Shirley Chapoton may expand in several directions, including golf and condominiums. Comstock Hill (on which the inn is perched) was once the site of both a fire tower and a dramatic toboggan run, both built in the 1930s. The single current building was cedar-built and completed in 1989. Right now, it's a charming and occasionally unorthodox country inn (somewhat difficult to differentiate from a B&B) with splendid views from the observatory atop the lodge. As for skiing, terrain and trails are unusually challenging. And though most ski areas are multi-season operations, this is perhaps the only one that reopens come spring as an elegantly formal croquet club.

Address: P.O. Box 365, Lewiston, MI 49756
Tel/fax: (517) 786-2000
e-mail: info@lakeviewhills.net
Internet: www.lakeviewhills.net
Location: North-central Lower Peninsula
Airport: Traverse City, 85 miles
Train: None nearby
Memberships and Awards: Cross Country Ski Areas Association, Great Lakes Nordic Ski Council, United States Croquet Association
Medical: Montmorency Medical Clinic, 5 miles
Accommodations: 14 rooms commemorate Northern Michigan history, each with individual decor—Victorian style, Tudor, colonial, wicker, oak, and walnut. Bedrooms are furnished with antiques, cable TV, chamber pots, and private baths. Ski-in/ski-out. Two-night minimum.
Guest Capacity: 30
Conference Capacity: 30
Rates: $$ (includes breakfast and use of trails)
Credit Cards: Visa, MasterCard, Discover
Season: Christmas holidays–end February; annual snowfall 122"
XC Skiing: While theoretically 33% Easier, 33% More Difficult, 33% Most Difficult, LakeView Hills has a remarkable amount of tough skiing on 22 kms of snowmobile-groomed trail, spread over six routes. Except for one arterial that allows both skating and classic, all trails are built for diagonal stride. A mix of ridges and valleys endows the area with a number of nosedives, though problems come as much from narrow trails and limited runouts as from loss of elevation. It's wise to observe the proper direction of travel, as meeting someone coming the other way around a downhill bend can be overstimulating (there speaks the voice of experience). The deciduous forest allows almost constant views of both interior valleys and far lakes. Access road crossings. Instruction on weekends; rentals available at the Ski Hut, a moment's walk from the inn. Daily trail fee. Altitude range 1,239'–1,442'.
Maps: A diverting hand-drawn, photocopied handout is available. Routes are labeled C (for "Piece of Cake"), S (for "So-So"), and R (for "Radical").
Activities and Entertainment: On-site: library, hot tub, sauna, Small fitness center, good conversation; downhill skiing may be added soon. Nearby: Gaylord is about 35 minutes away, with alpine, museums, shopping.
Children's Programs: LakeView isn't designed or operated for a family experience, but it's a great place for couples with reasonable skiing ability.
Dining: Breakfast specialties include home-baked quiche and banana pancakes; snacks are always available in the kitchen. For dinner, Lewiston has pleasant pizza places and a good steakhouse 10 minutes north, but it's no match for Garland, about the same driving time to the south.
Special Nordic Distinction: LakeView Hills is the highest point in lower Michigan; consequently, these are among the trickiest trails in this part of the state.
Summary: It's entertaining and inevitable to compare LakeView Hills with near neighbor Garland. Both are entrancing, though for different reasons; each wishes it could arrange a small topographic exchange.

Shanty Creek
Bellaire, Michigan

Shanty Creek resulted from the merger of two alpine-based ski areas, Schuss Village and Summit Village. Despite differences in altitude and architecture, they complement one another. This is serious snow country, with frequent lake effect dumps. Shanty Creek skiing exploits that fact in distinctive ways. For instance, golf course routes often depart from cart paths in order to reach the best terrain and snow. Another unusual trait is three major access points to the trails. The Nordic Center is located at Schuss, the lower-elevation trailhead; the building includes rentals, instruction, and day care. Instruction is also available at aptly named Summit. A third trailhead has no services. Summit views are dominated by Lake Bellaire in the background, and a large green golf ball–shaped water tower in the foreground.

Address: 1 Shanty Creek Road, Bellaire, MI 49615
Tel/fax: (800) 678-4111 or (616) 533-8621; fax: (616) 533-7001
e-mail: info@shantycreek.com
Internet: www.shantycreek.com
Location: Northwestern Lower Peninsula
Airport: Traverse City, 35 miles
Train: None nearby
Memberships and Awards: Cross Country Country Ski Areas Association, Great Lakes Nordic Ski Council, *Snow Country* magazine's Top 10 XC Resorts in the Midwest, *Ski* magazine's Top Three Resorts in Midwest
Medical: Burns Clinic, 3 miles
Accommodations: Rooms in the Summit Conference Center are pleasantly convenient to the main lodge amenities, including full kitchen and Jacuzzis. Non-smoking rooms available. Trailhead is a minute's walk away.
Guest Capacity: 2,000
Conference Capacity: 1,000
Rates: $
Credit Cards: Visa, MasterCard, American Express, Diners Club, Carte Blanche, Discover
Season: End November–late March; annual snowfall 200"

XC Skiing: The 30-km system spreads over 12 trails, with the latter split between Schuss and Summit. 40% Easier, 40% More Difficult, 20% Most Difficult. Everything is snowcat-groomed two-way single track with a skate lane. Among the toughies is Mountain Creek Trail, with one of the most remarkable sequences of ridge and gully in North America—a Black Diamond, but thrilling rather than terrorizing. There's delightful flow over golf courses, with more advanced routes in deciduous forest. Watch the many road crossings, and don't hit the turkeys. Slopes are almost undiscovered by telemarkers. Daily trail fee, which includes limited use of lifts. Altitude range 675'–1,115'.
Maps: Cross-country trails are on reverse of alpine map.
Activities and Entertainment: On-site: 43 alpine slopes (Shanty Creek sometimes builds up its own mountain), ice skating, snowshoeing, bonfire sleigh rides, fitness center and spa (what is aromatherapy?), live entertainment weekends, various shops plus hair salon at Summit. Nordic Ski and Feast Festival. Music hotbed (especially jazz) Traverse City is less than an hour's drive; there's a casino en route.
Children's Programs: Day care at both Villages; babysitting, rentals.
Dining: Northwest Michigan planked whitefish is the specialty of the Summit's Lakeview Dining Room. Dare to try one of Michigan's own wines. Ivan's Mountainside Grill at Schuss serves regional cuisine.
Special Nordic Distinction: Summit may be the only American hilltop ski resort; both XC and alpine trails head downhill. Shanty Creek compensates by running frequent shuttle buses between the Villages, with stops at several trailside points, so you don't have to spend the afternoon regaining altitude lost in the morning.
Summary: Views, skiing, lodging, staff, and dining create a quality product.

Bearskin Lodge
Grand Marais, Minnesota

It's simply not accurate to say that the magnificent Gunflint Trail recreation area is lost in the Great White North; nor is it quite true that there are more moose than people. It's not uncivilized, merely remote—and for skiers from the Twin Cities of Minneapolis/St. Paul, seeking solitude and romance, these attributes are a boon. Bearskin Lodge manages to blend the best of wilderness (beauty, serenity) and civilization (fine dining, not just baths but hot tubs). Along with Maplelag, it's the best known XC area in the state. Owner-operators Dave and Barb Tuttle are expatriate Kentuckians who have been running Bearskin virtually since leaving college. (She did work for a time as a speech therapist, while Dave was persuading her to move north and marry him.) They bought the resort in 1973 (it had been a summer fishing operation since 1925) and started building trails in 1975. The whole region has been heavily glaciated, which adds to skiing fun and landscape variety. This is boreal forest—virgin white pine, aspen, birch—with an active wildlife population, including the shy timber wolf. On the ride from Grand Marais, avoid close encounters with moose.

Address: 124 E. Bearskin Road, Grand Marais, MN 55604-9701
Tel/fax: (800) 338-4170 or (218) 388-2292; fax: (218) 388-4410
e-mail: ski@bearskin.com
Internet: www.bearskin.com
Location: Northeastern Minnesota
Airport: Duluth, 140 miles
Train: None nearby
Memberships and Awards: Cross Country Ski Areas Association, Gunflint Trail Association, *Snow Country* magazine's Top 10 XC Areas in the Midwest
Medical: Cook County Hospital, 27 miles
Accommodations: Lodging is in handsome handcrafted lakeside log cabins, kept fastidiously clean, all with kitchens. Long-time guests get possessive, return to the same

cabin every year. Ski-in/ski-out. Two-night minimum weekends.
Guest Capacity: 70
Conference Capacity: 50
Rates: $-$$$ (includes instruction, use of trails)
Credit Cards: Visa, MasterCard, Discovery
Season: Thanksgiving–April 1; annual snowfall 125"
XC Skiing: Dave snowcat-grooms 70 kms in cooperation with Golden Eagle Lodge (some claim he pats errant flakes into place by hand)—single track plus skating lane, double track plus skating, and some double track alone; more one-way than two-way. 25% Easier, 50% More Difficult, 25% Most Difficult. 1.5 kms lighted. Four warming shelters. Road crossing. Daily instruction in skating and classic styles. Excellent rental inventory. Daily trail fee. Altitude range 1,750'–2,000'.
Maps: It's among the best around—detailed, graphic, with precise trail descriptions, a section on geology, even an explanation of how to read contour lines.
Activities and Entertainment: On-site: snowshoeing, ice skating, hot tubs. Nearby: sleigh rides, dog sledding at Gunflint Lodge.
Children's Programs: Equipment.
Dining: Bearskin benefits from a chef rather than a cook. Examples: walleye in parchment, chicken in phyllo. Beer and wine available.
Special Nordic Distinction: Classic (so to speak) Midwestern skiing but on a grander scale than most. Trails have been very well thought out, sinuous at times but with good runouts on downhills. If you want an advanced trail, try Bear Cub World Cup. Try snowcat "co-piloting" (learn about these wondrous machines' care and complexities).
Summary: A grand destination, with *very* reliable Lake Effect snow. Though most visitors are Minnesotans, the Tuttles never discriminate against out-of-staters. (Hear that sweet Kentucky drawl and you'll know why.)

See color photos, page 92

Bemidji Region
Minnesota

Bemidji is a community committed to XC skiing—or more accurately, to making the sport accessible and *fun* for both visitors and residents. There are six nearby distinctive trail systems that welcome the public, totaling more than 80 kms and another 50 kms 30 miles from town. It's also home to the Minnesota Finlandia Ski Marathon, one of the longest-established major races in the Midwest. Held each February, the Finlandia is distinctive for being a grand event as much as a competition, including a Family Funday.

Address: Bemidji Tourist Information Center, P.O. Box 850, Bemidji, MN 56619
Tel/fax: (800) 458-2223; fax: (218) 759-0810
e-mail: gayle@visitbemidji.com
Internet: www.visitbemidji.com
Location: North-central Minnesota
Airport: Bemidji/Beltrami, 3 miles from town
Train: None nearby
Medical: North Country Regional Hospital, in town
Accommodations: Bemidji has several properties catering especially to XC skiers, such as Ruttger's Birchmont Lodge (218/751-1630), with its own tracked trail. Newest among them is Jerry and Barbara Vanek's Beltrami Shores Bed and Breakfast, set on 17 acres above a lake. Three uniquely decorated bedrooms each have private bath; breakfasts are both tasty and hearty (wild rice pancakes, stuffed French toast). There's direct backcountry ski/snowshoe access to the Three Island County Park trails, or ½ mile by car to a trailhead. Two-night minimum. Non-smoking environment. Route 5, Box 201, Bemidji, MN 56601; (888) 746-7373 or (218) 586-2518.
Guest Capacity: 700 in region
Conference Capacity: Various facilities
Rates: $-$$
Season: Late November–early April; annual snowfall around 48"
XC Skiing: Minnesota State Ski Pass required. Altitude range 1,350'-1,550".
• *Buena Vista*: 25 km, skate and classic, snow-cat groomed. Substantial hills run over a continental divide (Hudson's Bay–Gulf of Mexico). Host site for the Minnesota Finlandia, home of the annual Logging Days festival in February.
• *C.V. Hobson Memorial Forest*: 7 flowing kms, all double-tracked. Unheated bathrooms.
• *Lake Bemidji State Park*: 11 mostly easy double-tracked kms, with heated bathrooms. Candlelit night tours. One nasty road crossing. State park vehicle permit required.
• *Montebello Trail*: 4.5 easy kms right in town; lighted; warming house; particularly popular among young local skiers (single track and skating).
• *Movil Maze*: 14 enticingly technical skating-plus-classic kms; unheated bathrooms.
• *Three Island County Park*: 20 gentle kms for skating and classic along the lovely Turtle River; two trailheads with portable toilets.
Maps: The Ski Club produces a clever and complete product.
Activities and Entertainment: Polar Daze in January, downhilling at Buena Vista, snowshoeing, ice fishing, ice skating, curling, art, music, and athletic events at Bemidji State University, local casinos, snowmobiling.
Dining: Union Station provides the best meals in town, specializing in maplewood-grilled meats, poultry, and seafood.
Special Nordic Distinction: Bemidji Area Cross-Country Ski Club is an all-volunteer organization that maintains the trails in the area. So what else is needed in a community devoted to winter? Somewhere to get your skis! The Home Place Bike and Ski Shop has skiing staff who know the region, conditions, *and* the equipment they handle.
Summary: When winter visits, you can be bitter, fatalistic—or follow the Bemidji example by embracing the season.

Cascade Lodge
Lutsen, Minnesota

Imagine the vastness of the Great Lakes, ocean-like but without the scent of salt. Then visualize the Sawtooths, a mountain range glacier-ground to ridges, still rising 1,200 feet above the lake. Cascade Lodge lies between the two, at a location with immediate highway access, gives Superior views (the very best are from Lookout Mountain, above the lodge) and has trails leading out the door. Cascade is a major player along the North Shore Mountains Ski Trail, comprising around 200 kilometers of regularly groomed routes; it's also part of a lodge-to-lodge system, where you do the skiing and your hosts transfer the luggage. Gene and Laurene Glader purchased the lodge in 1981 and have imbued it with genuine friendliness. They've also been instrumental in expanding and refining local trails, and purchasing a state-of-the-art European-made hydrostatic-drive snowcat with power tiller (the very best kind).

Address: 3719 W. Highway 61, Lutsen, MN 55612
Tel/fax: (800) 322-9543 or (218) 387-1112; fax: (218) 387-1113
e-mail: cascade@cascadelodgemn.com
Internet: www.cascadelodgemn.com
Location: Northeastern Minnesota
Airport: Duluth, 100 miles
Train: None nearby
Memberships and Awards: Cross Country Ski Areas Association, Mobil Two Star, AAA Double-Diamond
Medical: Cook County Hospital, 9 miles
Accommodations: Guests can stay in the lodge, Cascade House, motel units, or a cluster of cabins, six of which are handsome log structures; #12 is a gem, with kitchenette and Jacuzzi, set beside Cascade Creek. Ski-in/ski-out. No smoking in lodge. No minimum stay.
Guest Capacity: 110
Conference Capacity: 40
Rates: $–$$
Credit Cards: Visa, MasterCard, American Express
Season: Mid-December–mid-April; annual snowfall 75". If snow is lean at lake level, Gene can arrange round-trip shuttle to higher points.
XC Skiing: 65 kms of trail are mostly double-tracked, some single-tracked, primarily two-way. 45% Easier, 45% More Difficult, 10% Most Difficult. Trails to the east of Cascade River may be maintained by a less sophisticated snowcat than those around the lodge. Road crossings. Instruction in classic technique by reservation. Rental and retail. Minnesota State Ski Pass required. Altitude range 605'–1,881'.
Maps: On one side is an overview map of the North Shore network, an inset of the lodge area, and an introduction to the region; on the reverse is an unusually clear topo map. You needn't be concerned about getting disoriented, as marking and signage on the trails are good.
Activities and Entertainment: On-site: snowshoeing, snow play, frozen cascades. Nearby: alpine (Lutsen Mountains), ice fishing on local lakes, Kah-Nee-Tah Gallery just down the road, a variety of intriguing shops and galleries 10 minutes away in Grand Marais (visit the Blue Water Cafe for a meal or just good coffee; it's "the meeting place in Grand Marais"), snowmobiling, and the Grand Portage Casino.
Children's Programs: Instruction, equipment, pulks, sledding.
Dining: Steaks and broiled walleye pike are favorites at the lodge restaurant, pastas can be excellent, and fruit pies are delectable. Children's menu. B.Y.O.B.
Special Nordic Distinction: A three-sided shelter on Lookout Mountain has fine views of Lake Superior's changing moods to the south and Cascade Mountain to the north. "Joel + Amanda = True Love" is inscribed on wall.
Summary: This part of Minnesota provides scenic beauty as well as great skiing. Cascade Lodge is a natural nexus for enjoying North Shore trails or driving up to the Gunflint for a day.

See color photos, page 93

Golden Eagle Lodge & Nordic Ski Center
Grand Marais, Minnesota

The first thing to note along the Golden Eagle Lodge driveway is a sign, "Caution: Mosquito Nesting Sanctuary," which hints at the humorous nature of hospitality here. Hosts Dan and Teresa Baumann are pleasant and intriguing. Dan's family bought the small run-down fishing resort in 1976, when he was just 15. They spent years renovating before adding their own buildings. In 1980 the Baumanns began year-round operations, making the decision to attract skiers rather than the lucrative snowmobile market. All the Baumanns enjoy winter, including three children who often accompany their father grooming. Golden Eagle is family-oriented and low-key about everything but skiing. Dan has designed some very interesting trails, exploring a series of eskers to form up/down flow. As for manmade adaptations, part of Old Logging Camp Trail is a railroad bed, ideal for beginners. Glaciation has left behind the spectacular cliffs on the south side of many lakes. Among interesting sights: "Old Man's Beard" (a form of lichen) hanging from trees, and bald eagles.

Address: Gunflint Trail, 468 Clearwater Road, Grand Marais, MN 55604
Tel/fax: (800) 346-2203 or (218) 388-2203; fax: (218) 388-9417
e-mail: ccski@golden-eagle.com
Internet: www.golden-eagle.com
Location: Far northeastern Minnesota
Airport: Duluth, 148 miles
Train: None nearby
Memberships and Awards: Cross Country Ski Areas Association, Gunflint Trail Association
Medical: Cook County Hospital, 33 miles (Dan is a senior E.M.T. and fire chief)
Accommodations: The Baumanns built most of the nine pretty lakeside cabins. Most have showers rather than bath; all have kitchens. Dan does a lot of the interior finish work. Home-made cookies await on checking in. Two barrier-free cabins. Ski-in/ski-out. Several non-smoking cabins. Two-night minimum.
Guest Capacity: 62

Conference Capacity: None
Rates: $–$$$ (includes some instruction, naturalist tours, use of trails)
Credit Cards: Visa, MasterCard, Discover
Season: Late November–April 15; annual snowfall 125"
XC Skiing: Dan maintains almost half of the 70-km trail system, partnered with Bearskin Lodge. (A single 3,000' segment has to be groomed by snowmobile, as it's illegal to operate a vehicle over 60" long on Boundary Waters Canoe Area lands.) His snowcat grooms mostly double track, some single track with skate lane. Network is primarily one-way. Trails near Golden Eagle are more often two-way than at Bearskin. 25% Easier, 50% More Difficult, 25% Most Difficult. 2 kms lighted. Four warming shelters. Daily instruction in classic and skating; full-time naturalist. Ski and snowshoe rentals. Daily trail fee. Altitude range 1,798'–2,010'.
Maps: One of the most imaginative and informative maps anywhere (*see also* Bearskin Lodge).
Activities and Entertainment: On-site: snowshoeing, lighted ice skating, broomball rink, sledding hill, Nature Center Tipi, bird watching, night hikes, and stargazing with a naturalist. Nearby: sleigh rides (4 miles), dog sledding.
Children's Programs: Babysitting by reservation, instruction, equipment, snow play, crafts.
Dining: Teresa serves home-style meals by reservation, but more customarily, guests do their own cooking. B.Y.O.B.
Special Nordic Distinction: It seems inevitable that skiers inquire about the relationship between Golden Eagle and Bearskin Lodge. Call it synergy. The Tuttles and the Baumanns have been instrumental in evolving the co-operative development of the Gunflint Trail, from grooming to marketing.
Summary: City sophisticates may define this experience as "non-commercial." It's more accurate and heartfelt to think of it as home-spun, down-to-earth Midwestern hospitality at its best.

Golden Eagle Lodge & Nordic Ski Center, Minnesota

Giants Ridge
Biwabik, Minnesota

When Giants Ridge opened in 1984, Minnesota XC owners were perturbed because tax dollars had been devoted to a huge new *competing* nordic operation. Over the years they found the area didn't reduce their business significantly because it tended to attract elite skiers (it has hosted a number of World Cup races). Today the ski area has evolved into the Giants Ridge Golf & Ski Resort. There's still plenty of vertical change, but none of it's nasty; the new golf course has smoothed out trails to the north. Routes through the woods are extremely pretty; from the summit you can enjoy 40-mile views east over Wynne and Sabin Lakes into Superior National Forest.

Address: P.O. Box 190, Biwabik, MN 55708
Tel/fax: (800) 688-7669 or (218) 865-4143; fax: (218) 865-4733
e-mail: info@giantsridge.com
Internet: www.giantsridge.com
Location: Northeastern Minnesota
Airport: Duluth, 70 miles
Train: None nearby
Memberships and Awards: Cross Country Ski Areas Association, *Snow Country* magazine's Top 10 XC Areas in the U.S.
Medical: White Community Hospital, 10 miles
Accommodations: Rooms and villas with kitchens at the Villas at Giants Ridge are a moment's drive from skiing. Some units with private whirlpool and sauna; some non-smoking rooms. Two-night minimum weekends and holidays. P.O. Box 350, Biwabik, MN 55708; (800) 843-7434 or (218) 865-4155.
Guest Capacity: 190
Conference Capacity: Up to 400 at ski area
Rates: $–$$$
Credit Cards: Visa, MasterCard, Discover
Season: Thanksgiving–end March; annual snowfall 48"; 1 km snowmaking
XC Skiing: Snowcat grooming is very good on 65 kms of boulevard-like trail (width is more California-style than Midwestern). 40% Easier, 33% More Difficult, 27% Most Difficult. Only Oslo is double-tracked alone; everything else is double-tracked with skate lane. There's a mix of one- and two-way flow. 3 kms lighted—once wooded, now it's on the golf course, which can be windy/chilly. Groomed downhill practice area. On-call instruction is available in classic and skating. Excellent quality though not wide-ranging rentals in a building shared with alpine skiing (there is no independent XC facility). Daily trail fee. Altitude range 1,400'–1,800'.
Maps: With all the changes going on, maps have looked temporary. A recent one simply outlined trails and facilities without contour indications, but the other side gives written detail on each trail.
Activities and Entertainment: On-site: alpine, 6-km snowshoe trail, sleigh rides, snow play, snowmobiling. Nearby: ice fishing, ice skating, dog sled rides, U.S. Hockey Hall of Fame with a 107' hockey stick (Eveleth), 85' Iron Ore Miner Statue (Chisholm), Fortune Bay Casino (Tower), Hibbing Historical Society Museum.
Children's Programs: Day care, special trails, instruction, equipment, snow play.
Dining: This part of Minnesota doesn't have a plethora of fine dining establishments. For an excellent dinner, drive an hour northeast to Ely to the Chocolate Moose—an eclectic menu including good sesame chicken, eggplant asiago, nightly specials, home-made ice cream. Beer, wine, and root beer floats available.
Special Nordic Distinction: Giants Ridge has evolved (and improved) from essentially a race site to one with fine recreational skiing. For more downhill drop, ride a lift to the ridgetop; motor around on Summit, Gold, and Cedar; then zoom down Bronze to the base of the hill.
Summary: Today Giants Ridge offers great family emphasis while still playing host to major regional and national XC events.

Anchorage Region, Alaska

See description on page 33

Dennis Buller and ACVB

ACVB

Montecito-Sequoia Nordic Resort, California

See description on page 36

Royal Gorge Cross Country Ski Resort, California

See description on page 39

David Madison/Royal Gorge

Royal Gorge Cross Country Ski Resort, California

See description on page 39

David Madison/Royal Gorge

Royal Gorge Cross Country Ski Resort, California

See description on page 39

David Madison/Royal Gorge

David Madison/Royal Gorge

Tahoe Donner, California

See description on page 40

Larry Prosor

Larry Prosor

Latigo Ranch, Colorado

See description on page 51

Jim Yost

Jim Yost

Vista Verde Ranch, Colorado

See description on page 54

Teton Ridge Ranch, Idaho

See description on page 60

Karin Prescott

Karin Prescott

Bearskin Lodge, Minnesota

See description on page 77

Cascade Lodge, Minnesota

See description on page 79

Gene Glader

Richard Hamilton Smith

B Bar Guest Ranch, Montana

See description on page 110

Lee Juillerat

Izaak Walton Inn, Montana

See description on page 109

Kyle Brehm

Eric Hallett

Lone Mountain Ranch, Montana

See description on page 112

Janice Tate

Matt Nagel

Salmon Hills, New York

See description on page 135

Elinor Osborn

Rochester Democrat and Chronicle, Reed Hoffman

Blueberry Hill, Vermont

See description on page 140

Grafton Ponds Cross Country Ski Center, Vermont

See description on page 144

Trapp Family Lodge, Vermont

See description on page 152

Freestone Inn, Washington

See description on page 156

Methow Valley Sport Trails Association, Washington

See description on page 156

Don Portman

Sun Mountain Lodge, Washington

See description on page 158

Don Portman

Don Portman

The Hills Health Ranch, British Columbia

See description on page 181

Chris Harris

Don Weixl

Stokely Creek Lodge, Ontario

See description on page 188

Bill Howe

Anne R. Peterson

Gatineau Park, Québec

See description on page 194

J. David Andrews

J. David Andrews

Maplelag
Callaway, Minnesota

Some XC areas are called "world-class," others "classy." Maplelag defies classification. It's a cross-country ski area, site of the Minnesota Museum of Fish Decoys and numerous Elderhostels, a dealer for Snorkel stoves and hot tubs, and home of the Bottomless Cookie Jar and "The Plunge." "Maplelag" is a word owners Jim and Mary Richards coined that roughly translates as "Maple community," expressing their interest in Norway and their location in sugarbush country. Prairie begins just a few miles west, so the area holds the last dense forest and the last XC destination east of the Rockies. Even if you have the temerity never to visit, ask the Richards to send the fall/winter copy of *Tap Line*, the most amusing and amazing brochure (or is it a newsletter?) in the business.

Address: Route 1, Callaway, MN 56521
Tel/fax: (800) 654-7711 or (218) 375-4466; fax: (218) 375-4600
e-mail: maplelag@tvutel.com
Internet: www.maplelag.com
Location: Northwestern Minnesota
Airport: Fargo, 50 miles
Train: Detroit Lakes, 20 miles
Memberships and Awards: Cross Country Ski Areas Association, *Snow Country* magazine's Top 10 XC Areas in the Midwest
Medical: St. Mary's Hospital, 20 miles
Accommodations: At most XC destinations, you can predict what the lodging will be like—log cabins at a guest ranch in the Rockies, a classic inn in New England, and so forth. Then there's Maplelag, where accommodations include rustic historical structures like remodeled Finnish saunas, the two-story Great Northern and Northern Pacific, and two beautifully renovated cabooses. There's a stained-glass window in most rooms. Linen rental available. Ski-in/ski-out. Almost entirely non-smoking. No minimum stay.
Guest Capacity: 200
Conference Capacity: 225

Rates: $$ (includes meals, nibblies, use of trails)
Credit Cards: Visa, MasterCard, American Express
Season: December–March 15; annual snowfall 60"
XC Skiing: Jim grooms 48 kms of double track plus the 5-km Skater's Waltz; most is one-way. 30% Easier, 50% More Difficult (perhaps overstated), 20% Most Difficult. Most loops are gentle, like Sukkerbusk; Wavy Gravy has a good deal more up and down. Telemarking practice on Suicide Hill. Road crossings. Instruction in classic, skate, telemark. Midweek tours are available to nearby Tamarack Wildlife Refuge and Itasca State Park. Excellent ski and snowshoe rentals. Daily trail fee. Altitude range 1,477'–1,532'.
Maps: Top notch. Trail names tend to alliterate.
Activities and Entertainment: Snowshoeing, ice skating, fishing, dog sledding, outdoor hot tub, saunas (one with suits, one without), Turkish bath, bird watching (500 pounds of sunflower seeds distributed at feeding stations along the trails), wildlife viewing (deer, moose, bobcat, beaver, otter, wolf tracks), DJed dancing Saturday nights, massage therapy. Nearby: half an hour's drive takes you to Shooting Star Casino on White Earth Reservation.
Children's Programs: Babysitting, instruction, equipment, pulks, kicksleds.
Dining: Meals made from scratch are served in the lodge dining area, reserved for overnight guests. Food is international (Native American fry bread, Scandinavian smorgasbord, Greek salad), plentiful, and very good. B.Y.O.B.
Special Nordic Distinction: Though it's tempting to ignore the skiing, trails have a delightful lilt, and grooming is as professional as at huge and humorless resorts.
Summary: The Richards collect Norwegian folk art, old signs, home-made Scandinavian skis, metal lunch boxes, neon clocks, and railroad memorabilia. This labyrinth of activities, items, and architectural styles is carried off with taste, style, and warmth.

Pincushion Mountain Bed & Breakfast
Grand Marais, Minnesota

Some innkeepers cater to XC skiers, some participate themselves, but few indeed are so inspired by the sport that they build their own hostelries next to a trail system. Renaissance man Scott Beattie is among the latter. The B&B that he and wife Mary run is just 3 miles from Grand Marais, but enter the long, winding drive and you achieve immediate seclusion. The 44-acre property has a private trail connection to the Pincushion Mountain XC System, which runs along the ridge line of the Sawtooth Mountains, 1,000 feet above Lake Superior. Birch, pine, and aspen forest protect the area from wind. From upper floors, guests have 40-mile views east to Isle Royale. Don't be discouraged if there's little snow in town; that extra altitude pretty much assures you'll have good skiing at Pincushion.

Address: 968 Gunflint Trail, Grand Marais, MN 55604-9701
Tel/fax: (800) 542-1226 or (218) 387-1276
e-mail: pincushion@boreal.org
Internet: www.pincushionbb.com
Location: Northeastern Minnesota
Airport: Duluth, 115 miles
Train: None nearby
Memberships and Awards: Cross Country Ski Areas Association, Gunflint Trail Association
Medical: Cook County Hospital, 2 miles
Accommodations: Pincushion has a spacious dining and living room with fireplace, four pleasant wood-paneled bedrooms upstairs, each with private bath. Three have fine vistas of sunrise over the lake. Smoke-free environment. Ski-in/ski-out. Two-night minimum weekends.
Guest Capacity: 8
Conference Capacity: None
Rates: $ (includes breakfast, use of trails)
Credit Cards: Visa, MasterCard
Season: Mid-December–end March; annual snowfall 92"
XC Skiing: Twenty-eight km are maintained by a new snowcat; all trails were recently widened to accommodate the machine, and another beginner route was added in 1998. The surface is so smooth that only 6" of snow are needed to track. Almost everything is one-way; all nine well-marked trails are groomed for single track and skating. 25% Easier, 50% More Difficult, 25% Most Difficult. There are wonderful swoops from esker to esker, and long sections for double-poling on slight downhills. Spectacular view into the gorge of the Devil Track River. One km lantern-lit on Saturday nights on the B&B property. Guide service, moonlight tours. Classic and skate rentals with a mix of older and new Salomon bindings; new snowshoes. Minnesota State Ski Pass required. Altitude range 1,200'—1,450'. Rentals.
Maps: Well done, showing direction and difficulty though not length.
Activities and Entertainment: On-site: snowshoeing, sauna. Nearby: the Gunflint Trail and North Shore XC Systems, alpine at Lutsen Mountains, dog sledding. Grand Marais art galleries are slowly blossoming in winter.
Children's Programs: The B&B isn't designed for children younger than 12 years.
Dining: When the Beatties built Pincushion in 1986, Scott could barely recognize a stove; now (under Mary's tutelage) he helps create fine and filling breakfasts (wild rice vegetable frittata, oven-baked french toast with raspberry topping . . .). Dinner choices in Grand Marais include Sven & Ole's Pizza, but the Pie Place has not only intriguing dishes but also the right attitude: "Somehow our desserts lose their calories in cold weather." For goodies try the Loafer Bakery & Deli. Gunflint Tavern is a non-smoking pub with 10 tap beers and great spinach-wrap sandwiches.
Special Nordic Distinction: Grooming is for and by XC devotees. The lighted trail begins a dozen steps from the door. And where else will your innkeeper also be your PSIA-certified instructor and groomer?
Summary: Pincushion combines down-home comfort with nordic devotion. And if you're sufficiently vocal about the great skiing or food, Scott will let you play with his Lionel train set.

Izaak Walton Inn
Essex, Montana

It's encouraging to know Montana has more to offer than the Freemen and the Unabomber. Halfway between the towns of East and West Glacier along the old Great Northern Railroad lies tiny Essex (permanent population: 7), home to Izaak Walton Inn. It's on the edge of magnificent Glacier National Park; the groomed trails border the Great Bear Wilderness; and the famous Bob Marshall Wilderness is almost next door. The half-timbered three-story hotel that became Izaak Walton was constructed in 1939 to accommodate crews building an east–west railway. The inn is one of North America's more "intriguing" XC destinations. Managed with both whimsy and style by owners Larry and Lynda Vieulleux, this is America's only ski area with virtual doorstep railway delivery. The region is known for winter wildlife, though you may see tracks rather than the animals themselves.

Address: P.O. Box 653, Essex, MT 59916
Tel/fax: (406) 888-5700; fax: (406) 888-5200
e-mail: izaakw@digisys.net
Internet: www.izaakwaltoninn.com
Location: Northwestern Montana
Airport: Glacier International, 60 miles
Train: Essex, 400 yards
Memberships and Awards: Cross Country Ski Areas Association, Historic Hotels of the Rocky Mountain West, *Snow Country* magazine's Top 10 XC Areas in the Rockies
Medical: Kalispell Regional Hospital, 60 miles
Accommodations: All 33 recently redecorated lodge rooms (each with private bath) are thoroughly comfortable, but it's more entertaining to stay in one of the four wonderful cabooses, set on a hilltop overlooking the inn. All have mini-kitchens. Smoke-free environment. Minimum stay varies.
Guest Capacity: 100
Conference Capacity: 60
Rates: $–$$$ (five-day package includes all meals, trails, instruction, tours by both snowshoe and ski, and use of sauna, and truly, there's no sense in a shorter stay at this entrancing place)
Credit Cards: Visa, MasterCard
Season: Thanksgiving–mid-April; annual snowfall 235" (576" of snow fell in the great winter of 1972)
XC Skiing: Larry uses a vibrant red German snowcat plus a unique hybrid Bombathol to groom 30 kms of mostly one-way trail, undulating through pine forest along the Middle Fork of the Flathead River and up around photogenic Essex Creek. There's a mix of single and double track, all with skating. 50% Easier, 30% More Difficult, 20% Most Difficult. 1 km lit. Guided tours into Glacier. Instruction covers classic technique, skating, and telemarking; excellent rental gear. Daily trail fee. Altitude range 3,700'–4,060'.
Maps: Elevation changes are clearly drawn; trail descriptions on the reverse.
Activities and Entertainment: On-site: snowshoeing, ice-skating, sauna. Tubing hill in progress. Nearby: alpine at The Big Mountain, an hour away in Whitefish. Visit the Buffalo Cafe (try Buffalo Blend Coffee), take a tour of Montana Coffee Traders' factory.
Children's Programs: Special trails, instruction, equipment, pulks, snow play, kick sleds.
Dining: A favorite dinner entrée at the Dining Car is the Shortline—breast of chicken topped with huckleberry sauce—and the home-made cobblers have terrific taste and texture. Full alcohol license.
Special Nordic Distinction: Izaak Walton is set at a comfortable altitude, so you don't need a day to learn to breathe again. Temperatures are usually more moderate than in other parts of Montana. Keeping with Larry's impish sense of humor, the Bombathol has its own "cathouse."
Summary: Izaak Walton is known as "a place where time stands still and lets you catch up," which captures the staff's warmth and imagination. Where else can you play on a swing on your skis, take part in a Snow Rodeo, and kick back in the saloon, trading puns with your host?

See color photos, page 95

B Bar Guest Ranch
Emigrant, Montana

Winter ranches entwine beauty, vast landscapes, and the mystique of the American West. If you enjoyed *The Horse Whisperer,* you'll love B Bar Guest Ranch, right in the same country. Its 9,000 private and pristine acres lie an hour north of Yellowstone in Tom Miner Basin, a thousand feet above Montana's Paradise Valley. Nestled below the 10,000-foot peaks of the Gallatin Range, B Bar is home to a profusion of wildlife: moose, bighorn sheep, elk, wolves (they drift north from the Park), mountain lion, and the elusive wolverine. Owners Maryanne Mott and Herman Warsh are courtly people with a deep love of this land. They raise rare Suffolk Punch draft horses; visitors are invited to help with feeding, grooming, training, harnessing, and driving the teams. Come evening, guests gravitate to the Big Room, furnished with deep-cushioned chairs and couches, vivid Southwestern wall hangings, beautiful bronzes, and a player piano.

Address: 818 Tom Miner Creek Road, Emigrant, MT 59027
Tel/fax: (406) 848-7523; fax: (406) 848-7793
e-mail: guestranch@bbar.com
Internet: www.bbar.com
Location: Southwestern Montana
Airport: Gallatin Field, 65 miles
Train: None nearby
Memberships and Awards: Cross Country Ski Areas Association, Dude Ranchers' Association
Medical: Livingston Memorial Hospital, 45 miles
Accommodations: The ranch has six cabins (bedroom, bath, and living room downstairs, upstairs loft) and four rooms in the main lodge (elegant "dorms" upstairs, downstairs suites). All ski-in/ski-out. Non-smoking environment. Two-night minimum.
Guest capacity: 34
Conference Capacity: 34
Rates: $$$ (includes all meals and on-ranch activities)
Credit cards: Personal checks and cash only

Season: Mid December–end February; annual snowfall 110" at ranch level, more higher up.
XC Skiing: B Bar snowmobile-and-horse grooms 40 kms. Ranch buildings straddle a mile-wide valley surrounding meandering Tom Miner Creek; trails swing through willows and meadows, then sweep up to ridge tops through aspen, fir, and pine. Classic predominates (single and double track), though there's some double track plus skating. 45% Easier, 45% More Difficult, 10% Most Difficult. Three shelters; groomed downhill practice area. Instruction in all techniques; guide service. Snowshoe rentals. Open to day skiers weekends (trail fee). Altitude range 6,600'–8,000'
Maps: The tough, useful little handout superimposes trails on a topo, with difficulty ratings but no lengths; on reverse are tips to keep trips safe and comfortable.
Activities and Entertainment: On-site: snowshoeing, skijoring, sleigh rides, horseback riding, outdoor hot tub. Nearby: Chico Hot Springs, dog sledding, Yellowstone National Park, the railroad town of Livingston, and the university "city" of Bozeman.
Children's programs: Pulks, sledding, tobogganing. The ranch suggests families with small children bring a nanny.
Dining: Meals are served buffet-style. B Bar specializes in ranch-grown natural beef, home-baked breads, pastries, and desserts. There's a cornucopia cookie crock in an alcove near the barnwood-sided dining room. B.Y.O.B.
Special Nordic Distinction: An evolving naturalist program emphasizes geology and ecology—photography, bird and wildlife viewing, wildlife counts . . .
Summary: Soft-spoken cow boss Tini Starkweather, raised near the ranch, takes guests on the most extensive sleigh system in the known galaxy. At sunset, vast stretches of deep blue linger overhead, while to the east, towering white-based clouds tipped with scarlet stand over the Absaroka massif.

See color photo, page 94

B Bar Guest Ranch, Montana

Lee Juillerat

Lee Juillerat

Lone Mountain Ranch
Big Sky, Montana

Lone Mountain is the granddaddy of winter guest ranches—best known, most extensive trail system (and most vertical), and leading fly-fishing program. It's a peaceful valley enclave in a region dominated by burgeoning Big Sky Resort. The ranch was founded by two families some 70 years ago; Bob and Vivian Schaap celebrated 20 years of ownership in 1996. Today it's famous for both skiing and dining. Reach any skyline and you'll see 11,166-foot Lone Mountain Peak to the west, as well as the Spanish Peaks and the Gallatin and Madison Ranges. The west entrance to Yellowstone National Park is only an hour away.

Address: P.O. Box 160069, Big Sky, MT 59716
Tel/fax: (800) 514-4644 or (406) 995-4644; fax: (406) 995-4670
e-mail: lmr@lmranch.com
Internet: www.lmranch.com
Location: Southwestern Montana
Airport: Gallatin Field, 48 miles
Train: None nearby
Memberships and Awards: Cross Country Ski Areas Association, Special Places, Five-Diamond Award for dining, *Snow Country* magazine's Top 10 XC Areas in the U.S.
Medical: Big Sky Medical Clinic, 6 miles
Accommodations: 24 cabins of varied sizes all have fireplace or wood stove, and private bath. Ridgetop Lodge is ideal for groups (six rooms plus common room, recreation room, and whirlpool); it also has the finest views of any accommodations. Seven-day minimum stay.
Guest Capacity: 70
Conference Capacity: 50
Rates: $$$–$$$$$ (includes all meals, evening entertainment, a sleigh ride dinner, on-snow buffet lunch, airport transfers, use of trails)
Credit Cards: Visa, MasterCard, Discover
Season: Early December–early April; annual snowfall 200"; 2 kms of snowmaking
XC Skiing: Lone Mountain's 65 kms of track on 15 trails would seem best suited to experienced skiers (15% Easier, 75% More Difficult,

10% Most Difficult), particularly considering altitude and vertical gain, but novices *love* them. Twice-daily shuttles to upper trails. All are single track and skating; some are one-way. Quality of snowcat grooming is among the best. Lower trails are largely open, higher routes in coniferous forest. PSIA-certified instructors specialize in telemarking as well as track. Groomed instruction and downhill practice areas. Naturalist-led ski tours into Yellowstone and the Spanish Peaks. Extensive rental selection, top-of-the-line clothing shop. Daily trail fee. Altitude range 6,200'–8,240'.
Maps: On one side, a multicolor projection that accurately shows the amount of uphill; on the other, a detailed introduction to trails and winter activities.
Activities and Entertainment: On-site: snowshoeing, sleigh rides, massage, hot tub; lounge and library in the B-K Lodge. Nearby: guided fly fishing, alpine skiing, dog sledding, Yellowstone National Park ski tours.
Children's Programs: Snow play, instruction, rentals, pulks; day care available nearby.
Dining: Meals at Lone Mountain are the stuff of legend—Montana beef, venison, bison (all with wine suggestions) as well as health-conscious lighter fare. A very limited number of "outsiders" can reserve dinner. Sleigh-ride dinners at a backwoods cabin as well, with entertainers including the famous Walkin' Jim Stoltz. Non-smoking restaurant and bar. Weekly trail buffet lunch.
Special Nordic Distinction: For two decades, instructors and guides have been among the best in the business.
Summary: The word is "ambiance." This is a place where stuffy businessmen have amazed their families by starting snowball fights (remember, this is "cold smoke" powder!). The finest tribute to ranch attractions is the 80% return rate for former guests.

See color photos, page 96

Lone Mountain Ranch, Montana

Rendezvous Ski Trails
West Yellowstone, Montana

West Yellowstone has as lovely and lilting a trail system as can be found in North America, designed for skiers by skiers. Snow transforms Yellowstone National Park (literally next door) from a summer lemming run to the stuff of winter legend—geysers, fumaroles, colored pools, and thousands of wild beasties. (Montana's Department of Fish, Wildlife, and Parks lamented in 1994, "There are bison in [town], bison at school, . . . bison chasing people and bison chasing horses.") The definitive tribute is that November XC camps are beloved by elite racers, yet recreational skiers come to play all winter. Drawbacks: most accommodations and restaurants are unexceptional, and the town is quite properly called "Snowmobile Capital of the World." But skiing has played an important role in West Yellowstone's prosperity. Local devotees hope a proposed community center will provide a central base facility, lit trail, snowshoe loop, and ice skating.

Address: West Yellowstone Chamber of Commerce, P.O. Box 458, West Yellowstone, MT 59758
Tel/fax: (406) 646-7701; fax: (406) 646-9691
e-mail: wyww@wyellowstone.com
Internet: www.wyellowstone.com
Location: Southwestern Montana
Airport: Gallatin Field, 100 miles
Train: None nearby
Memberships and Awards: Official Training Site for U.S. Biathlon and Nordic Ski Teams
Medical: West Yellowstone Clinic
Accommodations: West Yellowstone Conference Center has 123 rooms with microwaves and mini-fridges, including 20 comfortable suites with Jacuzzis, two minutes' walk from the trailhead. 315 Yellowstone Avenue, West Yellowstone, MT 59758; (800) 646-7365.
Guest Capacity: 246 at West Yellowstone Conference Center
Conference Capacity: 500
Rates: $$
Credit Cards: Visa, MasterCard, American Express, Diners Club, Discover

Season: Mid-November–end March; annual snowfall 200". Nighttime temperatures can be bitter, but it's usually comfortably warm by late morning. Park opens mid-December.
XC Skiing: 38.5 kms (and still growing!) of specially designed trails are snowcat-groomed with compulsive care. Most are one-way, passing through lodgepole pine forest. You'll find a mix of double track (Riverside), single track and skate, and double track plus skate; skate lanes are extra-wide. 80% Easier, 20% More Difficult. There are long-distance views of the Gallatin and Madison ranges. Instruction in classic and skating through ski shop Freeheel & Wheel, also a top source for rentals. Biathlon range. Famous Thanksgiving ski camp. Two warming shelters. Daily trail fee. Altitude range 6,666'–6,880'.
Maps: Minute in size, incorporated into small brochure.
Activities and Entertainment: Around town: snowshoeing, dog sledding, ice skating, Grizzly Discovery Center, six-story IMAX Theater, live entertainment weekends. Nearby: snowmobiling (actually, in town, too). For park naturalist tours, Yellowstone Alpen Guides offers customized snowcoach tours.
Children's Programs: Child care, equipment, groomed kids' hill.
Dining: Freeheel & Wheel's Caffeine Cafe is undergoing a name change but continues to offer fresh-made coffees, goodies, smoothies, pizza, and ski conversation.
Special Nordic Distinction: "West" qualifies as "Best Groomed Town Around." A grooming equipment manufacturer lives virtually beside the trails and is responsible for maintenance. Volunteer Loop is the most underrated route in the system, delightful for anyone with a reasonable step turn. Try the Spam Cup Series.
Summary: Mind-bogglingly good snow customarily stays up to five months. Early November visitors often bring not only skis for trails on the South Plateau but also mountain bikes, running shoes, and roller blades.

Rendezvous Ski Trails, Montana

Wade Lake Resort
Cameron, Montana

Montana isn't exactly overrun with people, but even for the Treasure State this tiny resort is remote—and therein lies much of its charm. Wade Lake is accessible only over the snow, by ski or snowshoe, with luggage shuttle provided. Owners Dave and Laurie Schmidt formerly were telephone company executives in Northern California. They purchased the property and opened for winter in 1990, and they seem to thrive on quiet beauty. Now five cabins and a lodge, the resort was founded almost a century ago, devastated by the great 1959 earthquake, and rebuilt. Wade is one of a chain of lakes in the Gravelly Range, an area that enjoys both sun and dependable snow. It's a fascinating but character-building ski in and a wonderful, mostly downhill out. From either direction you'll pass the ghost town of Missouri Flats, a place tasting of melancholy, with wind sighing through the sagebrush. On a sweeter note, because it's partly ice-free throughout the winter, Wade Lake teems with wildlife—bald eagles, great gray owls, ducks, trumpeter swans, rainbow trout spawning, lots of moose, and river otters. Don't forget a camera!

Address: P.O. Box 107, Cameron, MT 59720
Tel/fax: (406) 682-7560
e-mail: wadelkmt@3rivers.net
Location: Southwestern Montana
Airport: Gallatin Field, 110 miles
Train: None nearby
Memberships and Awards: Montana Wildlife Viewing Site
Medical: Ennis Hospital, 40 miles
Accommodations: The cabins are simple but all have full kitchens and furnaces. Electricity courtesy of Wade Lake's own stream-powered generator. Bring bath towels; bedding is provided. Separate building for modern bathrooms and showers. No smoking in cabins. Two-night minimum. Need it be said?—ski-in/ski-out.
Guest Capacity: 12
Conference Capacity: None
Rates: $ (includes round-trip baggage transportation, use of trails)

Credit Cards: Personal check or cash only
Season: Christmas–early March; annual snowfall 60"
XC Skiing: Trails run through an interesting vegetative mix (old-growth fir, aspen, and lodgepole pine, and sagebrush-covered rolling hills along lakes and stream sides), with abundant backcountry telemarking opportunities. The forested areas are wind-protected. Dave grooms 35 kms by snowcat, spread over six trails; most is double track, the rest single track, and everything is two-way. 50% Easier, 50% More Difficult. Snowmobilers sometime use some of the trails, less frequently weekdays. No rentals—try Free Heel and Wheel in West Yellowstone or Northern Lights in Bozeman. Informal nature tours. Altitude range 6,100'–6,700'.
Maps: The Schmidts have superimposed trails on a detailed purple-shaded topo map; it works well and looks good.
Activities and Entertainment: On-site: wildlife viewing, snowshoeing, sledding, outdoor wood-fired hot tub with lake view. Nearby: fly-fishing, ice fishing.
Children's Programs: Winter visits aren't particularly convenient for families with small children, but there is a snow play area.
Dining: Guests should plan to make their own breakfasts and lunches but can arrange dinner by reservation. Laurie provides for vegetarian needs if informed ahead of time, but guests more frequently enjoy a single entrée such as seafood crêpes, prime rib, or scampi, with homemade pies. B.Y.O.B.
Special Nordic Distinction: Two complementary attractions are privacy (far more kms and animals than people) and comfort. It's far nicer than seeing the same country living in a tent.
Summary: Skis are your means of access and egress; wildlife, your greatest treat.

The Balsams Wilderness
Dixville Notch, New Hampshire

Historic, majestic, and grand in the style of the vast hotels that once graced the rugged White Mountains, the Balsams Wilderness deserves accolades for both beauty and longevity. Set amidst a 15,000-acre private estate, it's one of the great remote winter resorts on the continent. Think of the grandeur of Chateau Lake Louise combined with the 1:1 staff-to-guest ratio of Mohonk Mountain House. The hotel has continuously operated for more than 140 years, and it resembles a self-sufficient hamlet. (Electricity is generated by a bio-mass power plant; and if you need latex medical gloves, they're also manufactured on-property.) Nordic skiing is a prominent part of winter pleasure; in fact, the XC presence is unavoidable, as the XC center is in the hotel lobby. The Balsams opened for winter in 1966 and has developed one of the larger, finer, and least-used trail systems in the East—a very good area for novices and families.

Address: Route 26, Dixville Notch, NH 03576
Tel/fax: (800) 255-0600 or (603) 255-3400; fax: (603) 255-4221
e-mail: thebalsams@aol.com
Internet: www.thebalsams.com
Location: Far northern New Hampshire, about equidistant from Vermont, Maine, and Québec
Airport: Portland International Jetport, 120 miles
Train: None nearby
Memberships and Awards: Cross Country Ski Areas Association, *Snow Country* magazine's Top 10 XC Areas at Alpine Resorts in North America; architectural, culinary, lodging, and wine cellar distinctions
Medical: Upper Connecticut Valley Medical Center, 10 miles
Accommodations: The 212 guest rooms are comfortable rather than ornate, with private bath, memorable views, and radiators. Luxury suites are also available. The "new wing" exterior (completed 1918) resembles an abbey's tower. Winter rates are remarkably reasonable. Ski-in/ski-out. No minimum stay.

Guest Capacity: 420
Conference Capacity: 400
Rates: $$$–$$$$ (low season includes breakfast, dinner, nursery, use of trails)
Credit Cards: Visa, MasterCard, American Express, Discover
Season: Mid-December–early April; annual snowfall 250" (one of the most reliable seasons in New England)
XC Skiing: XC Director David Nesbitt grooms 76 kms by snowcat, two-way double track with a wide skating lane in the middle. There are effectively two different but linked networks. 32% Easier, 47% More Difficult, 21% Most Difficult. One warming shelter. Daily instruction in classic, skating, and telemark; guide service. State-of-the-art rentals, equipment retail. Daily trail fee. Altitude range 1,840'–2,723'.
Maps: The map is large, topographical, masterful, accurate, and entertaining.
Activities and Entertainment: At resort: alpine (trail as well as free shuttle connections), snowshoeing, horse-drawn wagon rides, dancing, movie theater, nightclub shows, billiards, family games, history tours, nature programs, daily events. Nearby: with this array of fun, why be concerned?
Children's Programs: Day care, equipment, pulks.
Dining: On the formal side; food and presentation are fantastic. Enjoy live music with dinner. The executive chef is a managing partner in the resort, which helps explain quality in cuisine.
Special Nordic Distinction: True to the tradition of attention to detail, the XC staff are extremely personable.
Summary: Dixville Notch is famous during presidential elections as the first town whose votes are tabulated. Nordic skiing should enjoy similar renown, but not just every four years. The hotel has magnificent architecture, absorbing history, varied activities, outstanding dining, and riveting scenery.

Bretton Woods Resort
Twin Mountain, New Hampshire

In financial circles, Bretton Woods is associated with the 1944 International Monetary Conference that established the gold standard and created the World Bank and International Monetary Fund. Historians may know it as home to the Mt. Washington Hotel, a National Historic Landmark that's almost the only survivor of nineteenth-century grand hotels in the region. The hotel reopens for winter in October 1999. To alpine skiers, Bretton Woods is a mid-sized, quiet, and pleasant area. But to nordic visitors, it's definitely Big Time. There's everything from golf-course-gentle to the deep Black Diamond 4-km Tim Nash. And by any measure, it's a beautiful locale, dominated by views of the Presidential Range to the east and the lordly Mt. Washington Hotel below. Among entertaining options are skiing up to the Top o' Quad Restaurant, or following ungroomed Ammonoosuc Spring to overnight at a mountain cabin. And since Ted Gardner worked here, there's another Von Ryan's trail. Racing has been scaled back in the past few years; in any case, competitions don't consume a great deal of the system. Recent trail work assures that 70 percent of the system can open with 6 inches of packed snow.

Address: Route 302, Bretton Woods, NH 03575
Tel/fax: (603) 278-3322; fax: (603) 278-3337
e-mail: skibw@brettonwoods.com
Internet: www.brettonwoods.com
Location: North-central New Hampshire
Airport: Manchester, 105 miles
Train: None nearby
Memberships and Awards: Cross Country Ski Areas Association
Medical: Littleton Hospital, 20 miles
Accommodations: The Bretton Arms is a National Historic Landmark with 31 guest rooms and three suites. Now a stylish country inn, it once housed the chauffeurs of wealthy guests in larger mountain hotels. Ski-in/ski-out. No minimum stay; (800) 258-0330.
Guest Capacity: 68

Conference Capacity: Yes
Rates: $$
Credit Cards: Visa, MasterCard, American Express, Discover
Season: Thanksgiving–early April; annual snowfall 170"
XC Skiing: Bretton Woods is famous for frequent light coatings of snow rather than massive dumps. It has a major trail system, broken into three distinct but interconnected segments, totaling 97 snowcat-groomed kms. All routes are single-tracked with a skate lane and two-way. 35% Easier, 40% More Difficult, 25% Most Difficult. A snowmobile trail following the old cog railway road runs through part of the Deception Trail System. Two road crossings. Biathlon range. One warming shelter. Instruction in classic, skating, and telemark; guide service by reservation. Daily trail fee. Altitude range 1,500'–2,700'.
Maps: The map on the reverse of the XC brochure is clear and useful.
Activities and Entertainment: At resort: alpine, snowshoeing, ice skating, sleigh rides, sports club (indoor pool, sauna, Jacuzzi, racquetball courts, exercise room). Nearby: North Conway shopping, much more alpine and XC, snowmobiling.
Children's Programs: Day care, special trails, instruction, equipment, pulks, snow play (nearby).
Dining: The Bretton Arms serves Northeastern specialties such as medley of fresh New England seafood on lobster fettucine. Full liquor license.
Special Nordic Distinction: Bretton Woods has predominantly beginner and intermediate terrain, but there's enough vertical change and trail length (you can create a 25-km outer loop) to stretch advanced skiers. They claim the largest groomed network in New Hampshire.
Summary: Spruce, fir, and hardwoods; beaver ponds, icy streams, meadow, and golf course—all with 6,288' Mt. Washington gazing down.

The Franconia Inn
Franconia, New Hampshire

The Franconia region has largely escaped winter tourism madness. Though there's considerable skiing history locally—first ski school and first aerial tram in America—and plenty of downhill and XC nearby, the seasonal pace of life is temperate. Franconia Inn seems to encapsulate that serene quality. Constructed in 1868, burned in 1930 and immediately rebuilt, it's a handsome building just up the road from the house where Robert Frost wrote "Stopping By Woods on a Snowy Evening." In a skiing sense, it's a composite of elements found at other areas. It shares Bretton Woods' snow patterns (lots of flurries dropping 2 to 4 inches, though there has also been a 4-foot storm). As at Green Trails Inn, trail width has been somewhat restricted by landholding patterns. And like Bear Valley, some of the best beginner terrain is on an airstrip. It's also the second site in New Hampshire to have a Von Ryan's Express. (Ted Gardner gave the name to routes at Loon and Bretton Woods as well.) But trails have their own character; most are old logging roads, doubling as bridle paths in warmer seasons. In summer the ski shop reverts to a barn (it retains a pleasant horsy scent all winter long). Best vistas are of the White Mountains, particularly 5,249-foot Mt. Lafayette.

Address: 1300 Easton Road, Franconia, NH 03580
Tel/fax: (800) 473-5299 or (603) 823-5542; fax: (603) 823-8078
e-mail: info@franconiainn.com
Internet: www.franconiainn.com
Location: Northwestern New Hampshire
Airport: Manchester, 95 miles
Train: None nearby
Memberships and Awards: AAA Three Diamond, Mobil Three Star
Medical: Littleton Hospital, 8 miles
Accommodations: All 35 remodeled rooms and suites have private bath. The huge "honeymoon suite" has its own Jacuzzi. Ski-in/ski-out. Some rooms designated non-smoking. No minimum stay.

Guest Capacity: 70
Conference Capacity: 100
Rates: $$ (includes breakfast and dinner, instruction, use of trails)
Credit Cards: Visa, MasterCard, American Express
Season: Mid-December–mid-March; annual snowfall 100"
XC Skiing: The inn has 65 kms of snowmobile-groomed trail, primarily narrow single track (one skating trail on the air strip). 33% Easier, 34% More Difficult, 33% Most Difficult. Ridge Run is a genuine experts-only, often left ungroomed for descent control. Groomed downhill practice area. Road crossings. One warming shelter. Instruction in classic technique. At last look, rental equipment was oldish. Daily trail fee. Altitude range 960'–1,600'.
Maps: 200' contour lines don't give a precise idea of terrain, but the rest of the map is clear and well organized.
Activities and Entertainment: On-site: snowshoeing, sleigh rides, lighted ice skating, lounge, outdoor hot tub, sauna, game room. Nearby: alpine (Cannon, Bretton Woods, Loon), Old Man of the Mountains (famed 40' cliff profile at Franconia Notch State Park, sculpture by Mother Nature), antique stores, New England Ski Museum at Franconia Notch, snowmobiling.
Children's Programs: Instruction, equipment.
Dining: The inn has two dining rooms, one intimate, the other larger and more active. The kitchen prepares particularly good chicken dishes, with substantial portions and big, rich desserts (baking is done on premises). Children's menu. Items on the breakfast menu are named after XC trails. Rathskeller Lounge downstairs.
Special Nordic Distinction: It's restful to find a destination that concentrates so much on classic technique. Ski to other inns for lunch.
Summary: Franconia Inn offers fine food, comfort, and no affectations.

Jackson Ski Touring Foundation
Jackson, New Hampshire

Jackson is the only area in the Northeast that rivals the Trapp Family Lodge in fame. The entire town has invested in nordic skiing: one of every three residents is involved in some way, from ski instruction to firewood delivery at trailside restaurants and inns. When the Foundation was developed in the early '70s, founders hoped the non-consumptive use of the land would maintain Jackson's beauty and character. The plan has succeeded beyond expectations—the village still has its covered bridge, old hotels, gurgling river, and classic white church. There are still unspoiled views of the White Mountains, Ellis and Wildcat River Valleys, and the Presidential Range, including Mt. Washington. And visitors are still primary beneficiaries. Thom Perkins, longtime Foundation director, feels that "we provide release and rejuvenation for our guests." It's true. Trails are built with care—45 kilometers can be groomed with only 6 inches of snow. There's also extensive, mapped backcountry skiing. New in '98: a grand 7,000-square-foot base lodge.

Address: P.O. Box 216, Jackson, NH 03846-0216
Tel/fax: (800) 866-3334 for lodging, XC information (800) XC SNOWS, (603) 383-9355; fax: (603) 383-0816
e-mail: thom@jacksonxc.com
Internet: www.jacksonxc.com
Location: East-central New Hampshire
Airport: Portland International Jetport, 70 miles
Train: Portland, 70 miles
Memberships and Awards: Cross Country Ski Areas Association, *Snow Country* magazine's Top 4 XC Areas in North America
Medical: Memorial Hospital, 5 miles
Accommodations: Eagle Mountain House is a venerable nineteenth-century–looking inn (rebuilt in 1916 after a fire), with 93 rooms and suites. Jacuzzi, health club, dining. Ski-in/ski-out. Non-smoking rooms available. No minimum stay. Carter Notch Road, Jackson, NH 03846; (800) 966-5779.
Guest Capacity: 186 at Eagle Mountain House
Conference Capacity: 150
Rates: $–$$
Credit Cards: Visa, MasterCard, American Express, Discover
Season: Mid-December–early April; annual snowfall 115"
XC Skiing: Thom and his staff snowcat-groom 87 kms on 31 trails. There's a mix of everything from single track to skate-only, but quality is very consistent. 39.5% Easier, 21.5% More Difficult, 39% Most Difficult. Ellis River is one of the most scenic and well traveled trails in the U.S. Five warming shelters plus access to 18 inns. Groomed downhill practice areas. Road crossings. Instruction in classic and skating. Top-flight rentals and retail. Daily trail fee. Altitude range 740'–4,000'.
Maps: Jackson's large topo map has the entire network on one side, specifics on the reverse.
Activities and Entertainment: Around town: snowshoeing, ice skating, sleigh rides. Nearby: alpine (Wildcat, Black Mountain, Attitash), Peter Limmer and Sons (custom boots), factory outlet shopping and vicious traffic in North Conway, Hartman Model Railway and Toy Museum, snowmobiling; much additional XC.
Children's Programs: Day care at Wildcat, babysitting locally, instruction, equipment, pulks.
Dining: Although there are a number of excellent restaurants right in town, try dinner at the Bernerhof in Glen, a few minutes south. It features many kinds of schnitzel as well as a cooking school.
Special Nordic Distinction: There's wide-ranging terrain, from golf courses to remote forested routes; other trails wind throughout town. Jackson has the most expensive segment of trail in the world: $425,000 for a 292' covered bridge and tunnel.
Summary: Jackson is an inspiring example of community commitment to "clean" recreation.

Loon Mountain
Lincoln, New Hampshire

Hollywood has left its imprint in the world of XC skiing, even in White Mountain National Forest of rural New Hampshire. You'll find that influence at Bretton Woods, Franconia Inn, and most recently Loon Mountain, where former XC director Ted Gardner created another signature trail called Von Ryan's Express, named after a World War II escape-by-train film. Loon has two trail systems separated by the alpine area, with the XC center unfortunately equidistant from both and contiguous to neither (weekend shuttle). The East Ridge system is overall less hilly and much more private (western trails encounter a lot of condos); the latter loops are changing as the alpine resort expands. Cross-country was introduced at the resort in 1986; some trails were built for skiing, others have been adapted from logging roads; Black Mountain used to be a railroad line.

Address: RR #1, Box 41, Kancamagus Highway, Lincoln, NH 03251-9711
Tel/fax: (603) 745-8111; fax: (603) 745-8214
e-mail: info@loonmtn.com
Internet: www.loonmtn.com
Location: North-central New Hampshire
Airport: Manchester, 90 miles
Train: None nearby
Memberships and Awards: Cross Country Ski Areas Association
Medical: Plymouth Hospital, 22 miles
Accommodations: For real fun, drive west to the century-old, 21-room Woodstock Inn, also a B&B and brew pub. Each room is decorated differently. Mostly shared baths in the Main House; across the road mostly private baths, three with private Jacuzzis, canopied beds; also outdoor Jacuzzi. Six non-smoking rooms. Two night minimum weekends, more some holidays. Main Street, North Woodstock, NH 03262; (603)745-3951.
Guest capacity: 67
Conference Capacity: Limited by other activities
Rates: $–$$ (includes stupendous breakfasts)

Credit cards: Visa, MasterCard, American Express, Discover
Season: Mid-December–mid-April; annual snowfall 125"
XC Skiing: Loon grooms 35 kms by snowcat, mixing one- and two-way; all single track with skate lane. 30% Easier, 47% More Difficult, 23% Most Difficult. Daily instruction in all disciplines; groomed teaching area is at West Ridge Trail System; guide service. Daily trail fee. Altitude range 900'–2,000' (high point is on Von Ryan's—several lovely swooping downhills).
Maps: The most recent version is both tiny and very cursory.
Activities and Entertainment: On-site: alpine, snowshoeing, ice skating, lift-served night tubing, fitness club (squash, racquetball, tanning, massage, saunas), Wildlife Theatre (encounter young mountain lions from a safe distance, as well as raptors, parrots, and snakes). Nearby: sleighrides, Indian Head (wonderful cliff profile), Lahout's Country Clothing and Ski Shop (ask and ye shall likely find), snowmobiling.
Children's programs: Day care, equipment; Children's Theatre and Cabaret.
Dining: The Woodstock Inn has two restaurants. The Clement Room is more formal, with a goodly range of dinner entrées; Woodstock Station is casual, with a startling 148-item menu.
Special Nordic Distinction: Serendipity (on the eastern system) is one of the most light and scenic trails in the region. It runs just above the Pemigewasset River for most of its length (there's a grand stone bench for perching and lunching, or you can use more prosaic picnic tables), with glimpses up into the Pemi Wilderness.
Summary: What Loon lacks in physical coherence, it makes up for with fine skiing and a well-balanced nordic program (excellent telemarking instruction).

Norsk Cross Country Ski Center
New London, New Hampshire

Come winter, the New London locale seems forgotten by Bostonians, who fly by in ignorance on Interstate 89, headed for such benighted regions as Vermont. At Norsk, there's little to fear of congestion in traffic or on trails. The center was named by John Schlosser after a stint of studying in Oslo. He and wife Nancy support their XC habit by teaching yoga in summer (she also runs a gardening company; he operates a canoe/kayak rental business). Nancy applies her skills to ski school, incorporating stretching and breathing exercise into warm-up. They opened Norsk in 1976 and have constantly refined since then. Trails spread over 2,500 acres, thanks to the generosity of 25 landowners, including the Ausbon Sargent Land Preservation Trust. The terrain is seldom abrupt, running over the Lake Sunapee Country Club course; through fields and dense forest; up, along, and over eskers. To the south stands Mt. Kearsarge (just under 3,000 feet), best seen from the Country Club. Trails have been very thoughtfully laid out (some follow old skid roads, others have been built for skiing) and are extremely well groomed. To limber up before the working day begins, the Schlossers ski to the center on their own access trail.

Address: P.O. Box 2460, New London, NH 03257
Tel/fax: (800) 426-6775 or (603) 526-4685; fax: (603) 526-9622
e-mail: info@skinorsk.com
Internet: www.skinorsk.com
Location: East-central New Hampshire
Airport: Manchester, 55 miles
Train: White River Junction, 40 miles
Memberships and Awards: Cross Country Ski Areas Association
Medical: New London Hospital, 4 miles
Accommodations: Lake Sunapee Country Club is right on site—in fact, the whole XC center converts to golf come spring. There's a motel option, but the eight inn rooms are much more pleasant (private bath), still inexpensive,

and right on the trails. No minimum stay. Same address as Norsk but a different number: (603) 526-6040.
Guest Capacity: 40
Conference Capacity: 100
Rates: $–$$ (includes breakfast, use of trails)
Credit Cards: Visa, Mastercard, Discover
Season: Late November–early April; annual snowfall 75"
XC Skiing: John snowcat-grooms 55 kms on 20 trails, primarily double track but also 20 kms of single track with skate lane; one-way. 25% Easier, 60% More Difficult, 15% Most Difficult. One warming shelter (Robb's Hut is well worth visiting, both for hot chocolate and to drop suavely, "Oh, yes, I took Freefall this time, no problem!"). Daily instruction in classic, skating, and telemarking; guide service. Complete and up-to-date rental department; wide range of equipment for sale. Daily trail fee. Altitude range 950'–1,150'.
Maps: Accurate, readable, and extremely entertaining. There's a dance theme to many trail names.
Activities and Entertainment: On-site: snowshoeing, snowshoe nature tours, and lots of special programs (Women's Ski Day, moonlight tours, Teenager Day, New London Chocolate Fest). Nearby: alpine (Mt. Sunapee), Colby-Sawyer College Sports Center, Nunsuch Cheeses (you guessed it, a dairy run by an ex-nun).
Children's Programs: Ski games (Saturday), narrow tracks, instruction, equipment, pulks—a thoroughly family-friendly area.
Dining: The Country Club restaurant serves more vegetarian meals in winter (interesting reflection on golfing diets) as well as clam chowder and a skier buffet.
Special Nordic Distinction: Norsk is a fly-in/fly-out destination (private airstrip on premises).
Summary: Norsk combines the best of accessibility, affability, professionalism, and humor.

Waterville Valley
Waterville Valley, New Hampshire

Waterville Valley is a modest-sized, self-contained, good-looking four-season resort that has taken XC very seriously indeed. Peaks rise high above an alpine valley, in the midst of the White Mountain National Forest. The tradition of recreation in the area began almost a century and a half ago with fishing and hiking. Today 770,000 acres of public land surround the resort. Trails take off from the Village Square, which houses the Nordic Center. More than a ski shop, this is a resource for equipment, information, instruction, and guided tours. Some XC routes have been adapted from logging roads, many built specifically for skiing. More distant North End trails often open first because of snow retention. Waterville has reduced its race schedule because competition interfered with recreational skiers' pleasure. All activities are strongly family-oriented.

Address: P.O. Box 540, Waterville Valley, NH 03215
Tel/fax: (800) 468-2553 for accommodations, (603) 236-4666 for XC information; fax: (603) 236-4174
e-mail: nordiccenter@waterville.com
Internet: www.waterville.com
Location: North-central New Hampshire
Airport: Manchester, 75 miles
Train: None nearby
Memberships and Awards: Cross Country Ski Areas Association, *Snow Country* magazine's Top 10 XC Areas in the U.S. at an Alpine Resort
Medical: Speare Memorial Hospital, 22 miles
Accommodations: The Golden Eagle Lodge is comfortable, handsome inside and out, extremely convenient, and very affordable. Sizable but not impersonal, it has 139 one- or two-bedroom suites with full kitchen. Whirlpool, swimming pool, saunas. Ski-in/ski-out. Some non-smoking rooms. Three-night minimum holidays. P.O. Box 540, Waterville Valley, NH 03215; (800) 910-4499 or (603) 236-4600.
Guest Capacity: 278
Conference Capacity: 75

Rates: $$–$$$ (includes valley shuttle, use of trails, ice skating, Escapades, and other neat stuff)
Credit Cards: Visa, MasterCard, American Express, Diners Club, Discover
Season: Mid-December–early March; annual snowfall 130"
XC Skiing: Waterville Valley uses snowcats to groom 70 kms, mostly double track with skating, on 22 trails. 50% Easier, 30% More Difficult, 20% Most Difficult; only toughest trails are one-way. Groomed downhill practice area. Some road crossings, though there are also some XC underpasses. Daily instruction in classic, skating. Top-of-the-line rentals, excellent retail. Daily trail fee. Altitude range 1,500'–2,250'.
Maps: The XC Center has a two-sided, four-color, very detailed yet pleasant rendering of placement and terrain, including contours and difficulty ratings; it doubles as the area hiking map. Outstanding!
Activities and Entertainment: At resort: alpine, snowshoeing, indoor ice skating, sleigh rides, athletic club (swimming pool, sauna, weight room, racquet sports). Winter Escapades include fireworks, live animal presentations. Otherwise, activities are limited in immediate vicinity.
Children's Programs: Narrow tracks, instruction, equipment, pulks—and snowcat rides!
Dining: For lunch, sample the Jugtown Sandwich Shop on the Town Square. William Tell restaurant is worth the 7-mile drive for Swiss cuisine (Zürcher Ratsherren Topf) and excellent desserts.
Special Nordic Distinction: Snowshoeing, skiing, even hiking emphasize humans' relation to the environment. Weekly women's ski group. Ski up to Bob's Lookout for best views both up and down the valley.
Summary: There's a wide gamut of terrain and a lot for families to do in a lovely mountain environment.

Woodbound Inn
Rindge, New Hampshire

The number of country inns involved with XC skiing is remarkable—Blueberry Hill, Woodstock, Craftsbury, Mountain Top, The Old Tavern—but they're not entirely confined to northern or central New England. Woodbound is a couple of minutes above the Massachusetts border, which can be a mixed blessing: great for access, questionable at times in terms of snow. The inn began as a farmhouse in the early 1800s and was converted to a hostelry in 1892. It was owned by three generations of the Brummer family, from 1934 through the mid-1980s, an era that saw rail travel give way to roads. It has stayed relaxed under the ownership of the Kohlmorgen family. Both brothers used to work for Marriott, and they've upgraded service and facilities considerably since 1994. If you stay in a cabin, across Contoocook Lake ("Lake Sunshine") you'll see Mt. Monadnock (3,165 feet), reputed to be the most climbed mountain in the U.S. The XC system isn't large but is thoroughly suited to anyone a little doubtful about his or her abilities. Lucky skiers will see beaver along the Bullet Pond loop; those with good nerves may look forward to occasionally encountering moose. Judging by tracks, bear are also in the region in winter.

Address: 62 Woodbound Road, Rindge, NH 03461
Tel/fax: (800) 688-7770 or (603) 532-8341; fax: (603) 532-8341 ext. 213
e-mail: woodbound@aol.com
Location: Southwestern New Hampshire
Airport: Manchester, 40 miles
Train: Milford, 18 miles
Medical: Monadnock Community Hospital, 12 miles
Accommodations: Guests can select from rooms in the main inn, the Edgewood building (added in 1983), or 11 one- or two-bedroom cabins with fireplace, refrigerator, and lakeside seclusion. Ski-in/ski-out. Some non-smoking accommodations. No minimum stay.

Guest Capacity: 84
Conference Capacity: 175
Rates: $ (includes breakfast, dinner, use of trails)
Credit Cards: Visa, MasterCard, American Express
Season: Mid-December–early March; annual snowfall 72"
XC Skiing: Woodbound maintains 18 kms of single track by snowmobile; most people ski them both ways. 40% Easier, 30% More Difficult, 30% Most Difficult. Only 8" of packed snow are necessary to open most trails. Instruction available weekends; guide service by appointment. Three-pin rentals. Daily trail fee. Altitude range 750'–900'. The self-guided nature tour is better snowshoed than skied.
Maps: Though it's better than in the past, unfortunately the ski/hiking map is a blurred photocopy. It does have difficulty ratings but lacks contour lines.
Activities and Entertainment: On-site: snowshoeing, lighted ice skating, groomed sliding hill (it used to have a tow and alpine skiing), Playbarn (video games, jukebox, Ping Pong). Nearby: alpine (Temple Mountain), sleigh rides, New England Marionette Opera, galleries, antiques, craft shops, Boston.
Children's Programs: Equipment, snow play.
Dining: The range of entrées includes prime rib au jus and poached salmon Marie. Alcohol available in lounge.
Special Nordic Distinction: Particularly pleasant for beginners, skiing here includes a number of wide uncrowded trails.This may be the only destination in the Americas where a couple can make special arrangements to ski to a beautiful outdoor altar (Cathedral of the Pines), marry, and ski back to a country inn for their honeymoon.
Summary: Woodbound is very relaxed, decidedly inexpensive, and only 90 minutes from Harvard Square.

Enchanted Forest Cross Country Ski Area
Red River, New Mexico

Yes, indeed, New Mexico does have high peaks and winter. Set in the Sangre de Cristo mountains near the genuine Old West town of Red River, Enchanted Forest isn't a self-contained full-service resort, but it is unquestionably a XC destination, popular with New Mexican skiers as well as downhillers from Taos and Angel Fire. The Miller family, who own a store in town and run the ski operation five minutes up the road, have a pronounced sense of fun, as witnessed by the number of entertaining events they schedule each year: the January un-Super Bowl Race, and Mardi Gras in the Mountains (part of a townwide celebration), a treasure hunt, and the famous Just Desserts Eat & Ski "gorge fest," all in February. This is a high and wide country of meadows and aspen, fir, pine, and spruce, with views of two wilderness areas, including 13,161' Wheeler Peak, the highest point in the state; the Moreno Valley; and the Red River Valley. Trails are fun, grooming excellent, and snow usually forgiving.

Address: P.O. Box 219, Red River, NM 87558
Tel/fax: (505) 754-2374; fax: (505) 754-2375
Internet: www.redrivernm.com/enchanted
Location: North-central New Mexico
Airport: Albuquerque, 176 miles
Train: Raton, 80 miles
Memberships and Awards: Cross Country Ski Areas Association, New Mexico Special Olympics Commendation
Medical: Holy Cross Hospital, 40 miles
Accommodations: Telemark Bed & Breakfast is eight minutes from the trails, right on the Red River. Congenial hosts Martha and Sigi Klein created a class act: six rooms decorated in Tyrolean style, all with balconies; southwest hangings, big hewn beams. Outdoor hot tub. Non-smoking environment. Two-night minimum weekends. (505) 754-2534, fax (505) 754-2905.
Guest Capacity: 16
Conference Capacity: None
Rates: $ (includes breakfast)

Credit Cards: Visa, MasterCard
Season: Thanksgiving–Easter; annual snowfall 240"
XC Skiing: John and his crew snowcat-groom 30 kms of single track plus skating. 30% Easier, 40% More Difficult, 30% Most Difficult. Excellent instructors (with the ability to laugh at themselves) cover classic and skating; shuttle from Millers Crossing. The best selection of rental and retail equipment is at the store in town; some rentals at the XC center. Daily trail fee. Altitude range 9,600'–10,040'.
Maps: It's not a complex product. Instead of contour lines, there are numerous elevation markings. The whole family has contributed to trail names, with the distinctive Miller sense of humor frequently emerging. Visitors have come simply because names tickled their fancy: "Not Much" is a real shortie, as is "Not Much More"; "Face Flop Drop" is self-explanatory, as is "Yet Another Great View."
Activities and Entertainment: On-site: skiing! Pet/snowmobile trail takes off from the shared XC parking lot. Nearby: alpine (Red River) and saloons in town; an hour down the road are Taos Pueblo and Taos Ski Valley.
Children's Programs: Instruction, equipment, pulks. You'll see young grandson William Goins skiing when he's not downhilling at Red River.
Dining: Southwestern cuisine is at its best in New Mexico. For a sampling of this delicious stuff, visit the Sundance Restaurant—big menu, lively food, wine and beer license, super *sopapillas.*
Special Nordic Distinction: Beware the altitude, which is a superlative reason to stop occasionally to watch the snowflakes grow. Gunfighter Cullen Baker (inventor of the "fast draw") was a Miller; chat with John about his famous (infamous?) ancestor.
Summary: Enchanted Forest is New Mexico's only XC destination.

The Bark Eater
Keene, New York

Joe Pete Wilson is one of America's seminal XC figures. Founding father of Cross Country Ski Areas Association, he grew up in a farming family, the third generation working the same fields that today host skiers. Since then he has been a race car driver, real estate mogul, and Olympic XC racer (he also competed in biathlon and bobsledding). Currently he's an innkeeper, zealot polo player, and raconteur par excellence. He's also an aesthete, as you will note from selected antiques furnishing every room. Once a farmhouse that served as a stage stopover, the inn is nearly two centuries old. (Joe Pete will assure you he's not quite that aged.) "Bark Eater" comes from an Iroquois term for their longtime foes, the Algonquin. Visitors enjoy great views of the Adirondacks' 4,000-foot peaks, especially from the polo field that doubles as instruction area. The trail system is quite private—most skiers are overnight guests. For additional skiing, it's a 10-minute drive to the XC areas around Lake Placid, including Olympic site Mt. Van Hoevenberg.

Address: P.O. Box 139, Keene, NY 12942
Tel/fax: (800) 232-1607 or (518) 576-2221; fax: (518) 576-2071
e-mail: info@barkeater.com
Internet: www.barkeater.com
Location: Northeastern New York
Airport: Burlington, 75 miles
Train: Westport, 25 miles
Memberships and Awards: Cross Country Ski Areas Association
Medical: Keene Health Clinic, 2 miles
Accommodations: Ski-in/ski-out. No smoking in buildings. Two-night minimum weekends and holidays. Guests can stay in the Inn (seven cozy rooms, shared baths); the beautifully renovated and decorated Carriage House (four rooms, private baths); or the Log Cottage (two large rooms and two spacious suites), slightly removed from other buildings.
Guest Capacity: 37
Conference Capacity: 20

Rates: $–$$ (includes breakfast with wonderful country sausage, use of trails)
Credit Cards: Visa, MasterCard, American Express, Discover
Season: Christmas vacation–end March; annual snowfall 90"
XC Skiing: Joe Pete uses a snowcat to maintain 20 kms of single track plus skate lane, on seven trails; most are two-way. 40% Easier, 40% More Difficult, 20% Most Difficult—there are really only two challenging hills; many trails were recently widened. The system is divided by Alstead Mill Road. Instruction in classic and skating. Groomed downhill practice area. Some rentals are on the antique side. Daily trail fee. Altitude range 900'–1,250'.
Maps: As might be expected, the map is fun, effective (with a novel way of indicating difficult ratings), and artistic, with a rendering of the inn across the top.
Activities and Entertainment: On-site: snowshoeing, sleigh rides, ice skating, and vigorous horseback riding program. Nearby: alpine skiing at Whiteface, Lake Placid events.
Children's Programs: Equipment, snow play.
Dining: Bark Eater serves breakfast but no midday meal. Dinner is available by reservation; single entrée specialties include poached salmon, shrimp and scallops with wine sauce over linguine. (No hats or boots at the table—save those wood floors!) B.Y.O.B.
Special Nordic Distinction: First-time visitors often come for pleasant beginner terrain and great intermediate cruising. They return for Joe Pete's engaging stories and personality.
Summary: Winter in this lovely high-mountain valley ain't what it used to be. (Depending on your longevity, that can refer to anything from the early 1900s to the late 1970s.) Don't worry about the snow, there's snowmaking up the road at Mt. Van Hoevenberg; there's always opportunity to hike or horseback ride. At the Bark Eater, you will be marvelously diverted.

Friends Lake Inn
Chestertown, New York

Until recent days, a winter visit to Friends Lake Inn in Adirondack Park would have been more likely motivated by fondness for fine wines and dining than interest in skiing. But with improvements in trails, grooming, equipment, and the XC center building, things have changed dramatically. Friends Lake began in the 1860s as a boardinghouse, became an inn in 1890, and by the time Sharon and Greg Taylor purchased it in 1983, was in dire need of repair. They reduced the number of rooms from 40 to less than half that number, changing ambiance from frowzy to elegant. Greg was a ski company rep and a stonemason; he's now a wine merchant. Sharon worked as a civil engineer. (Both were downhill racers and first operated Friends Lake as a ski camp—quite an intriguing start for an inn that has the reputation as one of New York's most romantic restaurants.) They introduced XC in the mid-'80s, eventually developing a 25-trail system with lots of short connectors and loops. You often need to be able to carry off a snowplow. Cardiac Hill is aptly named (one of several Double Black Diamond Severe-Adrenaline routes), though there are gentle options to regain that altitude loss.

Address: Friends Lake Road, Chestertown, NY 12817
Tel/fax: (518) 494-4751; fax: (518) 494-4616
e-mail: friends@netheaven.com
Internet: www.friendslake.com
Location: East-central New York
Airport: Albany International, 75 miles
Train: Saratoga, 50 miles
Memberships and Awards: Cross Country Ski Areas Association, *Wine Spectator*'s Grand Award, AAA Three Diamonds
Medical: Chestertown Health Center, 5 miles
Accommodations: The inn has narrow halls but 17 very nice rooms and junior suites, with canopy beds, all with private bath. Many have private Jacuzzis. Ski-in/ski-out. Smoking in bar only. Two- or three-night minimum weekends and holidays.

Guest Capacity: 34
Conference Capacity: 25
Rates: $$–$$$$ (packages can include breakfast, dinner, use of trails, and other effete delights)
Credit Cards: Visa, MasterCard, American Express
Season: Mid-December–end March; annual snowfall 106"
XC Skiing: 32 kms of snowmobile- and snowcat-maintained trail tend to follow wide old logging roads; most are two-way. There's some double track, some skating. Until 1996, coniferous overhang minimized snow reaching the trails; though this created a pretty pattern (reaching a clearing was like emerging into a pool of light), bare earth was rather hard on skis. 10% Easier, 60% More Difficult, 30% Most Difficult (believe it!). Groomed downhill instruction area. Modern rentals for both kids and adults. Snowshoes, too. Daily trail fee. Altitude range 1,000'–1,400'.
Maps: A new map is a definite improvement but still lacks contour indications and is on the condensed side.
Activities and Entertainment: On-site: snowshoeing, ice skating, sleigh rides (Christmas only). Nearby: alpine (Gore Mountain), antique shops.
Children's Programs: Thus far, more oriented toward couples than families. Equipment, pulks.
Dining: The dining rooms serve delights such as salmon, duck, and venison, with homemade patés and breads. Full liquor license (over 1,200 wine selections, microbeers on tap). Annual Wilderness Ski and Fondue Party, Gourmet Ski Fest.
Special Nordic Distinction: There's a nice mix of ski trails with dedicated snowshoe routes.
Summary: In no way have the culinary arts slipped, and accommodations have become still more lavish. Finally skiing is moving toward the same quality.

Garnet Hill Lodge
North River, New York

George Heim was a Naval intelligence officer for 20 years before he became an innkeeper. He purchased Garnet Hill Lodge in 1977 and has fashioned one of the East's great XC areas. Of course, there were certain natural advantages, such as frequent winter squalls and storms (1995–96 saw a 145-day season). Then there's the visual context: Central Adirondack forests, lakes, and mountains, including the highest peaks in New York. But the quality of Garnet Hill (which incidentally is both a hill and the site of a former garnet mine) is as much a result of human endeavor as geology or weather. Trails are among the most carefully evolved and well groomed in the region, so moderate slopes won't panic beginners, and a 4-inch snowpack allows 20 kilometers of skiing. Support facilities are excellent—not ultramodern (much of the resort was built in the 1930s) but efficient as well as welcoming. And staff are genial, responsive, and generally have a keen sense of humor.

Address: 13th Lake Road, North River, NY 12856
Tel/fax: (800) 497-4207 or (518) 251-2444; fax: (518) 251-3089
e-mail: mail@garnet-hill.com
Internet: www.garnet-hill.com
Location: Northeastern New York
Airport: Albany International, 95 miles
Train: Ft. Edward, 55 miles
Memberships and Awards: Cross Country Ski Areas Association, New York Cross Country Ski Association, *Snow Country* magazine's Top 10 XC Areas in North America
Medical: North Creek Health Center, 10 miles
Accommodations: Guests can stay in the Log House (built in 1936 but thoroughly modernized; nicest rooms have balconies with views far over Thirteenth Lake) or in four other buildings (two rooms in the Tea House have Jacuzzis). Ski-in/ski-out. No TV, phones, or smoking. No minimum stay.
Guest Capacity: 54

Conference Capacity: 100
Rates: $$–$$$ (includes a lesson, use of trails)
Credit Cards: Visa, MasterCard
Season: Thanksgiving–early April; annual snowfall 150"
XC Skiing: Garnet Hill grooms 55 kms of trail by snowcat. Trails are either single- or double-tracked; all have skating, mostly two-way. 25% Easier, 50% More Difficult, 25% Most Difficult. Old Faithful is a great beginner loop starting near the ski shop. Two-km lighted trail. Road crossings. Groomed downhill practice area. Two shelters. PSIA-certified daily instruction in all disciplines (you can buy your lesson's videotape—this is a service, not blackmail!); guided tours, such as Gore Mountain to Garnet Hill. Ski shop has excellent equipment for rent and sale. Daily trail fee. Altitude range 1,260'–2,000'.
Maps: One side of a contour map shows all trails, the other covers the close-in core. It works well.
Activities and Entertainment: On-site: snowshoeing, ice skating, sauna, hot tub, snow play; spring skis to the Sugar House. Nearby: alpine (Gore Mountain), outlet shopping, Adirondack Park Visitor Interpretive Center.
Children's Programs: Special trails, narrow tracks, instruction, equipment, pulks, snow play. Special programs weekends and holidays. Babysitting by arrangement.
Dining: Meals are unpretentious and savory, with a slight Italian flavor. Mary Jane Freebern creates great pastries and desserts. Wines and beer available.
Special Nordic Distinction: To offset the vertical, Garnet Hill offers a shuttle service (reserve ahead!) and may install a surface lift. Another innovation: 1.5-hour introduction to trails and free ski clinics most weekends and holidays.
Summary: Garnet Hill is comfortable, sightly, fun, and family-friendly. If you (and he) have a free moment, sit and chat with George about how he found Garnet Hill.

Garnet Hill Lodge, New York

Frost Valley YMCA
Claryville, New York

It's a little-known fact that the YMCA oper-ates outside cities. The organization also runs unusual cross-country ski destinations in the Catskills and the Rockies, particularly suited for families, groups, and folks on a budget (though the latter doesn't connote reduction of quality). Frost Valley is located in the Catskills, with views of Slide Mountain, high-est peak in the range. The property covers 6,500 acres, most of it in hill and deciduous forest; there's a second small center within easy driving distance, particularly suit-ed for small conferences. In the midst of 200,000 acres of state forest, Frost Valley is only two and a half hours from NYC but feels both remote and wild. The property evolved around Forstmann Castle, an interesting structure built in 1915 as a replica of the owner's childhood home in Germany. Sold to a group of YMCA trustees in 1957 for a boys' camp, in 1968 it became an independent YMCA. While busiest in summer, Frost Valley is a full-service winter operation, with em-phases on fitness, wellness, and environmen-tal education. In spring you may see eagle, osprey, and sometimes bear tracks.

Address: 2000 Frost Valley Road, Claryville, NY 12725-9600
Tel/fax: (914) 985-2291; fax: (914) 985-0056
e-mail: fwasiak@frostvalley.org
Internet: www.frostvalley.org
Location: Southeastern New York
Airport: Stewart International, 80 miles
Train: None nearby
Memberships and Awards: Cross Country Ski Areas Association
Medical: Community General Hospital, 30 miles
Accommodations: Accommodations are avail-able in 45 cabins and 16 lodges. Rooms are clean and simple, dining is communal. The newer lodges are more comfortable and very presentable, with post-and-beam construc-tion. Each building has four bedrooms (sleeps four to six on bunks), with private bath and meeting room. Ski-in/ski-out. Non-smoking environment. Two-night minimum.
Guest Capacity: 700 at the YMCA
Conference Capacity: 700
Rates: $ (includes meals, instruction, use of trails; linens additional charge)
Credit Cards: Visa, MasterCard
Season: Mid-December–mid-March with the grace of the weather gods; annual snowfall 50"
XC Skiing: Frost Valley maintains 25 kms by snowmobile. Flatter trails in the valley are two-way. There's a grooming mix: single track, skate loop, single track with skating, and dou-ble track. Some routes stretch out along river bottom near the XC shop, but there are also impressive hills. 20% Easier, 40% More Difficult, 40% Most Difficult. Groomed down-hill practice area. Two warming shelters. Road crossings. Daily instruction in classic, skating, and telemarking; guide service on request. Rentals. Daily trail fee. Altitude range 2,100'–2,400'.
Maps: The simple map is based on a topo and includes ratings and tours.
Activities and Entertainment: On-site: snow-shoeing, ice skating, tubing/tobogganing, ice fishing, sugaring, hiking, and extremely diverse programming (astronomy, arts and crafts, winter ecology, Native American lore, snow sculpture, animal tracking, Elderhostel). Nearby: alpine (Hunter and Belleayre).
Children's Programs: Equipment, snow play, plus activities noted above.
Dining: Meals are enjoyed family-style, with impressive breakfast bar and salad bar. Emphasis is on healthy food and cooking—no deep-fat frying, for example. There's also an on-site bakery.
Special Nordic Distinction: This isn't a high-snowfall region, but trails can be enjoyed by snowshoe or foot as well as by ski.
Summary: Fun and family-oriented.

Lake Placid Region
New York

Talk with a longtime racer and you will eventually hear of the incredible finish of the men's 50-km event at the 1980 Olympics, where Finnish giant Juha Mieto lost by less than 0.001 second. But there's a great deal more to enjoy around Lake Placid than competition. The region is a XC hotbed, with four distinct but connected trail networks. Lake Placid enjoyed a skiing history decades before these Games and has marvelous mountain scenery, including 5,344-foot Mt. Marcy, highest point in New York.

Address: Lake Placid/Essex County Visitors Bureau, 216 Main Street, Olympic Center, Lake Placid, NY 12946
Tel/fax: (800) 447-5224 or (518) 523-2445; fax: (518) 523-2605
Internet: www.lakeplacid.com
Location: Northeastern New York
Airport: Albany International, 120 miles
Train: Westport, 30 miles (shuttle)
Medical: Adirondack Medical Center, 8 miles
Accommodations: Lake Placid Lodge is on a secluded cove with a terrific view of Whiteface. It has first-class-bordering-on-opulent rooms and cabins. Ski-in/ski-out. P.O. Box 550, Lake Placid, NY 12946; (518) 523-2700.
Guest Capacity: 6,500 in region
Conference Capacity: Several locations
Rates: $$–$$$$$ (includes full breakfast)
Season: Early December–late March; annual snowfall 180"
XC Skiing: Visitors can purchase a single ticket for all areas. Altitude range 1,600'–2,100'.
- *Cascade Cross Country Center* has 20 kms of gentle, wind-sheltered classic and skating trail, 3 kms lighted. Rental and retail, restaurant, bar, instruction and guided tours. Linked to both Jackrabbit Trail and Mt. Van Hoevenberg system. Daily trail fee. (518) 523-9605.
- *Jackrabbit Trail* runs from Saranac Lake east almost all the way to Keene. It's named for Herman "Jackrabbit" Johannsen, a historic figure in North American XC skiing.

Portions are groomed, including connectors with the ski centers. (518) 523-1365.
- *Lake Placid Lodge/Whiteface Club* grooms 20 kms of classic and skating, much of it on an open golf course. Instruction, rentals; backcountry skiing. Jackrabbit Trail connector. Daily trail fee. (518) 523-2551.
- *Lake Placid Resort* has 25 kms of track, most including skating. Best views of the Adirondacks from any XC center. Jackrabbit Trail connector. Instruction, clubhouse. Daily trail fee. (518) 523-2556.
- *Mt. Van Hoevenberg* grooms 50 kms for both classic and skating, much of it severely advanced. Up to 5 kms of snowmaking. Biathlon range. Rentals, instruction, cafeteria. Daily trail fee. (518) 523-2811.

Maps: There's an all-encompassing Jackrabbit Trail map plus individual area maps.
Activities and Entertainment: Alpine (Whiteface), snowshoeing, sleigh rides, bobsled and luge rides, ice rinks, ice fishing, dog sledding, toboggan chute, horseback riding, rock/ice climbing, snowmobiling, tours of Olympic facilities. Folk music festivals. Lake Placid Winter Olympic Museum.
Dining: Consider dining at Lake Placid Lodge, where chefs trained in England create "French American cuisine with an Adirondack flavor." Results are delicious.
Special Nordic Distinction: Mt. Van Hoevenberg has the distinction of being the only American site for two Winter Olympics: 1980 and 1932.
Summary: It's curious how many skiers speak of Lake Placid and how few have actually visited. It's interesting to speculate how many of those visitors ever spread ski wings and flew outside the Mt. Van Hoevenberg Stadium.

Lapland Lake Cross Country Ski & Vacation Center
Northville, New York

Three threads run through all activities and facilities at Lapland Lake: a sense of humor, meticulous attention to detail, and affection for all things Finnish. Founder Olavi Hirvonen was born in Montréal, "grew up on skis" in Finland, and came to the U.S. in 1949. Carpenter, waiter, and bartender in New York City, he eventually moved north and made the 1960 XC Olympic Team at age 29. In 1978 he purchased the 300 acres that's now Lapland Lake, surrounded by state forest in the southern Adirondacks. He has created a wonderously, sinuous trail system, winding through pine forest. Even the tougher downhills have good runouts, and surfaces are so smooth that the network can open with only 6 inches of packed snow. Olavi (gravely thoughtful) met Ann Hirvonen (full of laughter) skiing at Lapland. Their daughter, Leila, is a dedicated classic *and* skate skier. Together they have created one of the most friendly and animated XC areas anywhere, as you'll see at events such as Lumipossu Day and the annual St. Urho's Festival (a spoof on St. Patrick's Day).

Address: 139 Lapland Lake Road, Northville, NY 12134
Tel/fax: (800) 453-SNOW or (518) 863-4974; fax: (518) 863-2651
e-mail: lapland@klink.net
Internet: www.laplandlake.com
Location: East-central New York
Airport: Albany, 60 miles
Train: Amsterdam, 30 miles
Memberships and Awards: Cross Country Ski Areas Association, *Snow Country* magazine's Top 10 XC Areas in the East, Rossignol Demo Center
Medical: Nathan Littauer Hospital, 24 miles
Accommodations: Lapland has 10 housekeeping cottages (*tupas*), simple and meticulously maintained. Blankets and pillows are supplied, linens can be rented. No TVs or phones. Ski-in/ski-out. Smoke-free environment. Two-night minimum weekends, three-night minimum holidays.

Guest Capacity: 72
Conference Capacity: 50
Rates: $$–$$$ (includes use of trails)
Credit Cards: Visa, MasterCard, Discover
Season: November–early April; annual snowfall 128" (118-day seasons are the norm)
XC Skiing: Olavi fastidiously grooms 38 kms, primarily single track with skate lane, some double track with skating. 30% Easier, 56% More Difficult, 9% Most Difficult, 5% Expert. The great majority are one-way. Four-km lighted trail. PSIA-certified instruction in classic and skating; guide service. Three teaching areas; groomed downhill practice area. Excellent rental and retail fleet includes snowshoes. Daily trail fee. Altitude range 1,350'–1,600'.
Maps: It lacks contours but is clear and lively.
Activities and Entertainment: On-site: snowshoeing, ice skating and Finnish ice games, reindeer sleigh rides, snowcat rides, wood-burning sauna, reindeer appreciation, massage therapy, kicksleds, sledding hill, tubing, Olavi's birthday celebration on December 26. Nearby: alpine skiing (Gore and Royal Mountains), wilderness snowshoe tours.
Children's Programs: Special trails, narrow-groomed, instruction, equipment, pulks, snow play.
Dining: Lunch daily, dinner Friday and Saturday evenings. Lapland Lake serves traditional Finnish specialties (*lohilaatikko, kaalikaaryleet*) as well as vegetarian selections, homemade soups, chicken and fish dishes. Wine and beer license.
Special Nordic Distinction: Everything is well organized and clean; everything has a Finnish flavor (buildings, restaurant dishes, skis, events, trail names, sauna, and of course reindeer names).
Summary: Lapland has hands-on management, from grooming to food preparation; the benefits are obvious. It's exceedingly popular with women and families.

Lapland Lake Cross Country Ski & Vacation Center, New York

Nancie Battaglia

Craig Murphy

Mohonk Mountain House
New Paltz, New York

Mohonk Mountain House was built by Albert and Alfred Smiley in the 1860s (previously there was a tavern on the site) and has stayed in the family for over 130 years. Little has changed since 1910 (rooms still have steam heat), and responsible stewardship has been honored since Albert wrote, "I have treated this property . . . as a landscape architect does his canvas, only my canvas covers 7 square miles." The land once included a sawmill, dairy farm, barns, power house, and ice house. It's a grand hotel on the scale of The Balsams—a Victorian/Edwardian turreted confection with 261 rooms, lounges, parlors, library, 200 balconies, 150 fireplaces, period furniture, and polished woodwork. Set in the midst of the Shawangunk Mountains, the resort is surrounded by a 21,000-acre natural area, including private preserves and Minnewaska State Park. *Mohonk* means "lake in the sky" and, as you might guess, stands nearly on the apex of a mountain. Ski along lovely old carriage roads or up to Sky Top Tower. The latter offers some of the most spectacular views in this part of the world—50 miles in five states. And if the ski season is curtailed, there's very active programming, from swing-dancing to chocolate-lovers weekends.

Address: Lake Mohonk, New Paltz, NY 12561
Tel/fax: (914) 255-1000, reservations (800) 772-6646 or (914) 255-4500; fax: (914) 256-2100
Internet: www.mohonk.com
Location: Southeastern New York
Airport: Stewart Airport, 30 miles
Train: Poughkeepsie, 13 miles (pickup available)
Memberships and Awards: Cross Country Ski Areas Association, National Historic Landmark
Medical: Vasser Brothers Hospital, 15 miles
Accommodations: Enjoy your choice of 30 different room types. Tower rooms have (naturally) the finest views. No TVs. Ski-in/ski-out. Certain minimum stay requirements.

Guest Capacity: 550 (about same number of staff)
Conference Capacity: 300
Rates: $$$$$ (includes all meals, afternoon tea, use of trails, rentals)
Credit Cards: Visa, MasterCard, American Express, Diners Club, Discover
Season: Christmas–Presidents' Week; annual snowfall 80"
XC Skiing: Effectively, two networks—farther one is partly a golf course; both total 70 kms Some routes run along cliff faces. For the most part, trails are converted 14'-wide carriage roads; all grooming is carried out by snowmobile. The majority of trails are two-way. 30% Easier, 30% More Difficult, 40% Most Difficult (mostly based on distance). Several road crossings. Busy ski school on weekends. Rentals. Daily trail fee. Altitude range 943'–1,552'.
Maps: Mohonk has an excellent map, with a sensible trail-rating system.
Activities and Entertainment: On-site: snowshoeing, ice skating, snow play, skiing past gazebos, fitness center (Nautilus, yoga, aerobics, saunas), spa (reflexology, facial renewal), classical music concerts, theme programs, Barn Museum, Greenhouse. Nearby: XC (the abandoned bed of the Ontario & Western Railroad is a popular trail), Widmark Honey Farms, house museums, Rivendell Winery.
Children's Programs: Mohonk Kids' Club, instruction, equipment, snow play, and a repertoire of nature and exercise activities.
Dining: Choose from two menus, the customary wide-ranging treats or Sound Choice (reduced in fat, cholesterol, calories, and sodium). Alcohol available in dining rooms. Jackets required for gentlemen at evening meal.
Special Nordic Distinction: This may be the only ski shop that doubles as a summer art studio. If snow is sparse, still plan to visit—just hike instead of ski!
Summary: It's astounding to find such a treat 90 minutes from downtown Manhattan.

Salmon Hills
Redfield, New York

Wind sweeping east strips moisture from Lake Ontario then lifts, chills, and drops snow as it reaches the Tug Hill highland. Though this rolling glaciated terrain never reaches 2,000', storms deliver Sierra-like dumps. Two hundred years ago this was farming country; now it's mostly timber clinging to glacial till, with dramatic transitions in forest types. There's a magic climatic transition, climbing from the town of Pulaski up to Redfield—snow country! In December 1996 Hans and Liz Giuliani opened something new in the ski world: Salmon Hills, a trails-based year-round resort, centered around the Northeast's first yurt village (modern nomadic huts—light, airy, snug, unique!). They've devoted 800 acres to recreation in a region long dedicated to dairy farming and forest products. Hans grew up in Puerto Rico, Liz is originally from Iowa, but both love winter and have created a family-friendly destination. Plans are still evolving; right now a new log lodge and social center complement the yurts.

Address: 100 Noble Shores Drive, Redfield, NY 13437
Tel/fax: (315) 599-4003, (888) 976-SNOW for conditions and events; fax: (315) 465-6863
e-mail: LizExplor@aol.com
Internet: www.greatsalmonwilderness.com
Location: North-central New York
Airport: Syracuse, 50 miles
Train: Syracuse, 50 miles
Memberships and Awards: Cross Country Ski Areas Association, Key Fischer Nordic Center
Medical: Pulaski Community Health Center, 13 miles
Accommodations: Salmon Hills has new motel rooms, but it's far more fun to stay at the yurt village, all with bathrooms, several with showers (bring linen and towels). Trailside yurts available by time-sharing. Non-smoking environment. Every unit is ski-in/ski-out; some have 2-night minimum stay.
Guest capacity: 60

Conference Capacity: 60
Rates: $ (includes trails, guiding)
Credit cards: Visa, MasterCard, American Express, Discover
Season: Thanksgiving–mid April; annual snowfall 350"
XC Skiing: Salmon Hills snowcat-grooms 35 kms, 2 kms lighted. Virtually everything is one-way, single track plus skating, a little double track plus skating. Longest trail is 15 kms. 40% Easier, 40% More Difficult, 20% Most Difficult. Routes include numerous loops and connectors. Groomed downhill practice area, one trail opened to dogs. Backwoods yurts. Strong women's program, including seniors. Instruction in classic, skating, and tele. Ski and snowshoe rentals, retail. Guided tours. Daily trail fee. Altitude range 900'–1,200'.
Maps: The initial hand-drawn photocopy was complex and difficult to read; a refined product is in the works.
Activities and Entertainment: On-site: snowshoeing, telemarking, snow play, dog sledding, archery, outdoor hot tub. Nearby: alpine skiing (Snow Ridge), Wild Herb's Tattoos, ice-laden Salmon River Falls (higher than Niagara!), ice fishing, casino, karaoke at the Lake Effect Tavern, snowmobiling.
Children's Programs: Equipment, instruction, pulks, tubing on tow-served Alvin's Avalanche, Campfire Singalongs.
Dining: Yurting guests can cook their own meals; on-site dining is evolving (the blueberry cobbler is stupendous), beer and wine license soon. Fresh fish dinners are delish at characterful Century House (once a post office, later an undertaker's) in nearby Redfield. Salmon Hills sells designer maple syrup, when it isn't shipped east as "Vermont's Finest."
Special Nordic Distinction: "Lake effect snow" takes on a new dimension when it drops 7' in two days.
Summary: Hans and Liz have taken to skiing like swans to water. Expect hospitality, marvelous fun, constant growth and innovation.

See color photos, page 97

Mt. Bachelor Cross Country Center
Bend, Oregon

Mt. Bachelor Ski & Summer Resort isn't a XC area that you're likely to see on a whim. It's not a gourmand's paradise, like the inns of Québec. It doesn't provide the luxurious ski-in/ski-out lodgings of Colorado guest ranches. And it lacks the all-in-one "village" convenience of some other alpine destinations. In fact, Mt. Bachelor is that strange creature, a major western downhill ski area with no lodging. Why? The U.S. Forest Service controls most of the territory "Mt. B." uses, and regulations require that this federal land be used for recreation, not development. Were it otherwise, the XC operation would be swamped instead of merely busy. As 'tis, it's perhaps the most popular alpine-affiliated area in the country, with close to 30,000 visitors in a brisk year. Its magnetism comes from *splendid* skiing and utterly reliable snow—qualities particularly welcomed by families splitting their time between downhilling/snowboarding and skinny skiing. It's a destination for any XC devotee, not just for national caliber racers. Most of the continuously rolling terrain is suited to intermediates, with abrupt transitions from meadow into towering pine forest.

Address: P.O. Box 1031, Bend, OR 97709-1031
Tel/fax: (800) 829-2442 or (541) 382-2607; fax: (541) 382-4251
e-mail: MTB@bendnet.com
Internet: www.mtbachelor.com
Location: Central Oregon
Airport: Bend/Redmond, 40 miles
Train: Chemult, 60 miles
Memberships and Awards: Cross Country Ski Areas Association, Rossignol Demo Center, *Snow Country* magazine's Top 10 XC Areas in the West, U.S. XC Team Training Center
Medical: St. Charles Medical Center, 25 miles
Accommodations: Inn of the Seventh Mountain is a XC favorite because of proximity (14 miles to the trails), pleasant condominiums, reasonable prices, heated outdoor pool, hot tubs, and sauna. Largely non-smoking rooms. Multi-day stays required on holidays. 18575 S. Century Drive, Bend, OR 97702; (800) 452-6810.
Guest Capacity: 1,000 at the Inn of the Seventh Mountain
Conference Capacity: 375-plus
Rates: $–$$$ (inexpensive package includes ice skating, shuttle and use of trails)
Credit Cards: Visa, MasterCard, American Express, Diners Club, Discover
Season: Mid-November–mid-April; annual snowfall 300"
XC Skiing: Mt. Bachelor maintains 56 kms by snowcat, primarily skating and double track; the area is known for excellent grooming. (Bend has a vocal XC population; suspected deficiencies are usually pointed out with some asperity.) 5% Easier, 87% More Difficult, 8% Most Difficult. Groomed downhill practice area. Special clinics: weekend-long programs for women; fall camps; and innovative daily coaching in skating, classic, and telemarking; nature tour. Excellent rental and retail department. Daily trail fee. Altitude range 5,730'–6,380'.
Maps: Compact, graphically vivid, useful.
Activities and Entertainment: On-site: alpine, snowshoeing (including nature walks), Oregon Trail of Dreams Training Camp (*serious* dog sledding). Nearby: High Desert Museum, Museum at Warm Springs; in spring whitewater float trips.
Children's Programs: Day care just across the parking lot, special trails, instruction, equipment (classic and skating), pulks, snow play.
Dining: Josiah's Restaurant at the Inn of the Seventh Mountain serves American cuisine with a Northwest flavor; entrées such as hazelnut salmon or Tuscany roasted chicken breast.
Special Nordic Distinction: Try trails to the north and see Three Sisters Wilderness Area, with peaks over 10,000'.
Summary: Mt. B. is a skier's ski area, with great downhilling a moment's walk away. This is a place to visit when you've learned to love the sport.

Sundance
Sundance, Utah

The Sundance Nordic Center is part of a 6,000-acre resort owned by Robert Redford. Driving there from Salt Lake City, the Wasatch mountains to the east are a magnificent wall of bent and folded rock. Redford purchased a tiny downhill area in 1969 and has created an aesthetic gem. His public pledge to "recreation, the arts, and a commitment to the environment" has been admirably fulfilled. It's still small, and Redford maintains privacy by limiting the number of lift tickets sold each day. The village core is cohesive, landscaped with an eye to enhancing the natural beauty of trees, stream, and mountain backdrop. The Nordic Center is several minutes' drive along a winding, climbing, narrow road, but there's frequent shuttle service. The high alpine valley sits almost in the shadow of 12,000-foot Mt. Timpanogos (roughly translates from Ute as "rocky running river") and encompasses meadows and aspen groves. The center building is a yurt (sightly structure filled with light, which has a low impact on the environment). Trails climb into a natural amphitheater, an invitation to powder-play.

Address: R.R. 3, Box A-1, Sundance, UT 84604
Tel/fax: (800) 892-1600 or (801) 225-4107, XC center (801) 223-4170; fax: (801) 226-1937
Internet: www.sundance-utah.com
Location: North-central Utah
Airport: Salt Lake City International, 50 miles
Train: Salt Lake City, 50 miles
Memberships and Awards: Cross Country Ski Areas Association, Rossignol Demo Center
Medical: First Med, 10 miles
Accommodations: Guests can choose between elegant-rustic cottages in the resort base area or private homes a short distance away. Cottage suite has living room, fireplace, full kitchen. Some smoking rooms. Five-night minimum Christmas holiday.
Guest Capacity: 200-plus in cottages
Conference Capacity: 300
Rates: $$$$$ (includes lodging, breakfast)

Credit Cards: Visa, MasterCard, American Express
Season: December 1–April 1; annual snowfall 320"
XC Skiing: Sundance snowcat-grooms 15 kms with loving care. 30% Easier, 40% More Difficult, 30% Most Difficult—but this is customarily Wasatch powder, fluffy-dry and forgiving. Almost everything is two-way; some double track but the majority single track with skating. A great morning route is over to Elk Meadows, over Kennecott to Middle Earth, and back down. Talk with XC Director Sam Palmatier about trail names, which include those of Redford's grandchildren. And look for avalanche chutes above Stewart Falls Trail (the resort closely monitors snow stability). Outstanding rentals. 3 kms lit, four nights/week. PSIA-certified instructors for track, skating, and telemarking. Daily trail fee. Altitude range 6,610'–7,200'.
Maps: Based on an aerial photo; there's little indication of length.
Activities and Entertainment: At XC area: snowshoeing (separate 10 kms), astronomer-led programs. At resort: a wide variety of weekend entertainment, the famous Sundance Film Series, arts programs (painting, photography, organic crafts), dog sledding, shopping, new fitness center. Nearby: fly-fishing, ice skating, sleigh rides, snowmobiling.
Children's Programs: Sundance is child-friendly: special narrow tracks, "terrain gardens," instruction, equipment; nanny service at resort.
Dining: The elegant Tree Room typically offers a choice of entrées such as red snapper and pepper steak. Emphasis is on organic, fresh, regional products. Non-smoking public buildings. Owl Bar has Sundance Kid history.
Special Nordic Distinction: Utah's claim to "the best snow on earth" often holds true.
Summary: Neither alpine slopes nor XC trails are ever crowded. It's a place that's very relaxed, with a sense of community.

Ruby's Inn Nordic Center
Bryce, Utah

The English language doesn't contain enough nouns or adjectives to describe the span of geologic wonders at Bryce Canyon National Park. Red limestone has been worked by time, temperature, and water to create intricate and ever-changing forms—needles, spires, fins, spills, arches, caps, windows, columns, cliffs, hoodoos. (The clever folks in Utah Tourism have labeled the region "Color Country.") Flaming sunsets must be seen to be believed, with views from some vantage points stretching 200 miles into Arizona and New Mexico. Bryce was declared a National Monument in 1923 and a National Park four years later. Set on the Paunsaugunt Plateau, one looks down into the park, a series of bowls rather than one continuous canyon. Unlike most of Yellowstone and Yosemite, all roads are kept open in winter, and machine grooming for XC trails is not permitted within park borders.

Address: Box 17, Bryce, UT 84764
Tel/fax: (800) 468-8660 or (435) 834-5341; fax: (435) 834-5265
e-mail: jean@rubysinn.com
Internet: www.rubysinn.com
Location: Southwestern Utah
Airport: Salt Lake City International, 260 miles
Train: None nearby
Memberships and Awards: Cross Country Ski Areas Association
Medical: Garfield Memorial Hospital, 23 miles
Accommodations: Ruby's Inn has metamorphosed since it opened in 1920, changing both site and size. Today it's a 369-room Best Western, with something of the feel of a hotel—for what motel has an art gallery or enormous general store? Rooms have TVs and phones. Ski-in/ski-out. Non-smoking public buildings, some smoking rooms. No minimum stay.
Guest Capacity: 700
Conference Capacity: 300
Rates: $–$$
Credit Cards: Visa, MasterCard, American Express, Diners Club, Discover

Season: Mid-December–early March; annual snowfall 84"
XC Skiing: A portion of the 30-km snowcat-groomed system takes off just across the road from the inn on the Old Bryce Town Trail (the "town" is closed in winter); or park just to the south on the Main Trail (sometimes shared with snowmobiles). There's an evolving mix of single track, double track, and skating. In theory it's 50% Easier, 30% More Difficult, 20% Most Difficult, but, in fact, terrain is very moderate, running through ponderosa pine forest and across meadows. Wind is largely restricted to the Rim Trail, which has fantastic views of the eroded edge of the plateau. Groomed routes on Forest Service land join with ungroomed trails on Park Service property. Great backcountry touring, though downhills between rock needles can be inspiring. Instruction in classic and skating by appointment. Altitude range 8,000'–8,100'.
Maps: Incorporated into a small brochure, it shows both tracked and intersecting ski-set trails.
Activities and Entertainment: On-site: snowshoeing, sleigh rides, groomed dog trail, indoor swimming pools, hot tubs, annual Bryce Canyon Winter Festival in February. Nearby: Park Visitor Center, snowmobiling (not within Bryce), ice fishing, alpine skiing at Brian Head.
Children's Programs: Snow play, equipment.
Dining: Cowboy's Buffet and Steak Room has reasonable variety, including good pasta. Alcohol available in store.
Special Nordic Distinction: Summer is a madhouse at the park; crowds evaporate with the cold.
Summary: Bryce is best enjoyed during winter, a time of brilliant contrasts between snow and rock that has been twisted, shattered, crushed, caressed, weathered, hollowed, riven, scraped, polished—the sculpture of eternity. Forgetting a camera is a cardinal sin (and the inn's photo store can process film in an hour).

Ruby's Inn Nordic Center, Utah

Janet Reifert

Janet Reifert

Blueberry Hill Inn
Goshen, Vermont

Tony Clark was born in Wales, grew up in France, lived in Norway, and has been in the XC business most of his life, including a stint as a ski company representative. He founded Blueberry Hill in 1971, partly at the suggestion of Johannes Von Trapp, and has been a ski area owner ever since. The setting is an isolated and tranquil part of the Green Mountain National Forest, a region once hunted and fished by Abenaki Indians and later beloved by Robert Frost. The inn is a restored 1813 farmhouse that reflects Tony's own elegance, good cheer, and informality. One of its charms is a profusion of indoor flowers and plants—geraniums, ferns, jade trees—under a skylight along the walkway between rooms and inn proper.

Address: Goshen, VT 05753
Tel/fax: (800) 448-0707 or (802) 247-6735; fax: (802) 247-3983
e-mail: info@blueberryhillinn.com
Internet: blueberryhillinn.com
Location: Central Vermont
Airport: Burlington International, 55 miles
Train: Rutland, 20 miles
Memberships and Awards: Cross Country Ski Areas Association
Medical: Middlebury Porter Hospital, 15 miles
Accommodations: The inn contains an even dozen rooms, each with private bath and furnished with antiques. Ski-in/ski-out. No smoking in buildings. Two-night minimum weekends.
Guest Capacity: 32
Conference Capacity: 40
Rates: $$$ (includes meals and use of trails)
Credit Cards: Visa, MasterCard, American Express
Season: Mid-December–mid-March; annual snowfall 140"
XC Skiing: Blueberry Hill has a "big" 50-km network, groomed by snowcat; 30% Easier, 60% More Difficult, 10% Most Difficult. Primarily two-way, classic style predominates. Easier trails are on the west (XC center) side of Forest Service Road 32, but the more scenic routes are above the inn and require a certain amount of climbing. Romance Trail is the highest groomed route in Vermont. Gazing west from the top of Hogback Mountain, you can see the Champlain Valley as well as New York's Adirondacks. With a little luck, you'll also see peregrine falcons in the area. Several peripheral trails are shared with snowmobiles; there are also a number of wilderness paths. Full XC center (rentals, instruction, lounging area). Daily trail fee. Altitude range 1,400'–2,750'.
Maps: Sightly and extremely accurate (points were plotted by GPS). It's virtually impossible to get lost because every junction is numbered, with lowest numbers near the inn. For instance, if you're way out at intersection #43, just look for the sign indicating #42, and you're on the way home.
Activities and Entertainment: On-site: snowshoeing, sauna, massage, fun events. Nearby: several alpine areas (Middlebury Snow Bowl, Pico, Stratton . . .), profuse antiquing, the New England Maple Museum, walking in the town of Brandon, shopping in Middlebury. Dollhouse and Miniature Center at Fred's Carpenter Shop in Brandon.
Children's Programs: Instruction, pulks, equipment, sledding.
Dining: Guests who stay for a week or visit frequently find this a rounding experience. Dinner is a candlelit four-course event; sample entrée is black angus beef tenderloin stuffed with arugula and oyster mushrooms. B.Y.O.B.
Special Nordic Distinction: If anything, Tony *underestimates* the size of his trail system. Try a spin down Truck Hill, a wonderfully winding descent; but don't get distracted by its namesake to the right of an S-curve. Spring's major event—snow or no snow—is the infamous Pig Race.
Summary: Genial hosts Tony Clark and Shari Brown provide charm to complement New England's beauty.

See color photos, page 98

Burke Cross Country Ski Area
East Burke, Vermont

Stan Swaim would figure prominently in any XC Area Founding Parent list, with background at Bretton Woods and Cummington Farm (now a boys' prep school). Once an international bike racer and coach, he came to Burke in 1980, and (happily) skiing hasn't been the same since. Stan has no interest in sham or gloss (for confirmation, just listen to his recorded ski report). Focus is on quality of skiing, with sidelights on the environment and history—he can tell you of a sap bucket on one trail that's being absorbed into the trunk of a tree; on another you'll pass the foundations of an old homestead. The farmhouse that's the XC center connects to "The Tent," which has room to relax in while noshing on Betsy Swaim's good vegetarian chili. There is a series of easy loops to the west of the center; if you note a Black Diamond indicator elsewhere, it's best to believe it. Finest views are found up around McGill Fields; you can see the vast woods of the Northeast Kingdom, Willoughby Gap to the northwest, and peaks over 3,000 feet.

Address: R.R. 1, Box 62A, East Burke, VT 05832
Tel/fax: (800) 786-8338 or (802) 626-8338
e-mail: bam@together.net
Location: Northeastern Vermont
Airport: Burlington International, 85 miles
Train: White River Junction, 70 miles
Memberships and Awards: Cross Country Ski Areas Association
Medical: Northeastern Vermont Regional Hospital, 16 miles
Accommodations: The Old Cutter Inn has its own link to Burke's trail system. Originally a farmhouse, the Swiss Family Walther purchased the property in 1977. Nine rooms in the inn (five have private bath); there's also a pleasant separate suite in the Carriage House with fireplace and full kitchen. Some non-smoking rooms. Two-night minimum weekends. R.R. 1, Box 62, East Burke, VT 05832-9707; (802) 626-5152.
Guest Capacity: 37 at Old Cutter Inn

Conference Capacity: 40
Rates: $
Credit Cards: Visa, MasterCard, Discover
Season: December 15–April 1; annual snowfall 125"
XC Skiing: Stan maintains almost 80 kms by snowcat and snowmobile. Most routes are two-way, single track with skate lane; there's one classic-only. 30% Easier, 40% More Difficult, 30% Most Difficult (a lot of vertical on the trails to the southeast). Road crossings. Classic and skate instruction each weekend, weekdays by appointment. Goodly rental selection and retail, including snowshoes. Daily trail fee. Altitude range 1,100'–2,400'.
Maps: Burke has an attractive, functional map; difficulty ratings and contours but no trail lengths listed.
Activities and Entertainment: On-site: sleigh rides, rides with groomer. Nearby: alpine (Burke Mountain), horseback riding at Roan Farm (depends on weather and trail surface), Green Mountain Books & Prints, the cigar store Indian at Bailey's Country Store, Wednesday auctions in Lyndonville, Sugarmill Farm (a kind of maple museum), snowmobiling.
Children's Programs: Day care nearby (alpine area), equipment.
Dining: Fritz Walther at the Old Cutter Inn creates European recipes such as *Rahmschnitzel*; meat, fish, and chicken specials nightly. Nice wine list.
Special Nordic Distinction: Burke has perhaps the only snowcat fueled by liquid propane. Grooming quality stays excellent, and it puts out fewer noxious emissions than diesel or gas.
Summary: Burke is too often overlooked, despite an extensive trail system, reliable snow, expert operation, and Stan's sense of whimsy. Examples: the area is reputed to be a favorite of Bill "Snowshoe" Clinton, and there's a board for moose-sighting updates.

The Craftsbury Outdoor Center
Craftsbury Common, Vermont

Like Hazen's Notch, Craftsbury is located in the Northeast Kingdom, at equivalent altitude and with similarly reliable snow. However, it's a country of rolling highland, ridges, and open fields. Craftsbury Outdoor Center was founded in 1976 to provide year-round recreational programs with a training bent—running, hiking, sculling, skiing—using the facilities of a former boarding school. With the cooperation of 90 landowners, over the years it has created one of the largest track systems in the Northeast, flying over lake and pasture and through river valleys, linking several small towns. Today the center stages many non-competitive programs and events (orienteering, ice skating, nature tours, games, ice fishing), but there's still a leavening of serious coaching and racing.

Address: Box 31, Craftsbury Common, VT 05827
Tel/fax: (800) 729-7751 or (802) 586-7767; fax: (802) 586-7768
e-mail: crafts@sover.net
Internet: www.craftsbury.com
Location: North-central Vermont
Airport: Burlington, 70 miles
Train: Montpelier, 35 miles
Memberships and Awards: Cross Country Ski Areas Association, *Snow Country* magazine's Top 10 XC Areas in the Northeast
Medical: Northeastern Vermont Regional Hospital, 32 miles
Accommodations: The Outdoor Center has comfortable, rustic, and very affordable housing right on site, but if you enjoy a classic New England inn with fine food, on the outskirts of a lovely hilltop hamlet, try the Inn on the Common—16 beautifully appointed rooms in three buildings. Ski-in/ski-out. Some non-smoking rooms. Two-night minimum Presidents' Day weekend. P.O. Box 75, Craftsbury Common, VT 05827; (800) 521-2233 or (802) 586-9619.
Guest Capacity: 32
Conference Capacity: 36 at the Inn, 90 at the Center

Rates: $$–$$$ at the inn (includes breakfast, dinner, and use of trails)
Credit Cards: Visa, MasterCard, American Express
Season: Early December–mid-March; annual snowfall 150"
XC Skiing: Craftsbury has a 100-km network, groomed by snowcat and snowmobile, all double track with skate lane, and most (in theory) one-way. 25% Easier, 40% More Difficult, 35% Most Difficult. (If that last figure intimidates, remember that you also have as much gentle stuff as most XC areas have kilometers.) Two warming shelters. Instruction covers all techniques and skill levels. Good rentals. Daily trail fee. Altitude range 1,200'–1,500'.
Maps: Outstandingly clear and sturdy.
Activities and Entertainment: On-site: snowshoeing (20 km), ice skating, weight and conditioning rooms, sauna, massage. Nearby: alpine (Jay Peak, Burke Mountain), Bread and Puppet Theater Museum, Fairbanks Museum and Planetarium (home of the unusually accurate weather reports heard on Vermont Public Radio), snowmobiling. This is Bag Balm country (factory in Lyndonville).
Children's Programs: Babysitting by reservation, instruction, equipment, pulks; many special weekends for families.
Dining: Go no farther than the Inn on the Common, with entrées familiar and exotic (sautéed monk fish and shrimp), accompanied by fine wines. For lunch, consider hearty buffet-style meals at the Center.
Special Nordic Distinction: Great variety in both terrain and activities. Some trails need only a few inches of snow to open for skating, such as the straight shot across Little Hosmer Lake (for obscure reasons, larger than Big Hosmer). "Snow guarantee" from the Inn and nordic center: skiable cover or money back. Best views of the Lowell Range are from the high east side of the trail system.
Summary: Craftsbury is another destination with racing antecedents. It still can hone those skills but has expanded its menu of attractions.

The Equinox
Manchester Village, Vermont

No Vermont area excels The Equinox at winter diversity. There's an absorbing mix of skiing, programs (Land Rover Driving School, British School of Falconry), and history. The building's vast pillared frontage is complemented by a handsome, meandering interior. Originally a two-story tavern built in 1769, today the resort incorporates a half-dozen building styles and 17 architectural changes. Owners have invested $43 million in refurbishing and expanding the 2,300-acre property, centerpiece of a beautiful village of rambling clapboard residences, most built in the 1860s and 1870s. Marble sidewalks remind of its past as a lavish summer retreat. Mount Equinox, tallest peak in the Taconics, provides the town's scenic backdrop.

Address: P.O. Box 4, Historic Route 7A, Manchester Village, VT 05254
Tel/fax: (800) 362-4747, XC (802) 362-4700, ext. 870; fax: (802) 362-7777
e-mail: reservations@equinoxresort.com
Internet: www.equinoxresort.com
Location: Southwestern Vermont
Airport: Albany, 75 miles
Train: Rutland, 33 miles
Memberships and Awards: Cross Country Ski Areas Association, AAA Four Diamond, Historic Hotels of America, National Register of Historic Places
Medical: Northshire Medical Center, 3 miles
Accommodations: The Equinox has 183 rooms, townhouse accommodations, and suites, with private baths and data ports. Generous-sized rooms have trees or plants; some designated non-smoking. Three- or four-night minimum holidays.
Guest capacity: 360
Conference Capacity: 360
Rates: $–$$$$$$ (low-season package covers rentals, trails, instruction)
Credit cards: Visa, MasterCard, American Express, Discover, Diners Club
Season: Late November–early March; annual snowfall 72"
XC Skiing: The Touring Center snowcat-grooms some 35 kms on 20 trails, almost all one-way. 40% Easier, 40% More Difficult, 20% Most Difficult. Open terrain lies below the XC Center, another network on forested lands of the Equinox Preservation Trust. Both have splendid views of the Green Mountains and the white-steepled First Congregational Church. Outstanding rental/retail shop, with lounge. Instruction in classic and skating; guide service. Daily trail fee. Altitude range 1,100'–2,200'.
- The *Gleneagles Golf Course* system varies from flat to downrolling-exciting. There are several teaching areas in roughly 20 kms of double track plus skate lane, with several rest huts along the way. Trails can be breezy; two road crossings.
- The *Mount Equinox* system provides 15 kms of packed timbered trails, often narrow-twisting, for skating and snowshoeing. Expect deeper snow and vertical. Groomed routes go partway up the 3,800' mountain.

Maps: Two maps, simple for the Golf Course trails, a complex multi-season product for Mount Equinox.
Activities and Entertainment: On-site: snowshoeing, ice skating, Fitness Spa and Vermont Sports Medicine Center, swimming, lighted ice rink, ice fishing, fly fishing museum, shopping at 12 specialty stores. Nearby: Orvis fishing headquarters and shooting school, horseback riding, sleigh rides, arts and crafts centers, paddle tennis, alpine (Bromley, Stratton), astounding numbers of factory outlets, and snowmobiling.
Children's programs: Equipment, instruction, babysitting, pulks, snow play. holiday "Winter Olympics."
Dining: Colonnade Restaurant is elegantly formal; historic Marsh Tavern has grand desserts. House label wines from California.
Special Nordic Distinction: Two different joyous ski experiences.
Summary: The Equinox joins a select few as a lovingly-restored grand XC hotel.

Grafton Ponds Cross Country Ski Center (The Old Tavern)
Grafton, Vermont

Many New England villages have attempted to maintain their architectural integrity. Grafton has gone a unique step further, burying phone and power lines. Two covered bridges reinforce the antique aura. Truly it has the feel of bygone days, to the point where cars look almost out of place. Founded around 1763, life revolved around agriculture until the advent of mills and quarries. In 1830 its population was several times the current figure. Grafton's centerpiece, the Old Tavern, opened in 1801 and was visited by notables such as Daniel Webster, President Grant, and Rudyard Kipling. It was restored by the Windham Foundation in 1965, with addition of modern plumbing and heating. The XC center is located about ½-mile away, at the foot of Bear Mountain. It has a sizable and growing trail system, supported by a 1,500-square-foot addition that tripled the size of the base building. The entire operation has been built specifically for skiing.

Address: Grafton, VT 05146
Tel/fax: reservations (800) 843-1801 or (802) 843-2231, XC (802) 843-2400; fax: (802) 843-2245
e-mail: tavern@sover.net
Internet: www.old-tavern.com
Location: Southeastern Vermont
Airport: Albany International, 75 miles
Train: Bellows Falls, 12 miles
Memberships and Awards: Cross Country Ski Areas Association, *Historic Hotels of America*, *Andrew Harper's Hideaway Report's* Top 4 Hideaways in U.S.
Medical: Grace Cottage Hospital, 8 miles
Accommodations: Overnight guests have several alternatives—The Old Tavern's main building, cottages, or guest houses. No TVs or phones in the rooms. No minimum stay.
Guest Capacity: 132
Conference Capacity: 55
Rates: $–$$ for rooms (midweek package includes full breakfast)
Credit Cards: Visa, MasterCard

Season: December–March; annual snowfall 100"; 5 kms snowmaking
XC Skiing: XC director Colin Lawson snowcat-grooms 30 kms on a dozen or so loops (network is still evolving and always improving), generally two-way double track with skate lane. 25% Easier, 50% More Difficult, 25% Most Difficult. Simplest terrain is in the valley in open fields and atop the mountain on Big Bear, from which you can look down into Grafton. There are some radical climbs, though descents tend to be more gradual. Groomed downhill practice area. Instruction in classic, skating, and telemarking; guide service. Modern rentals. Daily trail fee. Altitude range 500'–1,500'.
Maps: New version is much more detailed and useful; contains good descriptions.
Activities and Entertainment: On-site: snowshoeing, ice skating, snow play. Nearby: alpine, paddle tennis court with heated floor (near center), craft and antique shops, North America's sole ski-in/ski-out cheese factory (try the Classic Reserve Cheddar); Green Mountain Gringo Salsa, 4,000 stuffed bears at Hugging Bear Inn & Shoppe (both in Chester).
Children's Programs: Very family-friendly: tubing hill, snow park, equipment, special kids' festivals.
Dining: Innkeeper Kevin O'Donnell sets an excellent candlelit table in rooms with old portraits on the walls. Specialties include jumbo shrimp and andouille sausage, pan-seared mignons of Denver venison. Lighter fare (fish, fowl) is an option. Pub/lounge. All dining rooms are non-smoking.
Special Nordic Distinction: The Windham Foundation, a philanthropic organization dedicated to historic preservation, provides annual funds to expand and upgrade the skiing at Grafton Ponds. (Irrelevant but fascinating: this non-profit *chooses* to pay taxes).
Summary: Grafton Ponds and the Old Tavern offer intriguing history, assurance of snow, and extremely reasonable prices.

See color photos, page 99

Green Mountain Ski Touring Center
Randolph, Vermont

When you visit Randolph, you're seeing more than the home of Vermont Castings stoves—you're visiting Morgan horse country. And when you're a guest at Green Mountain Stock Farm, you're in the middle of equine history; some of the sturdy breed will be grazing nearby. Victorian-era Three Stallion Inn is the heart of the property. Back in the 1700s, the grounds were part of an extensive farm. Innkeepers Al and Betty Geibel have been managing partners of the property since the mid-1980s, about the same time XC was introduced. Today the 1,300 acres are slowly being developed into 10- to 20-acre lots. Trail easements aren't just part of property planning, they're an intrinsic attraction, as is the golf course across the road. The latter converts into flowing terrain in winter, part running along a branch of the White River. Skiers pass along old carriage roads, through pine, birch, and maple forest. You may pass a sugar house, or see beaver on Trail #4. Higher trails tend to be more open (and windier). Best lookout points are the meadows of trails #10 and #2, from which you can gaze down on a church steeple; while on the southwest horizon, you may find Killington and Rochester Gap, about 40 miles away.

Address: RFD #2, c/o Three Stallion Inn, Stock Farm Road, Randolph, VT 05060
Tel/fax: (800) 424-5575 or (802) 728-5575; fax: (802) 728-4036
e-mail: tsi@3stallioninn.com
Internet: www.3stallioninn.com
Location: Central Vermont
Airport: Burlington International, 50 miles
Train: Randolph, 1.5 miles (pickup)
Medical: Gifford Memorial Hospital, 2 miles
Accommodations: 17 tasteful rooms in two buildings, all individually decorated and with private bath. No phones, TV, or keys. Ski-in/ski-out. Smoke-free environment. Multi-night minimum holidays only.
Guest Capacity: 32
Conference Capacity: 80

Rates: $$ (package includes some meals, use of facilities and trails)
Credit Cards: Visa, MasterCard, American Express, Discover
Season: Late November–end March; annual snowfall 80"
XC Skiing: Al grooms 50 kms by snowmobile—some double track, some skating and single track, some single track alone. There's a mix of one- and two-way routes. 40% Easier, 40% More Difficult, 20% Most Difficult (but pretty good width on the downhills). Road crossings. Instruction may be available by reservation. Rentals. Daily trail fee. Altitude range 600'–1,500'.
Maps: The new map was plotted with assistance from a GPS—it's accurate within 6 inches!
Activities and Entertainment: On-site: snowshoeing (trail follows a summer mountain bike race course), small fitness center converted from a harness shop, sauna, indoor and outdoor hot tubs. Nearby: alpine (many areas), snowmobiling, Chandler Music Hall in Randolph, Green Mountain Chocolate Company, Simon Pearce Glass Blowing and Factory Store, sugaring tours at the Vermont Technical College Farm, Dartmouth College and its great bookstore.
Children's Programs: Equipment.
Dining: The restaurant is well known in Vermont, with entrées like sautéed lamb loin with raspberry mint sauce. Morgan's Pub is a pleasant bar/lounge with its own menu.
Special Nordic Distinction: Distinguished novice and intermediate terrain. And since all the trails have numbers to date, why not leave your own imprint on the area by suggesting memorable names to the Geibels?
Summary: Another "find." It's very convenient to Interstate 89, yet intervening hills muffle traffic sounds. P.S.: Don't confuse Green Mountain with Green Trails in neighboring Brookfield.

Green Trails Cross Country Ski Center
Brookfield, Vermont

It's high time more people enjoyed Green Trails, which, incidentally, is the only XC center where you can purchase an antique clock or have it repaired or restored. The inn has several unique features, including the skills of owners Sue and Mark Erwin, former corporate executives. She managed a gas utility company's office information services; he worked for a toy company specializing in Halloween costumes. They purchased the 17-acre estate in 1995. Accommodations are divided between two buildings, one built in the 1840s as a private home, the other an eighteenth-century guest house. Green Trails is just across the road from the longest floating bridge east of the Mississippi, buoyed by 380 barrels and always a little disconcerting to cross. It's a pretty place set in a snow pocket of the Vermont highlands; the relaxed pace fits a region that retains much of the sleepy beauty of pre–combustion engine times.

Address: By the Floating Bridge, Brookfield, VT 05036
Tel: (800) 243-3412 or (802) 276-3412
e-mail: greentrails@quest-net.com
Internet: www.quest-net.com/gti
Location: Central Vermont
Airport: Burlington, 50 miles
Train: Randolph, 13 miles
Medical: Gifford Medical Center, 13 miles
Accommodations: 14 rooms are all furnished with antique (but firm and comfortable) beds; mix of private and shared baths. The Stencil Room is quite spacious and has a private whirlpool. Ski-in/ski-out. No smoking in buildings. No minimum stay.
Guest Capacity: 28
Conference Capacity: 20
Rates: $–$$ (includes breakfast and use of ski equipment)
Credit Cards: Visa, MasterCard
Season: Mid-December–mid-March; annual snowfall 96"
XC Skiing: Mark snowmobile-grooms seven trails totaling 35 kms; some are single track and some double. They're often on the narrow side and thus one-way, partly because the land belongs to neighbors who prefer not to have turnpikes cut across their property. (Brookfield residents love to ski!) 40% Easier, 40% More Difficult, 20% Most Difficult. There are a couple of road crossings, but this is hardly a high-traffic area. Green Trails has a pleasant blending of meadow and wood, with the classic Vermont mix of hard and soft woods; skiers sometimes see deer, snowshoe hares, even moose. Excellent ski school area—instructor available by reservation. The rental fleet is not quite up-to-date but the snowshoe fleet is new. Daily trail fee. Altitude range 1,500'–1,800'.
Maps: XC maps can range from childlike impressions to graphic marvels. The most intriguing may be the profusely illustrated yet surprisingly accurate two-part creation by a famous *New Yorker* cartoonist.
Activities and Entertainment: On-site: snowshoeing, ice skating, sledding. Nearby: alpine skiing (Norwich University Ski Area), sleigh rides; local sugaring operation in March; January Ice Harvest Festival.
Children's Programs: The inn welcomes children over age 10. Equipment available.
Dining: While Green Trails has a B&B element (outstanding buttermilk waffles), the Erwins unhesitatingly recommend the fine dining at Ariel's Restaurant and Village Pub, right across the street. The owner is CIA-trained (no puns, please!); restaurant menu changes monthly.
Special Nordic Distinction: More suited to intermediates than beginners. The higher you go (especially behind the inn), the better views get from trails such as Top Flite. Green Trails also specializes in showshoeing.
Summary: New Englanders "standoffish"? Not here! Brookfield is in the running for friendliest town in Vermont, and the Erwins are among the most gracious of hosts, ever willing to sit and chat.

Hazen's Notch Cross Country Ski Center
Montgomery Center, Vermont

Cloud hangs over ridge and mountain like a white powdered wig clinging to a British magistrate's dome. . . . Austrian Rudi Mattesich, who helped "grow" nordic skiing in America and lived in nearby Troy, memorialized Vermont's Northeast Kingdom in his watercolors. Val Schadinger also enjoys the region enormously, though peaks don't rival those of his native Austria. He arrived as an alpine instructor at Jay Peak, bought property, and in 1978 was persuaded to start grooming trails in this farming and timber country near the Québec border. Since then his life has revolved around skiing, even to meeting wife Phyllis at Hazen's Notch. (The locale is named for a gap in the Green Mountains that was a military road in the 1770s.) This is grand, flowing ski country. Trails are mostly wooded; there are fields near the parking area. Views are striking: to the north, a beautiful over-meadow sweep to Jay Peak and Big Jay; to the south, the horizon is filled with Haystack and Burnt Mountains. Higher routes tend to lie to the south, though little is truly difficult; here you'll find glacial erratics (boulders) such as Coyote Rock.

Address: Route 58, Box 730, Montgomery Center, VT 05471
Tel/fax: (802) 326-4708
e-mail: hazens@together.net
Location: North-central Vermont (winter access only from the west, which helps maintain tranquility)
Airport: Burlington International, 60 miles
Train: St. Albans, 30 miles
Memberships and Awards: Cross Country Ski Areas Association
Medical: Northwest Medical Center, 30 miles
Accommodations: In 1991 the Schadingers opened a small B&B in a 130-year-old renovated farmhouse (Val did the remodeling). It's very simple, clean, and pleasant. There are three bedrooms upstairs, one with private bath, a living room downstairs warmed by wood stove. Ski-in/ski-out. No-smoking environment. No minimum stay.

Guest Capacity: 6
Conference Capacity: None
Rates: $ (includes breakfast)
Credit Cards: Personal checks and cash only
Season: Early December–early April; annual snowfall 150"
XC Skiing: Val grooms 50 genuine kms by snowmobile (remember: he *likes* grooming), all two-way. 30% Easier, 60% More Difficult, 10% Most Difficult—almost all single track, a little double track, with a smidgen of skating. Wonderful groomed downhill practice/play area (Sugar House) on the southern trail system. Road crossings but little traffic. Instruction/guide service next door to the B&B, run by mountaineers Rolf and Sharon Anderson, founders of the Hazen's Notch Association; rentals with 75-mm bindings. Daily trail fee. Altitude range 1,000'–1,700'.
Maps: The simple photocopied handout gives a feel for the land; it's best used in conjunction with the newer Hazen's Notch Association contour map.
Activities and Entertainment: On-site: snowshoeing. Nearby: alpine (Jay Peak), antique shops, wooden toy manufacturer Montgomery Schoolhouse, seven covered bridges, snowmobiling, and Québec. (You could reach Ripplecove Inn in a couple of easy hours.)
Children's Programs: No services.
Dining: John Zachadnykjon has a predilection for purple: boulders, dress, decor, stove, meals. This *sounds* eccentric (he's a canny publicist), but it's worth indulging him because Zack's on the Rocks is one of the finest restaurants in Vermont—a mere 30-second drive or short walk from the B&B. The interior is reminiscent of a French country restaurant. Among entrées: Chicken Banana.
Special Nordic Distinction: If Vermont has snow, you'll find it around Jay Peak. Other enticements: the land's beauty and serenity, Val's vigor and sense of fun.
Summary: Hazen's Notch is one of the finest skiing finds in New England.

The Hermitage
Wilmington, Vermont

Vermont is renowned for the colors of autumn leaves, Grade A light amber maple syrup, cheddar cheeses, and alpine ski resorts whose ownership changes annually. It's also famous for historic lodges that offer cross-country skiing. It's not yet known (outside of a tight circle of nordic oenophiles) that at one inn, you can rent skis and purchase a bottle of fine wine on the same tab. Jim McGovern, wine connoisseur and owner of The Hermitage, has cleverly placed a nice selection in the same room as the rental equipment, just across from made-on-property jams and jellies. A one-time carpenter and bartender turned gourmet chef, McGovern is an enthralling character. In 1971 he purchased the former farmhouse and has both refined and expanded the property. Among the intriguing elements are hundreds of handmade duck decoys; resident hunting dogs; acclaimed dining; and prints, paintings, and lithographs of artist Michael Delacroix. As for the skiing, there are easy close-in loops like Ice House, progressing into intermediate and, finally, advanced runs. You may encounter otter, sometimes beaver; listen for coyote calls in the evening.

Address: Box 457, Wilmington, VT 05363
Tel/fax: (802) 464-3511; fax: (802) 464-2688
e-mail: hermitage@sover.net
Internet: www.hermitageinn.com
Location: South-central Vermont
Airport: Bradley International, 90 miles
Train: Brattleboro, 25 miles
Memberships and Awards: Cross Country Ski Areas Association, *Wine Spectator*'s Grand Award, Vermont Innkeeper of the Year
Medical: Deerfield Valley Health Center, 5 miles
Accommodations: The Hermitage began in the 1700s as a farmhouse; today the entire property contains 29 rooms, in two locations. The Main House has four upstairs rooms with private bath and fireplace, furnished with antiques, all with private bath. Ski-in/ski-out.

Phone, cable TV. Two- to three-night minimum weekends and holidays.
Guest Capacity: 58
Conference Capacity: 200
Rates: $$–$$$ (includes breakfast, dinner, use of trails)
Credit Cards: Visa, MasterCard, American Express, Diners Club
Season: December 25–April 1; annual snowfall 150"
XC Skiing: The Hermitage maintains 40 kms, groomed largely by snowcat. 40% Easier, 40% More Difficult, 20% Most Difficult; primarily two-way double track. Terrain on the inn side of the road is significantly hillier and more secluded than to the east, though this more open area has better views of Haystack Mountain. Two routes are shared with snowmobiles. Instruction in classic. Goodly rental selection. Daily trail fee. Altitude range 2,000'–2,900'.
Maps: At first look, primitive; at second, also rather endearing, though it gives little hint of topography.
Activities and Entertainment: On-site: snowshoeing, sporting clays, sauna, sugaring in spring. Nearby: alpine (Haystack, Mt. Snow), sleigh rides, ice skating, ice fishing, snowmobiling, crafts, antiques, Adams Petting Farm, North River Winery in Jacksonville (weekends).
Children's Programs: Equipment only.
Dining: The Hermitage motto: "Time is the essence of good food." Among delicacies: game birds, fresh seafood. Day skiers don't consume the entire 40,000-bottle cellar, so there's always wine for dinner as well as cognacs, ports, and Madeiras. Smoking and non-smoking dining rooms.
Special Nordic Distinction: Some trails are located within the Hunting Preserve; they may be closed at times. Bonne chance!
Summary: It's pleasant to find an inn meeting the needs of an inherently sophisticated clientele ("I'll have a modest red with my Swix, please.").

Highland Lodge
Greensboro, Vermont

Cross-country areas in the Northeast Kingdom aren't truly cheek-by-jowl; they're actually spread out over almost 2,000 square miles. But the trails at Highland Lodge do link with Craftsbury's, though the relationship is one of cooperation and contrast rather than child and parent. Just above Caspian Lake, Highland was originally an 1860s farmhouse that took in boarders; it converted to lodging in 1926. In 1954 the property was purchased by two families who had summered in the area. Today it's run by David and Wilhelmina Smith, second-generation innkeepers. David still has a certain presence on entering a room, though he seems more natural as a host and a dowser than a former trial lawyer. With the help of 50 landowners, the Smiths opened for winter in 1972. This is still farming country; most times you won't pass either structures or skiers along the trails, though some peripheral routes are shared with snowmobiles. The network is laid out for views; circle Barr Hill to enjoy Jay Peak to the north, rolling hills to the south, Mt. Mansfield to the west, and Burke Mountain to the east.

Address: R.R. 1, Box 1290, Greensboro, VT 05841
Tel/fax: (802) 533-2647; fax: (802) 533-7494
e-mail: HLodge@connriver.net
Internet: www.pbpub.com/vermont/hiland.htm
Location: Northeastern Vermont
Airport: Burlington, 70 miles
Train: Montpelier, 35 miles
Memberships and Awards: Cross Country Ski Areas Association
Medical: Copley Hospital, 20 miles
Accommodations: Highland offers 11 Victorian-style rooms with private baths in the lodge (gorgeous sunsets over the lake), and four winterized cottages with kitchenettes and gas-log stoves (more convenient, if less fragrant, than wood-burners). Smoking permitted only in cottages. Ski-in/ski-out. No minimum stay.
Guest Capacity: 38

Conference Capacity: 30
Rates: $$–$$$ (includes breakfast, dinner, use of trails)
Credit Cards: Visa, MasterCard, Discover
Season: December 20–March 15; annual snowfall 147"
XC Skiing: David maintains about 65 kms of trail, around 16 kms of which is track-set by small snowcat and snowmobile; the balance is packed up to 16' wide. He track-sets when there's a reasonable amount of fresh snow. Wind can make resetting futile; some years see drifts the height of Shaquille O'Neal. There's a mix of one- and two-way flow. Easy Rider is a thrilling/chilling ¾-mile downhill. Road crossings. Classic instruction available daily; guide service. Three-pin rental equipment. Daily trail fee. Altitude range 1,500'–2,100'.
Maps: On one side is a map of buildings and nearby trails (easiest are between lodge and lake); the reverse shows the entire network. Contours are useful, but neither trail lengths nor difficulty ratings are mentioned.
Activities and Entertainment: On-site: snowshoeing, sledding. Nearby: alpine (Burke Mountain, Stowe), Host Farm in Greensboro (watch the milking), Cabot Creamery (taste the cheeses).
Children's Programs: Babysitting by reservation, instruction, equipment, indoor play room, snow play.
Dining: Look for regional cuisine and products, such as grilled chicken breast with red wine sauce and Vermont lamb. Desserts are home-made, including cryptic but delicious Ishkabibble. Beer and wine license.
Special Nordic Distinction: There's a small maze of trails for kids (and adults) in the pine and fir woods behind the cottages. In summer the XC center is a playhouse.
Summary: Highlands isn't a secret Spandex hideout, nor is there pretense to high-tech grooming. Much of visitors' delight comes from Willie's warmth and David's exuberant sense of humor.

Mountain Top Inn and Resort
Chittenden, Vermont

Mountain Top is one of those Eastern inns that perennially appears in everyone's Top 10 XC Resorts in the Galaxy, with a rank similar to that of Woodstock and Trapp Family Lodge. It has the whole ball of wax—altitude, ambiance, terrain, facilities, mountain scenery, even snowmaking and reasonable prices. President Eisenhower visited during the '50s, which should draw every nostalgic Republican. But it still doesn't get great numbers of skiers, meaning those who do come don't have to flail elbows to get out the door and onto the trails. The 1,000-acre resort is surrounded and protected by public land. It was established in 1945 on the site of a former stage road, rebuilt in 1977 after a fire, and has been refurbished by former Californians Mike and Maggie Gehan, who bought the inn in 1995. The XC facilities have also developed a new polish, as affable XC manager Don Cochrane—a resort fixture since 1973—will be glad to explain. This is a mountain, and almost every trail has some ups and downs. Happily, a couple of the easiest routes are close to the inn; Morning Glory gets both snowmaking and the day's early sun. There are views everywhere, cloud and shadow racing across the mountain landscape—you'll see guests stopping to look out from the inn's glass-enclosed staircase or from the dining room. Chat with Don about the best trail for your energy and ability—Turkey Track, Debonis Cutback, newer and aptly named Nosedive, or the long loop around Chittenden Reservoir.

Address: Mountain Top Road, Chittenden, VT 05737
Tel/fax: (800) 445-2100 or (802) 483-2311, XC (802) 483-6089; fax: (802) 483-6373
e-mail: info@mountaintopinn.com
Internet: www.mountaintopinn.com
Location: Central Vermont (check that atlas!)
Airport: Burlington International, 70 miles
Train: White River Junction, 30 miles
Memberships and Awards: Cross Country Ski Areas Association, *Snow Country* magazine's Top 10 XC Areas in North America
Medical: Rutland Hospital, 12 miles
Accommodations: Guests can choose between housekeeping cottages or 33 lodge rooms; most of the latter overlook the 700-acre reservoir. Phone but no TV. Ski-in/ski-out. No minimum stay.
Guest Capacity: 150
Conference Capacity: 100
Rates: $$-$$$ (includes facilities, use of trails)
Credit Cards: Visa, MasterCard, American Express
Season: Thanksgiving–Easter, annual snowfall 110"; 3 kms snowmaking
XC Skiing: Don grooms 70 "real" kms of single track and skate lane, on 31 trails. 30% Easier, 40% More Difficult, 30% Most Difficult; most are two-way. Two warming shelters. Instruction in all disciplines. Good selection of rental and retail equipment (the latter mostly racing skis). Daily trail fee. Altitude range 1,400'–2,000'.
Maps: It can be complex to correlate descriptions and map because of the number of trails.
Activities and Entertainment: On-site: snowshoeing, ice skating, sleigh rides, sauna, and a *great* snow play area just below the dining room; Charlie James Cocktail Lounge. Nearby: alpine (Killington), ice fishing, Maple Museum, Green Mountain National Forest Interpretive Center, ice climbing, Texas Falls (snowshoes needed), outlet shopping, antiquing.
Children's Programs: Equipment, pulks, snow play.
Dining: Not a vast number of entrées, but they're prepared well (salmon en papillotte, Yankee pot roast). Full liquor license.
Special Nordic Distinction: Views are as fine as any in this part of the world; after fresh snow, picture-postcard lovely in every direction.
Summary: It has been quite a transformation—from turnip farm to resort.

Ole's (Inn at the Round Barn)
Warren/Waitsfield, Vermont

John Howard is a skier/management consultant; partner Jim Despres a former racer who has run XC operations since the early '90s. Jennifer White has made skiing her professional passion, first at Blueberry Hill, then managing Waterville Valley. With other ski business luminaries, they're building a remarkable area whose trails swing through field and wood and across the snowbound runways of a private airstrip. Ole's was founded in the late 1970s by Norwegian Ole Maseson. The element transforming it from a day place into a destination is a new connection (completion late 1999) with the Inn at the Round Barn.

Address: Sugarbush-Warren Airport, P.O. Box 1653, Warren, VT 05673
Tel: (802) 496-3430
e-mail: jthvt@madriver.com
Location: North-central Vermont
Airport: Burlington International, 45 miles
Train: Waterbury, 15 miles
Memberships and Awards: Cross Country Ski Areas Association, Rossignol Demo Center
Medical: Mad River Valley Medical Clinic, 3 miles
Accommodations: The Inn at the Round Barn is an 85-acre B&B with chambers ranging from comfortable to sumptuous. The 12-sided barn (mailbox is a miniature replica) houses the Green Mountain Cultural Center. Great breakfasts! Ski-in/ski-out. Non-smoking buildings; various minimum stays. RR1, Box 247, Waitsfield, Vermont 05673, (802) 496-2276.
Guest capacity: 23
Conference Capacity: 23
Rates: $–$$$ (includes lodging, breakfast, all trails; midweek multi-day package)
Credit cards: Visa, MasterCard, American Express
Season: Early December–late March (shorter season at The Round Barn); annual snowfall 250"
XC Skiing: Ole's has 50 kms maintained by snowmobile, largely two-way, running through farm-meadow and forest. In the timber, mostly single track and skating; in the open, double track and skating. With a route leading down to the Round Barn, the network will total 75 kms—30% Easier, 50% More Difficult, 20% Most Difficult. Great views, including Northfield Mountain and Sugarbush. Road crossings. Instruction in classic and skating; guided tours. Rental/retail department, with both skis and snowshoes; showers. Daily trail fee. Altitude range 1,000'–1,575'.
Maps: Most recently, a simple handout with contour indications and concise trail summaries.
Activities and Entertainment: At Ole's: separate and shared snowshoe trails, Heidi's DinerSoar Deli; at The Round Barn: snowshoeing rentals and tours, 60' lap pool. Nearby: NATO (North American Telemark Organization) headquarters, alpine skiing (Mad River, Sugarbush), day spa, horse trekking, sleigh rides, ice skating, Mad River Canoes, Cabin Fever Follies, Vermont Teddy Bear Factory in Shelburne, snowmobiling.
Children's Programs: Instruction, kick sleds, pulks, equipment, day care (Sugarbush).
Dining: Few restaurants are as lively as John Egan's Big World. Named for a famous "extreme skier" who is also a partner, the bar is built of skis and snowboards. Culinary specialty is wood grilling. Stop at Waitsfield's Bridge Street Bakery for goodies: a delectable array of pastries, breads, breakfasts, and bagels, served warmly.
Special Nordic Distinction: John, Jim, and staff are constantly "sophisticating" trails. Jennifer has helped make the area extremely popular with women. New Warren Pinnacle trail is a major racing site.
Summary: Ole's sees an interesting mix of guests: a little wool, a good deal of lycra; leisurely couples, racers in training; women's groups on skis, and an increasing number of snowshoers. The Millennium Connection to The Round Barn adds a whole new flavor.

Trapp Family Lodge
Stowe, Vermont

It's safe to say that XC skiing would never have achieved its current stature or character without Trapp Family Lodge. The von Trapps not only were among the first to arrive at the ski area concept, they also had the prestige to legitimize the idea. The lodge is still the most famous XC area in North America, with a major trail system and all conceivable associated facilities (rental, retail, instruction, lounging areas, fine dining, accommodations, ski-in/ski-out Austrian Tea Room and Gift Shop). In addition, there are grand views of the Stowe Valley and Worcester Range. But the essence is that 'orrid cliché, "ambiance." There's an admirable mix of Austria and Vermont: Tyrolean architecture (probably the only such XC area in the U.S.) amidst 2,800 acres in the Green Mountains. Although Trapp's is a self-sufficient destination, it's only minutes away from the town of Stowe and legendary alpine skiing on Mt. Mansfield, the highest point in the state.

Address: 700 Trapp Hill Road, P.O. Box 1428, Stowe, VT 05672
Tel/fax: (800) 826-7000 or (802) 253-5719; fax: (802) 253-5740
e-mail: info@trappfamily.com
Internet: www.trappfamily.com
Location: North-central Vermont
Airport: Burlington International, 38 miles
Train: Waterbury, 10 miles
Memberships and Awards: Cross Country Ski Areas Association, *Gourmet* magazine's top fine hotel award
Medical: Copley Center, 9 miles
Accommodations: 93 rooms in the lodge, 100 guest houses. All options are ski-in/ski-out. Non-smoking rooms available. Minimum stay varies with weekends and holidays.
Guest Capacity: 186
Conference Capacity: 100
Rates: $$–$$$$$ (includes instruction, use of trails)
Credit Cards: Visa, MasterCard, American Express

Season: December 15–April 1; annual snowfall 140"
XC Skiing: Trapp grooms 55 kms by snowcat, primarily double track with skate lane, basically two-way. 15% Easier, 75% More Difficult, 10% Most Difficult. Two warming shelters. Road crossings. Groomed downhill practice area. XC director Charlie Yerrick heads up a fine team of instructors for skating, classic, and telemarking; guide service. National award of Retailer of the Year gives an idea of rental and retail quality. Daily trail fee. Altitude range 1,100'–2,500'.
Maps: It's enormous, graphic, accurate, and and water-resistant. Another covers the entire Stowe region. Detailed contours, excellent annotations on wilderness trails.
Activities and Entertainment: On-site: snowshoeing, sleigh rides, ice skating, maple sugaring, nature tours, indoor pool and fitness center, sauna. Nearby: alpine (Stowe), much antiquing, the town of Stowe (dancing, bars), Ben & Jerry's Ice Cream factory (tours and a free sample), Vermont Distillers (Mad River Vodka), January Winter Carnival, Stowe Canoe and Snowshoe Company (you may already have some of their snowshoe-like furniture), snowmobiling.
Children's Programs: Instruction, equipment, pulks, snow play; new Mountain Kids program.
Dining: Trapp's has several dining areas. The main restaurant features constantly changing entrées such as scaloppine of veal sauté with roasted peppers, fresh romaine-wrapped seabass.
Special Nordic Distinction: This is country with very little flat land. A combination of good trail design and careful grooming makes most hills palatable to novices. Trails connect directly to another 80 groomed kms of the Mt. Mansfield and Topnotch networks.
Summary: Trapp Family Lodge could live quite easily on its *Sound of Music* fame. It has chosen instead to continue refining the entire winter experience.

See color photos, page 100

Viking Ski Touring Centre
Londonderry, Vermont

History speaks here. Viking is one of the oldest XC areas in North America and has played a momentous, if quiet, role in the sport and business of nordic skiing. It was founded in 1970 by the Allaben brothers, who also helped establish both Cross Country Ski Areas Association and Professional Ski Instructors of America. In addition, the Allabens pioneered inn-to-inn skiing in Vermont, though consecutive poor winters ended the effort. Viking was also one of the earliest areas to install trail lighting. When Stan and Lee moved to warmer climes, the area was purchased by former ABC sales executive Irving Gross and since has been run by Malcolm and Dana McNair (the latter has an irrepressible sense of humor). In this modern age of "cross-country," Viking has kept "ski touring" in its name, perhaps because they've never added skating. It should still be considered among the sweetest skiing systems around. Virtually everything is in pine and hardwood forest, which restricts views of the Green Mountains, whose crest lies a few miles to the west. Several easier routes are close to the center, including lighted loops; most are intermediate, but advanced trails like Helga's Way are the real thing. Much of the network has a Scandinavian theme (Norseman, Odin's Run, Ygdrasil).

Address: R.R. 1, Box 70, Londonderry, VT 05148
Tel/fax: (802) 824-3933; fax: (802) 824-4574
e-mail: info@vikingnordic.com
Internet: www.vikingnordic.com
Location: South-central Vermont
Airport: Albany International, 90 miles
Train: None nearby
Memberships and Awards: Cross Country Ski Areas Association
Medical: Mountain Valley Medical Clinic, 3 miles
Accommodations: Viking has a four-room B&B in a farmhouse dating from the 1860s; two rooms have private baths. Handsome pine flooring, table fashioned from church pews. Four couples can rent the entire place and have evening cooking privileges. Ski-in/ski-out. No smoking in buildings. Two-night minimum. If no snow, payment can be refunded.
Guest Capacity: 8
Conference Capacity: 20
Rates: $$ (includes breakfast, use of trails)
Credit Cards: Visa, MasterCard
Season: Mid-December–early April; annual snowfall 90"
XC Skiing: Viking grooms 30 kms with a small snowcat, all double-tracked, primarily one-way. 3 kms lighted. Best guess is 20% Easier, 60% More Difficult, 20% Most Difficult. Several road crossings. Instruction in classic and telemarking (private, video, and kids' lessons by appointment); guide service by appointment. There's an excellent rental/retail selection where you can "try before you buy." Daily trail fee. Altitude range 1,200'–1,600'.
Maps: It's a useful and attractive item, giving a feeling for hills and forest, with local advertising on the back.
Activities and Entertainment: On-site: snowshoeing, ice skating. Nearby: alpine (Bromley, Stratton), sleigh rides, Fudge Shop, Priory, Vermont Country Store, Weston Toy Works (weekends only), snowmobiling; art galleries, antiques, and factory outlets in Manchester.
Children's Programs: Instruction, equipment, pulks.
Dining: The 30-seat Olympic Cafe serves up veggie chili and soups on weekends. For an elaborate dinner, try Mistral's at Toll Gate. A dozen miles on the way to Manchester, the restaurant has a long-standing reputation as expensive but well worth it. Specialties includes salmon-stuffed lobster.
Special Nordic Distinction: Not only is Viking an historic area, it's one of the few totally committed to classic technique.
Summary: Longtime guests return in part for the nostalgia; *everyone* visits for the trail quality.

Woodstock Inn & Resort
Woodstock, Vermont

The town of Woodstock has been called "one of America's half-dozen prettiest villages." If there's a commercial core to maintaining this vision, it hardly matters. The Woodstock Inn is probably the most famous structure in town, still owned by Laurance Rockefeller, who has played a vital role in preserving village beauty. Woodstock Resort holds most of the land used for XC trails, including the golf clubhouse that converts into a fine ski center. On-site restaurant, bar, and huge fireplace. Beginners can rent equipment here and enjoy 10 kilometers of inviting terrain at the base of the Mt. Peg network, whose other narrower trails tend to be fairly precipitous. The entirely separate Mt. Tom network presents the whole skiing spectrum; it also possesses much the finer views—Ascutney to the south, New Hampshire to the east, Killington to the west, and town steeples below. Trails, including old carriage roads, lead through a complex forest mix (site of Vermont's first tree farm)—sugar maple, birch, spruce, hemlock, white, red, and Scotch pine. There's a pretty white pine cabin partway up Mt. Tom that's a good lunch destination.

Address: Fourteen The Green, Woodstock, VT 05091
Tel/fax: (800) 448-7900 or (802) 457-1100, XC (802) 457-6674; fax: (802) 457-6699
e-mail: email@woodstockinn.com
Internet: www.woodstockinn.com
Location: East-central Vermont
Airport: Lebanon Regional, 16 miles
Train: White River Junction, 15 miles
Memberships and Awards: Cross Country Ski Areas Association, *Small Luxury Hotels of the World*, *Snow Country* magazine's Top 10 XC Areas in North America, AAA Four Diamond, Mobil Four Star
Medical: Ottauquechee Health Center, ½-mile
Accommodations: The 144 inn rooms are beautifully appointed; most are non-smoking. Two-night minimum weekends, longer on holidays.

Guest Capacity: 288
Conference Capacity: 225
Rates: $$–$$$ (weekday rate includes equipment, use of sports center, XC skiing, and alpine skiing at Suicide Six)
Credit Cards: Visa, MasterCard, American Express
Season: Early/mid-December–late March; annual snowfall 88"
XC Skiing: Woodstock snowcat-grooms 60 kms. 23% Easier, 54% More Difficult, 23% Most Difficult; some are double track, some skate only, some a mix of the two. Most are two-way. Two warming shelters. Instruction covers classic and skating; telemarking at nearby Suicide Six (first ski tow in the U.S.); guide service. Equipment rental and retail. Daily trail fee. Altitude range 700'–1,450'.
Maps: One of the great ones—photos, contours, commentary.
Activities and Entertainment: At resort (various points): snowshoeing, ski orienteering, ice skating, sleigh rides, lighted platform tennis, health and fitness center (swimming pool, hot tub), snow play. Nearby: alpine, snowmobiling, antique shops and galleries galore, Vermont Institute of Natural Science, three covered bridges in town, Dana House. Mountain Brewers in Bridgewater (every ale uses "trail" in its name).
Children's Programs: Instruction, equipment, pulks, snow play, kicksleds, sledding.
Dining: For a sense of the dining room's exquisite dishes, merely examine a selected vegetable—dauphinoise potatoes, truffled whipped potatoes, whipped Yukon Gold potatoes. Full license at Richardson Tavern, and fine wines.
Special Nordic Distinction: Ski director and Woodstock forester John Wiggin maintains the landscape with love. This is the first XC area to be incorporated into a National Historic Park.
Summary: Woodstock's nordic skiing has seen no dimming of reputation or quality with the years.

Sleeping Lady
Leavenworth, Washington

Add a new epicenter to the Northwest's XC repertoire. Founded in 1995 by Seattle's Harriet Bullitt (glider pilot, flamenco dancer, competitive fencer) and committed to environmental excellence, Sleeping Lady is designed for conferences. The retreat lies on the outskirts of Bavarian-themed Leavenworth at the outlet of Icicle Valley; it's named for a prominent local mountain. Variously a Civilian Conservation Corps (CCC) camp, a dude ranch, and a Church camp, today the 69-acre resort is committed to nature, the arts, and healthful dining. Sleeping Lady's heart is vehicle-free, shaded by venerable Ponderosa pines.

Address: 7375 Icicle Road, Leavenworth, WA 98826
Tel/fax: (800) 574-2123 or (509) 548-6344; fax: (509) 548-6312
e-mail: info@sleepinglady.com
Internet: www.sleepinglady.com
Location: North-central Washington
Airport: Pangborn Field, 34 miles
Train: Wenatchee, 25 miles
Memberships and Awards: Good Enviro-Management Award, A.S.I.D. Washington State Cultural & Artistic Achievement Award
Medical: Cascade Medical Center, 3 miles
Accommodations: Clustered buildings provide graceful airy lodging, with varied room configurations; also a group cabin and honeymoon cabin. Fine touches like heated towel racks, polished fir furnishings, data-ports for skiers who can't escape business! Smoke-free environment. No minimum stay.
Guest capacity: 188
Conference Capacity: 188
Rates: $$$ (includes meals, trail fee)
Credit cards: Visa, MasterCard, Discover, American Express
Season: Early December–early March; annual snowfall 96"
XC Skiing: Four snowcat-groomed networks total 23 kms, double-tracked with skate lane; all one-way. 50% Easier, 30% More Difficult, 20% Most Difficult. Daily trail fee. Altitude range 1,200'–1,600'. Instruction. More trails further west at Lake Wenatchee State Park and Stevens Pass.

- *Icicle River Trail* (8 kms) starts a snowball's throw from Sleeping Lady. It winds through meadow and forest, beside a canal, across a spillway bridge (eagle and osprey wait for a fish-meal), at the base of spectacular peaks. Rentals.
- *Ski Hill Trail* (5 kms, 3 kms lighted). Rock-and-roll wooded terrain, with fine valley views. CCC Lodge is open for food and warmth.
- *Leavenworth Golf Course* (8 kms) has delightful ups and down, mostly open terrain, views of the confluence of Icicle Creek and the Wenatchee River. Clubhouse open for meals some days.
- *Waterfront Park* (2 kms) is a block below downtown and connects to the Golf Course, with interpretive trail above Wenatchee River.

Maps: Trail descriptions and programs on one side, map with area insets on the other.
Activities and Entertainment: On-site: snowshoeing, Winter Mystery Weekend, musical events, hot pool, sauna, massage. Nearby: alpine skiing (Ski Hill, Stevens Pass, Mission Ridge), dog sledding, sleigh rides, ice fishing, Aplets and Cotlets Factory, January Bavarian Ice Fest, Nutcracker Museum.
Children's programs: Equipment, pulks. Nearby: sledding, specialty kids stores.
Dining: Meals are served buffet-style, with a gourmet touch. Menus change frequently; favored dishes include grilled chicken minestrone and fresh fruit flan. Beer and wine at the Grotto Bar, sandwiches and goodies at O'Grady's Pantry by the trailhead.
Special Nordic Distinction: This is a classic example of local commitment to skiing (vibrant Leavenworth Winter Sports Club grooms trails, even raised funds for two snowcats).
Summary: Leavenworth offers the mountain setting; Sleeping Lady adds that extra fillip for a dynamic destination.

Methow Valley Sport Trails Association
Winthrop, Washington

Nearly 25,000 people visit Methow Valley each winter, but that figure becomes insignificant when you realize this is America's second most extensive trail system, certainly the largest that's community-supported. Here you can use the tracks for hut-to-hut *and* lodge-to-lodge trips, surrounded by a million acres of national forest and designated wilderness for backcountry touring. Add truly spectacular mountains (the Cascades may reach only 8,800 feet, but the valley floor is at 2,000 feet!) and the fact you have very little altitude acclimation, *et voilà!*: a nordic nirvana. There are several distinct but interconnected networks in the region. Mazama Trails are generally gentle, mostly lying along the Methow River toward the north end of the valley. They are linked to a larger and hillier network, mostly at higher altitude, in the Rendezvous system (Rendezvous Outfitters can transport baggage by snowmobile while you skate or stride between huts), which in turn meshes with the Sun Mountain Lodge system.

Address: Methow Valley Sport Trails Association, P.O. Box 147, Winthrop, WA 98862
Tel/fax: (509) 996-3287, reservations (800) 422-3048 or (509) 996-2148; fax: (509) 996-3282
e-mail: mvsta@methow.com
Internet: www.methow.com/-mvsta/
Location: North-central Washington
Airport: Pangborn Field, 98 miles
Train: Wenatchee, 95 miles
Memberships and Awards: Cross Country Ski Area Association, *Snow Country* magazine's Top 10 XC Areas in the U.S.
Medical: Twisp Medical Clinic, 8 miles
Accommodations: Freestone Inn at the Wilson Ranch has inn rooms, lakeside lodges, and renovated cabins with hardwood floors, stone fireplaces, and kitchenettes. Ski-in/ski-out. No smoking in rooms. Three-night minimum holidays and major weekends. 17798 Highway 20, Mazama, WA 98833; (800) 639-3809.

Guest Capacity: Valley-wide capacity 900; 56 at the Wilson Ranch
Conference Capacity: 80–100, new facility
Rates: $–$$$
Credit Cards: Visa, MasterCard, American Express, Diners Club, Discover
Season: December 1–April 1; annual snowfall 72" (it falls dry and stays around)
XC Skiing: 200 kms of snowcat-groomed trail (the Sun Mountain network composes about one-third)—averaged out, that's 125 people per km per *season*. There's a combination single track, single with skating, double with skating. 43% Easier, 36% More Difficult, 21% Most Difficult. Loads of lodges and warming huts along the way. Instruction is available at Sun Mountain, the Wilson Ranch, and Winthrop Mountain Sports. Daily trail fee. Altitude range 1,500'–4,000'.
Maps: Developed from an aerial photo, there's a valley-wide map plus detailed mini-maps for the Rendezvous, Mazama, and Sun Mountain systems; now includes snowshoe trails.
Activities and Entertainment: Alpine (Loup Loup), heli-skiing, ice skating, snowshoeing, snowmobiling, sleigh rides, sledding, canoeing on the Methow River (bring your own craft), a beer pub, and a remarkable number of coffeehouses for only 4,000 residents. Snowmobiling is popular but takes place in other areas of the 40-mile-long valley.
Dining: It's hard to beat Sun Mountain Lodge, and the Freestone Inn's new restaurant has a grand reputation, but the Duck Brand Hotel and Restaurant is a local favorite in the Old West–theme town of Winthrop.
Special Nordic Distinction: You'll find genuine powder plus vast amounts of sunshine (residents of the Washington coast tend to forget that's possible). Avoid the thrill of meeting a cougar along the trails (not available by reservation).
Summary: Explore midweek discounts all over the valley, and plan on staying *at least* five days—anything less is self-deprivation.

See color photos, pages 101 and 102

Methow Valley Sport Trails Association, Washington

Don Portman

Don Portman

Sun Mountain Lodge
Winthrop, Washington

Sun Mountain Lodge is the crown jewel among the Methow Valley's barely discovered gem collection. Simple statistics imply a great deal. The resort encompasses 3,000 acres, is set 2,000 feet above the valley floor, is perched on a hill with 360-degree panoramic views, and has its own major trail system. Equally important, the facilities, staff, and architecture are all absolutely first-rate. Furthermore, Sun Mountain enjoys an extraordinary combination of great snow and deep sunshine (80 percent of winter days). Building exteriors are handsome but not ornate, and interiors are literally a showcase for regional arts and craftspeople. The original lodge was built in the early 1960s, renovated to the tune of $20 million, and has recently added luxury suites. The future may hold a small spa, expanded ski shop, kids' game room, and another restaurant. Since the North Cascades Highway is closed in winter and the region suddenly becomes less accessible from Seattle, Sun Mountain offers low-priced incentive packages from early January through early March.

Address: P.O. Box 1000, Winthrop, WA 98862
Tel/fax: (800) 572-0493 or (509) 996-2211; fax: (509) 996-3133
e-mail: smtnsale@methow.com.
Internet: www.sunmountainlodge.com
Location: North-central Washington
Airport: Pangborn Field, 90 miles
Train: None nearby
Memberships and Awards: Cross Country Ski Areas Association, AAA Four Diamond, Mobil Four Star, *Wine Spectator*'s Award of Excellence, Four Lips rating from *Best Places to Kiss in the Northwest*
Medical: Twisp Medical Clinic, 12 miles
Accommodations: Huge Mt. Robinson Guest Rooms and Suites include gas fireplaces, wet bar, and whirlpool baths with mountain views. Mostly non-smoking rooms. Ski-in/ski-out. Three-night minimum holidays.
Guest Capacity: 250 (includes Patterson Lake cabins)

Conference Capacity: 175
Rates: $$$ (multi-day stay includes breakfasts, dinners, and trail pass for all 200 kms)
Credit Cards: Visa, MasterCard, American Express, Diners Club
Season: December–late March; annual snowfall 84"
XC Skiing: The resort snowcat-grooms 65 kms on 22 trails through meadow, evergreen, and aspen. Most are single track with a skate lane, perhaps 15% double track and skating; almost all are two-way. 31% Easier, 39% More Difficult, 30% Most Difficult—there's a fairly tough connector to trails in the valley. Top ski school headed by former PSIA Nordic Demonstration Team member Don Portman (classic, skating, telemarking), also a well-known photographer. Guide service. Two warming shelters. Excellent rental department. Daily trail fee. Altitude range 2,000'–4,000'.
Maps: An admirable graphic presentation coordinates with overall Methow schema.
Activities and Entertainment: On-site: ice skating, sleigh rides, snowshoeing, sauna, exercise room, reflexology, three outdoor hot tubs. Nearby: alpine (Loup Loup), heli-skiing, snowmobiling (virtually no conflicts with skiers), dog sledding, and the rest of the Methow groomed trails, including guided hut-to-hut trips.
Children's Programs: Day care, snow play, instruction, rentals, pulks.
Dining: The award-winning cuisine includes entrées such as smoked kahlua hoisin Chinese BBQ duck breast (!) and salibut (poached layered salmon and halibut). Outstanding new wine cellar.
Special Nordic Distinction: Arrange a lesson with Don Portman, a superb skier and instructor as well as a founding father of the region's trails. He is reputed to have the lowest level of body fat in the Methow Valley.
Summary: Setting, service, fabulous food—and no weekday crowding.

See color photos, page 103

Sun Mountain Lodge, Washington

Don Portman

Don Portman

Justin Trails Nordic Ski Center
Sparta, Wisconsin

Like The Springs, Justin Trails lies in Wisconsin's "driftless region," among hills that weren't ground down or rounded by the last glacial epoch. Founded in 1985, owned and operated by Don and Donna Justin, both from local families, it's one of the smallest XC areas around—actually something of a farm-resort. Meter for meter, it has one of the most challenging trail networks in the Midwest. More important, it's also among the most entertaining, attractive as much as a "winter getaway" as for skiing. For many years a 213-acre dairy farm, the last Holsteins departed in 1996, the same year the restaurant opened. A former barn is now the "Cow Stadium." For seasonal updates, check the *Moos Letter*.

Address: 7452 Kathryn Avenue, Sparta, WI 54656
Tel/fax: (800) 488-4521 or (608) 269-4522
e-mail: justntrailsbb@centuryinter.net
Internet: www.justintrails.com
Location: Southwestern Wisconsin
Airport: LaCrosse Municipal, 30 miles
Train: LaCrosse, 32 miles
Memberships and Awards: Cross Country Ski Areas Association, First Place Honors from *Country Woman* for Oven French Toast with Nut Topping, 10 Most Romantic Inns (*Travel America* magazine), 10 Great Country Escapes for Families (*Family Fun* magazine)
Medical: Franciscan/Skemp Medical Center, 8 miles
Accommodations: Guests can choose among a B&B element in the four-bedroom 1920 farmhouse, two cottages, or two handsome cabins; the latter four have kitchenettes. Built in 1988, Little House on the Prairie is a hand-scribed log home with log queen bed, gas fireplace, skylights, small bathroom with shower, and a double whirlpool bathtub in the loft. Smoke-free environment. Ski-in/ski-out. Two-night minimum weekends and holidays.
Guest Capacity: 20
Conference Capacity: 25

Rates: $$ (includes breakfast, tubing, instruction, use of trails)
Credit Cards: Visa, MasterCard, American Express, Discover, Diners Club
Season: December 26–early March; annual snowfall 45"
XC Skiing: Don snowcat-grooms 12 kms on six trails, largely double track plus skating; longest is 3.5 kms 35% Easier (can be windy), 40% More Difficult, 25% Most Difficult. Higher trails are largely in forest. Best view is off Meadow Loop. Groomed dog trail. Instruction weekends and holidays. Ski and snowshoe rentals. Daily trail fee. Altitude range 840'–1,100'.
Maps: The serious one is included in the overall brochure; the hilarious impressionistic one is surprisingly accurate and useful.
Activities and Entertainment: On-site: snowshoeing, snow tubing on two hills, skijoring with your own dogs, massage by arrangement. Nearby: ice fishing, tours of an Amish cheese factory in Cashton, the Monroe County Museum in Sparta (Air and Space displays share with Bicycling), historic walking tour of Sparta.
Children's Programs: Day care (by reservation), rentals, snow play, farm animals including Pete the pygmy goat.
Dining: In 2000 a new restaurant opens; the old converts to a two-bedroom cabin. Dinner reserved for overnight guests. Country cooking includes vegetarian, such as fruit pizza, but also delicious chicken dishes. Homemade pies are delectable, as are breakfast muffins, coffee cake, banana bread. B.Y.O.B. to enjoy in your cabin.
Special Nordic Distinction: Bambi-eze is a very gentle loop; from there, skiers go up (and down). There are a number of diverting spots along the way (Harry's Dilemma requires a little history, but Reprieve and G-Force are self-explanatory).
Summary: Donna aptly calls it "one-stop shopping"—settle into your cabin, then play, laze, dine, and converse as the spirit moves.

Justin Trails Nordic Ski Center, Wisconsin

Eagle River Nordic
Eagle River, Wisconsin

Bert Kleerup is one of the more remarkable individuals in a business replete with complex characters. He and wife LaNora are owner-operators of Eagle River Nordic—known to some as the Nicolet North Trails—a 40-acre private core in the deep woods of a national forest, along the Continental Divide. (First-time visitors sometimes think it's a government operation and inquire why staff aren't wearing green uniforms.) The Kleerups built trails, then an earth-sheltered passive-solar base building, beginning in 1978. Their year-round business is a famous mail order catalogue carrying select XC equipment and clothing. Bert is known as "the scientist of skiing," with extremely strict standards of excellence—Eagle River tests literally all the skis they sell. As to skiing, Eagle River's priorities seem to be quality and fun. The trails are physically beautiful, passing among grand maples, ironwood, aspen, and hemlock. There's a wonderful teaching area beside the Center in a glacial sinkhole. Along the way you may see pine marten, otter, and pileated woodpeckers; more shy but still in the area are coyote, wolf, and cougar.

Address: P.O. Box 936, Eagle River, WI 54521
Tel/fax: (715) 479-7285, (800) 423-9730 for mail order; fax: (715) 479-2208
e-mail: ernordic@com
Internet: www.ernordic.com
Location: Northeastern Wisconsin
Airport: Rhinelander, 40 miles
Train: None nearby
Medical: Eagle River Memorial Hospital, 17 miles
Accommodations: The Inn at Pinewood is 10 minutes from Bert's place and attracts XC skiers. Once a boys' camp, then a boarding school, today it's a plush B&B, also occupied by Casey the macaw. Eight rooms in the inn, private baths and balconies, some Jacuzzis; small lodge also available. Non-smoking environment. Two-night minimum weekends, three nights holidays. P.O Box 459, Eagle River, WI 54521; (715) 479-4114.

Guest Capacity: 25
Conference Capacity: Small groups
Rates: $–$$ (includes a gala breakfast)
Credit Cards: Visa, MasterCard
Season: Early December–end March (can be substantially longer); annual snowfall 150"
XC Skiing: Bert grooms 50 kms by snowmobile, double track plus skate lane, on 15 trails; all but two trails are two-way. There's a connector to the U.S. Forest Service Anvil Trail system. 20% Easier, 70% More Difficult, 10% Most Difficult. Groomed downhill practice area. Road crossings. Daily PSIA instruction in classic, skating, and telemarking; guiding. The Kleerups retail most catalogue items—a purchase of some kind is hard to resist. Mostly waxable rentals. Daily trail fee. Altitude range 1,650'–1,800'.
Maps: Simple, contours. An examination of trail names hints at Bert's affection for both history and wordplay (Blue 22 refers to an old logging camp along the route, Dow Jones nicely expresses the trail's ups and downs).
Activities and Entertainment: Nearby: alpine (Ski Brule), indoor and outdoor ice skating, dog sledding (races, too), sleigh rides, copious snowmobiling (but talk with the folks living in West Yellowstone, Montana, about who *really* is the intergalactic capital of snowmobiling).
Children's Programs: Instruction, snow play.
Dining: Somehow northern Wisconsin produces excellent Italian food; in this instance, The Pasta Cottage draws on the talents of a former Chicago pizza chef.
Special Nordic Distinction: Eagle River has very little skiing that's genuinely difficult, but the constant rise and fall of the terrain quietly teaches you a lot about technique. Kids love it.
Summary: The Kleerups offer great skiing, particularly for novices and intermediates, complemented by an outstanding play ethic. Bert loves to tell stories; they're good ones, so indulge him.

Mecan River Outfitters & Lodge
Princeton, Wisconsin

Some XC operators seem born to the profession, others become involved in a more circuitous fashion. Paul and Leanne Harvey are of the latter kind. Born in Illinois, they've worked as everything from corn farmers to canoe outfitters, finally settling in a part of Wisconsin explored 300 years ago by Marquette and Joliet. Nearby Princeton bore the frontier stamp, becoming a major fur trading post. There's a taste of the past at Mecan River Outfitters, too—the very name probably means "trail" in Ojibwa. They opened for summer business in 1984, introduced skiing in 1986, and built the lodge in 1994. Today visitors can stay in the new red and white pine lodge (with an addition completed in 1997) or in rustic cabins. When you spend a morning skiing, a trail heading west may take you past the foundations of a barn built in the 1870s. The Harveys and their children observe an ethic of work and integrity that seems from an earlier age. For instance, Paul pulverizes crusty snow until it's comfortable for novices, or he closes the trails. The Harveys own 320 acres and have accommodating neighbors with adjoining land, mostly gentle terrain. Some trails are straight-line paths through neat rows of red pine, others move in more sinuous fashion through less controlled forest and across meadows.

Address: 720 State Road 23, Princeton, WI 54968
Tel/fax: (920) 295-3439
Location: Southeastern Wisconsin
Airport: Wittman Field, 35 miles
Train: Portage, 25 miles
Medical: Berlin Hospital, 25 miles
Accommodations: There are three simple log cabins (no electricity or running water). A more comfortable option is one of five comely rooms in the lodge; shared bathrooms. No TV or phones. Private Great Room for overnight guests. Ski-in/ski-out. No smoking in lodge. Two-night minimum.
Guest Capacity: 40
Conference Capacity: None

Rates: $–$$ (includes instruction and use of trails)
Credit Cards: Visa, MasterCard
Season: December 20–March 15; annual snowfall 40"
XC Skiing: 16 kms of trails follow fire lanes, farm roads, and some specifically designed routes. Three distinct areas, groomed by snowmobile; single track plus skate lane, or double track. 75% Easier, 25% More Difficult; almost everything is two-way. Soda Hills trail to the northeast has some significant ups and downs as well as the best views. Lessons in classic technique given weekends on groomed instruction area. The new ski shop carries accessories and updated rental equipment. Daily trail fee. Altitude range 525'–600'.
Maps: A simple, effective photocopied handout has printed hints as to terrain, vegetation, and sights ("Flat & Fields," "Rolling," "Forest," "Old Car").
Activities and Entertainment: On-site: sledding hill for overnight guests, snowmobiling (separate non-interfering route connects to state trail), bird hunting. Nearby: alpine skiing (less than an hour away), ice fishing, ice skating, Experimental Aircraft Association Museum in Oshkosh.
Children's Programs: Snow play, rentals.
Dining: Surprisingly varied menu, with 10 or more tasty entrées. Among house specialties are sautéed walleye with artichoke cream sauce, tournedos of beef with whisky peppercorn and Chateaubriand sauce. Onion rings are delish; home-made desserts. Full-service bar.
Special Nordic Distinction: Most terrain is suited to beginners. Mecan River is one of the few XC areas where you can ski and pheasant hunt the same day.
Summary: The Harveys are friends of the Palmquists, sharing a dedication to service and hospitality. It's difficult to believe a place this relaxed exists an hour from Madison, two hours from Milwaukee.

Minocqua Winter Park Nordic Center
Minocqua, Wisconsin

Minocqua Winter Park isn't a typical XC area. First, it's a public/private/non-profit partnership among the city, the land-owning corporation, and the managing foundation. Second, orientation is very clearly toward kids, families, and older-than-young Silver Striders, in addition to citizen racers. Third, high-frequency state-of-the-art rather than weekend/holiday grooming is a matter of pride, as expressed in the motto "We treat our snowflakes right!" It's interesting that such a sophisticated operation evolved in a Wisconsin community that has long been a magnet for snowmobilers. And skiing is *good*, ups and downs—some flowing, some precipitous—produced by moraines, kames, and eskers. Many trails have been built specifically for XC, others adopted from logging roads; all move through a forest interrupted only by tree plantations, a swath opened by a tornado in 1991, and peat bogs like Yukon Basin.

Address: 12375 Scotchman Lake Road, Minocqua, WI 54548
Tel/fax: (715) 356-3309
e:mail: xcskimwp@centuryinter.net
Internet: www.skimwp.org
Location: North-central Wisconsin
Airport: Rhinelander, 30 miles
Train: None nearby
Memberships and Awards: Cross Country Ski Areas Association, Rossignol Demo Center
Medical: Howard Young Medical Center, 12 miles
Accommodations: Booth Lake Landing specifically caters to cross-country skiers. While several buildings are available for rent, the handcrafted Log Home is particularly suited to small groups or large families—three bedrooms, two baths, full kitchen, living room with fireplace, and sun room. 8774 Do Di Lac Drive, Minocqua, WI 54548; (715) 588-7939. Two-night minimum.
Guest Capacity: 40 at Booth Lake Landing
Conference Capacity: None
Rates: $–$$

Credit Cards: Personal checks or cash only
Season: December–March 31; annual snowfall 90"
XC Skiing: Two snowcats—one of them new in '96—groom 75 kms on 23 one-way trails. There are 10 kms double-tracked; most trails are single plus skating; some double track and skating. 30% Easier, 50% More Difficult, 20% Most Difficult. Skijoring dog trail nearby. One shelter. Road crossings. PSIA Nordic Demo Team member Dan Clausen is just the fellow to introduce you to the whole technical gamut, including groomed downhills on 200' Squirrel Hill (formerly an alpine area, and certainly the best local lookout) next to the lodge. Excellent rentals; same equipment available for sale. Daily trail fee. Altitude range 1,500'–1,700'.
Maps: Minocqua has one of the better maps you'll find, noting vegetation, terrain changes, and views.
Activities and Entertainment: On-site: snowshoeing. Nearby: alpine (Big Snow Country and others), indoor ice skating, sleigh rides, ice fishing, Northwoods Wildlife Center, Ojibwa Museum and Cultural Center as well as Lake of the Torches Casino in Lac du Flambeau, snowmobiling, rollerskating, movie theater.
Children's Programs: Babysitting, special trails, narrow tracks, instruction, equipment, pulks—a *great* place for youngsters to learn winter is joyous. You'll find everyone from kids to grandmothers skating.
Dining: Mama's Supper Club has been run by the Chiolino family for three generations, dishing up dynamite Italian (or more accurately, Sicilian) food, with pizza the specialty. Full bar, lively atmosphere, very popular with skiers.
Special Nordic Distinction: There's a sense of fun at Minocqua that emerges in events such as an Australian Wine Tasting party. There are also environmental tours.
Summary: Perhaps more than any other Midwestern area, Minocqua is committed to pleasing families.

Palmquist's "The Farm"
Brantwood, Wisconsin

No Midwestern ski operators need take lessons in hospitality. One area in north-central Wisconsin, an hour west of Rhinelander, seems to epitomize the region's charm. Palmquist's "The Farm" combines gentle trails, skiing innovation, comfortable accommodations, delicious dining, welcoming hosts, and moderate prices. It's a hands-on family operation, supplemented by local friends and European students on an exchange program. The Palmquists ran a dairy farm until economics dictated diversification. Art and Toinie began taking in summer guests in the 1940s. Since the area was settled by Finns in the 1890s, skiing is part of local heritage; so it was natural to extend the lodging business to winter in the late '60s. Now son Jim and his wife, Helen, are the farm's workhorses, though visitors are sure to meet Art taking out sleigh rides and Toinie in the kitchen.

Address: N5136 River Road, Brantwood, WI 54513
Tel/fax: (800) 519-2558 or (715) 564-2558; fax: (715) 564-2558
e-mail: palmquistfarm@centuryinter.net
Internet: www.northcoast.com/pqfarm/ski
Location: North-central Wisconsin
Airport: Rhinelander, 40 miles
Train: None nearby
Memberships and Awards: Cross Country Ski Areas Association
Medical: Tomahawk Medical Center, 20 miles
Accommodations: Visitors can stay in the four-bedroom farmhouse or in cabins with fireplaces (one has its own wood-fired Finnish sauna—book early!). Handsome White Pine Inn, which would grace any Montana guest ranch, contains four suites with private bath and has a chainsaw-sculpted lumberjack on the front porch. No smoking in buildings. Ski-in/ski-out. Two-night minimum.
Guest Capacity: 50
Conference Capacity: 50
Rates: $$ (includes meals)

Credit Cards: Visa, MasterCard, Discover
Season: Mid-December–mid-March; annual snowfall 100"
XC Skiing: Jim Pisten Bully–grooms 35 kms of single track, single track plus skating, and double track, mostly two-way. 75% Easier, 25% More Difficult—terrain is exceedingly mild-mannered. Eight trails spread over a thousand acres, through meadow and cedar, birch, sugar maple, balsam, and spruce. The most talked-about route is sinuous "Snow Snake." Instruction in classic technique. Nearby: more XC at Minocqua Winter Park, Eagle River, Timms Hill, and Nine Mile Forest. Modern rental fleet. Daily trail fee. Altitude range 1,500'–1,560'.
Maps: The Ski Adventure Map doesn't need contour lines; it relates trails to ponds, buildings, and roads.
Activities and Entertainment: On-site: snowshoeing, sauna, kick sleds, sledding hill, ice skating, and horse-drawn sleigh rides. The Pickaroon Saloon hosts lively weekend entertainment. December holidays see a Christmas tree in every cabin and a New Year's Eve party.
Children's Programs: Equipment, pulks, farm animals to admire (horses, cattle, rabbits, chickens, cats, and Barney the Golden Lab).
Dining: The Farm produces savory Finnish specialties (ask for the creamed rice with raspberry sauce recipe). Buffet-style meals are well balanced; portions, generous.
Special Nordic Distinction: Jim has corrected nature's oversight by building hills up to 50 feet high; there's usually the option of a flatter route alongside. "Palmquist's Mountains" give a view of the whole locale. Most recent addition: a trail through the deer-feeding area, passing a herd of buffalo!
Summary: Exercise, fun, good companions, comfortable lodging, tasty vittles, and the beauty of snow-laden forest and meadow. The Farm's motto is: "Experience the warm side of a northwoods Wisconsin winter." That's an excess of modesty.

Paust's Woods Lake Resort
Crivitz, Wisconsin

Survival in the hospitality business can lead to painful decisions. For economic reasons, Woods Lake Resort used to be a snowmobile haven. Owners Dale and Judy Paust (both former teachers) made an inspired gamble, reserving trails for skiers exclusively (there's just one access route for snow machines). They seem to have won the wager, attracting couples, families, and clubs—even some experienced skiers preparing for the American Birkebeiner. The 3,000 acres have been in the family since Dale's grandfather acquired them in 1911. The land carries a mix of forest and meadow, with accommodations facing the lake. The resort is water-oriented in summer, skiing-dominated in the real season. Like Minocqua Winter Park, the area was hit by a tornado some years ago; deep scars remain, exposing impressive Big Buck Canyon. Happily, the storm spared some trailside showpiece white pines. Certain ski routes are former logging roads, many do double duty for summer hiking, but in no instance are there death-defying downhills. (The west end of Thunder Mountain Pass is probably the most difficult terrain, and it can be handled by a confident intermediate.) One of the pleasures is really stretching out on long straighter sections—not dull skiing at all because there are constant small changes to the flow. You may run into non-lethal wildlife at any time: deer, raccoons, turkeys, grouse, and porcupine—check for their prints.

Address: N10008 Paust Lane, Crivitz, WI 54114
Tel/fax: (800) 468-8025 or (715) 757-3722, fax: (715) 757-3722
e-mail: paust@exploringthenorth.com
Location: Northeastern Wisconsin
Airport: Green Bay, 70 miles
Train: None nearby
Medical: Crivitz Medical Center, 17 miles
Accommodations: Paust's has very simple cottages that include full kitchen facilities; some with shower, some tub/shower. Motel option preferred by snowmobilers. Ski-in/ski-out. Two-night minimum.
Guest Capacity: 65
Conference Capacity: 65
Rates: $ (includes breakfast, dinner, use of trails)
Credit Cards: Visa, MasterCard
Season: December 1–March 1; annual snowfall 50"
XC Skiing: Dale grooms almost 50 sweet kms of single track and skating lane with a small snowcat; all are two-way. 90% Easier, 5% More Difficult, 5% Most Difficult. Daughter Jennifer has designed a very interesting 26-station nature trail, discussing trees, brush, logging, and habitat. One warming shelter. Classic instruction. Modern rental fleet. Daily trail fee. Altitude range 900'–1,000'.
Maps: It's a sizable map, but lack of difficulty ratings and the number of loops can be confusing. However, good signage at intersections helps remedy concerns.
Activities and Entertainment: On-site: snowshoeing, ice skating, ice fishing, sleigh rides, sledding, picnics at the base of the fire tower; short snowmobile trail into the property doesn't interrupt skiing flow. Nearby: alpine (Pine Mountain).
Children's Programs: Equipment, snow play.
Dining: Overnight guests can order breakfast from the menu. Each dinner is home-cooked and changes daily. Judy requests advance notice for preparing vegetarian meals. Fine home-made pies (apple, cherry, wild blueberry), salad bar. Beer and wine license. A sizable teapot collection graces the dining room, which overlooks Woods Lake.
Special Nordic Distinction: Wonderfully gentle terrain that engenders a sense of security for learners.
Summary: As is so typical of the Midwest, the resort is relaxed, amiable, and inexpensive. The Pausts' sense of humor peers out unexpectedly, such as the parking meter in front of the lodge (yep, law-abiding citizens have been known to put in coins).

The Springs Golf Club Resort
Spring Green, Wisconsin

Parts of southern Wisconsin have a dramatically different appearance from the northern Midwest. It's a geologic anomaly, "the land the glaciers forgot." Frank Lloyd Wright spent much of his life in the region, evolving a vision of architecture in which structure harmonizes with nature. One of his associates, Charles Montooth, designed The Springs, an 800-acre resort that opened in 1993. Located near Taliesin, the working community that also served as Wright's summer residence, set among limestone hills and sometimes using that same rock in construction, it's a tribute to the human instinct for beauty. Taliesin apprentices even designed interior furnishings, from carpets to drapes. Come evening, you can look out from restaurant or room to watch deer feed. Winter outdoor activities are still evolving—instruction and snowshoeing may lie in the near future—but in the meantime the skiing is excellent, as is the tasteful opulence (for once, not a paradox).

Address: 400 Springs Drive, Spring Green, WI 53588
Tel/fax: (800) 822-7774 or (608) 588-7000; fax: (608) 588-2269
e-mail: springs@mhtc.net
Internet: www.springsresort.com
Location: South-central Wisconsin
Airport: Dane County, 35 miles
Train: Madison, 35 miles
Memberships and Awards: Just wait!
Medical: Iowa Co. Memorial Hospital, 17 miles
Accommodations: Each of the 80 spacious suites has a whirlpool tub, microwave, and refrigerator. To hint at the quality, guests find chocolate truffles instead of mints on their pillows. Non-smoking rooms available. No minimum stay.
Guest Capacity: 160
Conference Capacity: 350
Rates: $$ (package includes use of most indoor facilities, ski equipment, trails)
Credit Cards: Visa, MasterCard, American Express, Discover

Season: End December–early March; annual snowfall 30"
XC Skiing: The Springs has 16 snowcat-groomed trails, most designed specifically for skiing. All 35 kms are double-tracked with skating, a mix of one- and two-way. There's gentle running on a golf course next to the resort, but the climb to the hardwood-covered ridge just to the south is a stiff one. It's worth it for the views and for the descent into Hidden Valley, one of the prettiest trails in the Midwest. 25% Easier, 50% More Difficult, 25% Most Difficult. There's a scenic overlook on Redtail Run, with fine views of The Springs and further north to the Wisconsin River Valley. One warming shelter. Skate and track rentals. Daily trail fee. Altitude range 730'–1,070'.
Maps: Both trails and map are elongated; the latter doesn't express vertical change.
Activities and Entertainment: On-site: swimming, ice skating (rentals), eagle watching, racquetball, fitness center, spa (salt-glow treatments!). Nearby: alpine, pheasant hunting, sporting clays, cheese factory, Ho-Chunk Casino. To expand artistic horizons, visit galleries in Spring Green; and if you're looking for an experience that defies cultural definition, see The House on the Rock, with the world's largest carousel and seasonal collection of more than 6,000 Santas. The town of Mt. Horeb is home to trolls and the amazing Mustard Museum.
Children's Programs: Fine sledding hill, equipment, Kids' Night Out.
Dining: The Back Nine Steak and Chop House features fish, poultry, and aged steaks, complemented by an extensive wine list; desserts are fine and filling. The Grille on the Green presents lighter fare. The Springs is home to the original Ski for Chocolate.
Special Nordic Distinction: Ascents are reasonably gradual; the return trip can be exciting! Ridge trails are charmingly sinuous.
Summary: The Springs makes an ideal, uncrowded weekend destination.

Trail Farm
Westboro, Wisconsin

Three fundamental influences in the nordic ski business have been farming, alpine skiing, and glaciation. XC skiing at Trail Farm reflects all these strains. The skiing core consists of 480 quiet acres owned by the Meyer family; the rest is on county land. Some 10,000 to 20,000 years ago (geologists can be as imprecise as meteorologists), a vast ice field left a terminal moraine (hill) on the land, which a Finnish family farmed early in the century. After drought years, a tornado, and a tipping tractor, they sold the property to Dr. Walther Meyer in 1964. The Meyers installed two small tows on that sizable hill across from the farmhouse, and behold! had a private ski area. Some years later they had to shut down due to liability problems (one of the tows is still in use at a nearby camp). Its sequel was a "tree and recreational farm," now managed by Wally Meyer and his wife, Laurie. XC was introduced in 1990; the quiet and security have proven especially popular with groups of women and with families. Trails wander through cedar swamps as well as the dominant hardwood and red pine forest. Visitors can wax or warm up in an attractive building with wood stoves and many windows; only recently it was a dilapidated garage. The further out you go, the more likely you are to see tracks of timber wolf or bear.

Address: N9110 Meyer Drive, Westboro, WI 54490
Tel/fax: (715) 427-5460
e-mail: trlfarm@aol.com
Internet: www.sws-wis.com/TrailFarm
Location: North-central Wisconsin
Airport: Mid-Wisconsin, 75 miles
Train: None nearby
Medical: Medford Clinic, 15 miles (Dr. Meyer is on call in nearby Medford)
Accommodations: There are four choices in types of accommodation; the most pleasant for a family (actually pleasant by any criterion) is The Cabin, nestled in a pine grove above a small lake—two bedrooms, two singles in a loft, a private hot tub, full kitchen, wood stove, VCR, and phone. Ski-in/ski-out. Two-night minimum.
Guest Capacity: 60
Conference Capacity: 25
Rates: $$ (includes use of trails)
Credit Cards: Personal checks or cash only
Season: Mid-December–early March; annual snowfall 80"
XC Skiing: Wally and his father maintain 50 kms of two-way trail by snowmobile: single and double track plus skating. Dogs are OK as skiing companions if you call ahead. Informal instruction. Rentals are available through Pine Line Sports in Medford. Daily trail fee. Altitude range 1,630'–1,782'.
Maps: Incorporated into an all-season brochure, it shows spatial relations but gives little sense of size or of elevation change.
Activities and Entertainment: On-site: snowshoeing, ice skating, ice fishing (bass and bluegill), bird watching, sauna, outdoor hot tub, snow play. Nearby: alpine (Rib Mountain), snowmobiling, casinos, diverse nordic trails.
Children's Programs: Narrow tracks on request; formidable tubing fun on the 179' former alpine hill (don't mention this to neighbor Jim Palmquist at The Farm). 1,951' Timms Hill, the highest point in Wisconsin, is only a five-minute drive.
Dining: High View Inn is a 25-minute drive, sitting on a small hill overlooking Lake Isadore. Everything from menu to decor follows a nautical theme. Food is good and clientele are robustly genial.
Special Nordic Distinction: This is Midwestern skiing at its best—rolling hills and no terror; even steeper descents are long gradual runs.
Summary: No longer a farm, not quite a resort—the important qualities are gentle scenery, pleasing hosts, and seclusion.

Jackson Hole Region
Wyoming

Jackson Hole ("hole" is frontier lingo for "valley") stretches for 50 miles, surrounded by five mountain ranges, with the famous Tetons towering 7,000 feet above the Snake River. Some say they're the only range in the Continental U.S. that compares to the Canadian Rockies. The town of Jackson can be anything between lively and crowded; but since more than 90 percent of the valley is federal land, "civilized" encroachment is strictly limited. As to skiing, no single track network dominates. Most trails are easy, but there are some thrillers at Spring Creek Resort and Trail Creek Ranch. Teton Pass provides some of the most famous downhill skinny-ski terrain in the Rockies. And Jackson is the southern access point to Yellowstone National Park—worth at least a day's tour by snowcoach or snowmobile.

Address: Jackson Hole Chamber of Commerce, P.O. Box E, Jackson, WY 83001
Tel/fax: (307) 733-3316; fax: (307) 733-5585
e-mail: info@jacksonholechamber.com
Internet: www.jacksonholechamber.com
Location: Northwestern Wyoming
Airport: Jackson Hole, 8 miles north of town
Train: None nearby
Medical: St. John's Hospital in town
Accommodations: The Alpine House, owned and operated by former Olympic XC skiers Hans and Nancy Johnstone, offers seven guest rooms with balconies. Smoke-free environment, new outdoor hot tub. No minimum stay. P.O. Box 20245, Jackson, WY 83001; (307) 739-1570.
Guest Capacity: 14 at Alpine House, 4,861 in region, concentrated in town and at Teton Village (Jackson Hole Ski Area).
Conference Capacity: Numerous facilities
Rates: $ (includes breakfast)
Credit Cards: Visa, MasterCard
Season: Early December–early April; annual snowfall up to 500"
XC Skiing: There are five cross-country areas on the flanks of the Tetons. Altitude range 6,200'–8,000'.

- *Grand Targhee Nordic Center:* on the west, "sunny" side of the Tetons; 15 kms double-tracked with skating; some rock and roll terrain; instruction, including telemarking, rentals; superb snow. Daily trail fee. (800) TARGHEE.
- *Jackson Hole Nordic Center:* 22 kms, double-tracked with skating, largely meadow; instruction, rentals, guided tours. Outstanding telemarking program. Daily trail fee. (307) 733-2292.
- *Spring Creek Resort:* 20 kms, single-tracked and skating; some serious hill-thrills (vertical 900'); instruction, rentals, guided tours. Daily trail fee. (800) 443-6139, ext. 1103.
- *Teton Pines Cross Country Ski Center:* 14 kms double-tracked with skating—very gentle golf course; instruction, rentals, guided tours. Daily fee. (800) 238-2223.
- The *Jackson Hole Ski Club* grooms 15–20 kms, single-tracked with skating at Trail Creek Ranch, lovely flowing trails through meadow and wood. Parking can be a problem. Daily trail fee. (307) 733-6433.

Maps: Nordic activities map available through Skinny Skis (307/733-6094), regional activities through Chamber of Commerce.
Activities and Entertainment: Endless! Three alpine ski areas, dog sledding, sleigh rides through the National Elk Refuge, ice skating, power-shopping, snowmobiling, dinner sleigh rides, art galleries, the fabulous National Museum of Wildlife Art, Western Swing at the Cowboy Bar, Bill Briggs' country band at the Stagecoach Bar in Wilson, great wine cellar at Dornan's in Moose.
Dining: Fish Creek Inn in Wilson for breakfast; Snake River Grill in town for dinner.
Special Nordic Distinction: Skinny Skis is one of the finest specialty shops in the West. Rendezvous Ski Tours guides guests to backcountry yurts.
Summary: North America's youngest mountain range provides a backdrop for days of track skiing and gorgeous tours. Beware moose encounters!

Resorts, Lodges, and Groomed Trails

Canada

Canmore Nordic Centre
Canmore, Alberta

Selection as a XC Olympic venue is based on several criteria. Primary among them are reasonable altitude and a 100-kilometer radius from the host city. As a 1988 Olympic Game site, Canmore of course met those specifications—but as far as recreational skiers with an appreciation for beauty are concerned, that fact is almost irrelevant. The Nordic Centre has an absolutely stunning setting below beautiful, blocky mountains. Trails offer magnificent views of the Bow Valley with its gorgeous blue-green river. Since the Games, the Centre has diversified, fulfilling its promise as a national legacy that can please visitors seeking a scenic outing or world-class workout. Skiing is supported by an attractive, full-service day lodge.

Address: 1988 Olympic Way, Ste. 100, Canmore, AB T1W 2T6
Tel/fax: (403) 678-2400; fax: (403) 678-5696
Internet: www.env.gov.ab.ca
Location: Southwestern Alberta
Airport: Calgary International, 60 miles
Train: Calgary, 60 miles
Memberships and Awards: Cross Country Ski Areas Association, site of the 1988 Winter Olympic XC and Biathlon events
Medical: Canmore Hospital, 3 miles
Accommodations: The Lady Macdonald Country Inn is conveniently close to the trails (10-minute drive) and Trans-Canadian Highway. All 11 rooms have floor heating. Non-smoking environment. No minimum stay. 1201 Bow Valley Trail, Canmore, AB T1W 1P5; (800) 567-3919 or (403) 678-3665.
Guest Capacity: 22 at Lady Macdonald Country Inn
Conference Capacity: 22
Rates: $–$$ (includes a splendid breakfast)
Credit Cards: Visa, MasterCard, American Express
Season: November 15–March 3; annual snowfall 50"; 12 kms of snowmaking (probably the most extensive system in the world)
XC Skiing: Canmore uses a mix of snowcats and snowmobiles to meticulously maintain 72 kms of trail. (Early each winter they work with manmade snow, requiring special expertise.) Competition trails are one-way single track plus skate lane; gently flowing Banff Trail and Banff Trail Loops are two-way (effectively doubling distance), skate lane plus double-tracked for conviviality. 30% Easier, 25% More Difficult, 45% Most Difficult. 2.5-km lighted trail. Biathlon range. Fine instruction program for all levels in classic and skating; guide service. Excellent rental fleet at Trail Sports. Daily trail fee. Altitude range 4,511'–5,085', but this encompasses a lot of ups and downs and some neat freeway-like interchanges.
Maps: It's an excellent product in text and trail outline; trail profiles compensate for lack of contours. There's strong emphasis on recreational skiing.
Activities and Entertainment: On-site: snowshoeing, lockers and showers, sauna. Host site for the International Sled Dog Classic. Nearby: alpine skiing (Mt. Norquay and other major areas), snowmobiling. Canmore is 20 minutes from Banff, with famous outdoor hot springs, all types of shopping, and three museums.
Children's Programs: Instruction, equipment, pulks.
Dining: Head west to Banff to The Beaujolais, the only restaurant regionally with a reputation rivaling the Post Hotel in Lake Louise.
Special Nordic Distinction: An Olympic site with a gentle heart (as you'll see if you ski the Banff Trail, which runs through the middle of the network—great spectating during an event!). New terrain hill for teaching near biathlon range—lights, bicycle jump, banked curves with rolls. The Nordic Centre's Kick N Glide Café & Lounge has good lunches and a particularly fine salad bar.
Summary: Canmore was once maligned as a racers-only haven. With recent trail additions, it's extremely attractive for less experienced guests, who also have the chance to challenge themselves on Olympic trails. By any objective measurement, it's one of the most beautiful ski areas in the world.

Château Lake Louise
Lake Louise, Alberta

Since oracular *Snow Country* magazine long ago awarded a plaque to Château Lake Louise as one of the outstanding XC areas in Canada, there should be a new trophy: the Golden Binoculars, granted for Most Spectacular Lake and Mountain Scenery. The Château itself is one of the great hotels of the world in terms of majesty, quality, and diversity (it's a small village—you can even shop for furs, jewelry, and art). As throughout this region, the railroad played a role here: a surveyor for the Canadian Pacific Railroad discovered the lake in 1882. Named for a daughter of Queen Victoria, Lake Louise almost defies description. Suffice it to say that its beauty rivals both Yosemite and the drive from Banff to Jasper.

Address: Lake Louise, AB T0l 1E0
Tel/fax: (403) 522-3511; fax: (403) 522-3834
Internet: www.cphotels.ca
Location: Southwestern Alberta (minutes from B.C. and the Continental Divide)
Airport: Calgary International, 115 miles
Train: None nearby
Memberships and Awards: *Snow Country* magazine's Top 10 XC Areas in Canada
Medical: Mineral Springs, 33 miles
Accommodations: The Château has 489 bedrooms and suites. Try to book a room looking over the lake toward the Victoria Glacier and down to the skating/ice sculpture. Ski-in/ski-out. One-night minimum stay.
Guest Capacity: 1,000
Conference Capacity: 450
Rates: $$–$$$ (package includes huge buffet breakfast, instruction)
Credit Cards: Visa, MasterCard, American Express, Diners En Route, JTC
Season: Mid-November–mid-April; annual snowfall 168" (trails close due to lack of use long before they lose their snow)
XC Skiing: 152 kms are groomed locally, almost all double track; some single track and a skate lane, primarily two-way. Grooming is not up to commercial standards, largely because the Park Service won't permit specific XC trails to be built or a snowcat to maintain them. 75% Easier, 20% More Difficult, 5% Most Difficult (often defined by width rather than steepness, such as parts of the Telemark Loop). Daily instruction in skating, classic, and telemarking; guided tours (Skoki Lodge and Boom Lake shouldn't be missed). Rentals at Monod Sports in Château. Park entrance fee. Altitude range 5,012'–5,800'.
Maps: The Lake Louise regional map is splendid; the combination of photos, text, and artistic aerial views gives a taste of this incredible scenery.
Activities and Entertainment: On-site: snowshoeing, ice skating, Bavarian curling, broomball, ice sculpture awe, ice climbing (an excellent spectator sport), sleigh rides, dog sledding (multi-day trips available), tobogganing, gazing about with dropped jaw, indoor pool, hot tub, steam room, shopping. Nearby: alpine (huge Skiing Louise is just the nearest), heli-tours, ice fishing, Banff Hot Springs, backcountry tours, snowmobiling.
Children's Programs: Play room (complimentary for overnight guests) and babysitting, instruction, equipment, snow play. Pet-sitting can also be arranged.
Dining: The Chateau has several restaurants, ranging from the relaxed to the formal. The Post Hotel (member of Relais & Chateaux), less than 10 minutes away, has superb food and an extensive wine list.
Special Nordic Distinction: Couples, families, even sad and solitary individuals will enjoy the skiing; skate skiers find trails and grooming limiting.
Summary: It's entirely legitimate to come to Lake Louise for skiing, but it's an aesthetic felony not to explore the landscape. Historical note: the explorer who found Lake Louise also discovered Emerald Lake in British Columbia.

Jasper Park Lodge
Jasper, Alberta

In summer, the town of Jasper can resemble Bedlam; come winter, visitation drops to a very livable level—so much so that Jasper Park Lodge, a Canadian Pacific Hotels gem, drops rates to draw guests. Both the Lodge and nearby "railroad town" of Jasper are magnificently isolated, just east of the British Columbia border, in the midst of 4,200 square *miles* of Jasper National Park. Built in 1922, the Lodge has been visited by luminaries such as John Travolta, King George VI, Sir Arthur Conan Doyle, and Marilyn Monroe. The hotel is finally receiving recognition as a XC destination—a point of pride with management. Four routes gently turn through 903 gorgeous acres, around and sometimes across Lac Beauvert and Mildred Lake and along the east bank of the Athabasca River. The long drive from Calgary to Jasper is simply stunning. You pass Canmore, site of the 1988 Olympic cross-country and biathlon events. Next come Banff and Lake Louise, high spots for almost any trip. Then you have 140 savory miles to the town of Jasper, through two national parks. Perhaps no highway in the world compares to the Icefields Parkway. The scale is overwhelming—towering peaks mixed with hanging glaciers, the Columbia Icefields, frozen lakes and waterfalls, spectacular rock formations, wolf, bighorn sheep, mountain goats, wapiti, and moose. If you're inclined to leave the driving to others, there's train and bus service to Jasper.

Address: P.O. Box 40, Jasper, AB T0E 1E0
Tel/fax: (403) 852-3301; fax: (403) 852-5107
Location: West-central Alberta
Airport: Edmonton, 235 miles (Edmonton is closer, but Americans are more likely to get hassled at customs than when flying to Calgary)
Train: Jasper, 2 miles
Memberships and Awards: CAA Four Diamond, Four Diamond for Fine Dining
Medical: Jasper Hospital, 2 miles
Accommodations: Select among 442 rooms in cedar chalets and posh log cabins; suites have fireplaces, opulent bath towels, some Jacuzzis.

Unlike sister resort Château Lake Louise, lodging is very dispersed. Ski-in/ski-out. No minimum stay.
Guest Capacity: 1,000
Conference Capacity: 1,000
Rates: $–$$$
Credit Cards: Visa, MasterCard, American Express, Diners En Route, JTC
Season: December 15–March 15; annual snowfall 80"
XC Skiing: The Ski Centre snowcat-grooms 25 kms of trail on slightly rolling terrain, primarily single track winding about three lakes and the river, through woods and meadows. 50% Easier, 50% More Difficult. Rentals and instruction. Park entrance fee. Altitude range 3,400'–3,500'.
Maps: An aerial-type view with superimposed trails and buildings gives such fine detail that you can locate individual chalets.
Activities and Entertainment: On-site: snowshoeing, ice skating, ice fishing, sleigh rides, health club (hot tub, co-ed steam room, heated indoor/outdoor pool), shopping labyrinth, Elderhostels (from classical music to t'ai chi). Nearby: alpine (Marmot Basin), heli-skiing, heli-sightseeing and snowshoeing, "Journey into Wonder" ice walk at Maligne Canyon, Athabasca and Sunwapta Falls, shopping in Jasper, Jasper Museum, snowmobiling. There's a wide variety of ski trails and tours nearby. Reserve a ski, snowshoe, or nature tour with "Alpine Art" Jackson (403-852-3709), the region's CANSI-certified instructor.
Children's Programs: Day care, recreation center, equipment, snow play.
Dining: The lodge has four restaurants, offering a range in cuisine, costs, and formality. Dining at the Edith Cavell Room approaches the sublime.
Special Nordic Distinction: Trails aren't crowded, scenery is splendid; just don't run into an elk—they also enjoy packed snow.
Summary: It's difficult to describe the magnetism of the region. Jasper is romance incarnate. Bring a camera or regret it forever!

Terratima Lodge
Rocky Mountain House, Alberta

Terratima is both place and concept, creations of owners Claire and Larry Kennedy. The name comes from Latin ("earth") and Inuit ("greetings"); it translates into essence of peace and a tonic to the spirit. Guests drop luggage, cares, and car by the entrance and for the rest of the vacation ski and snowshoe. Set in sunny eastern foothills of the Rockies, there's no other XC area within 150 miles. Terratima has grown since 1974 from a ski-hostel to a low-key resort. The lodge has played a remarkable role in Canadian skiing history, as home to Alberta's first groomed trails and host to the first Canadian Ski-Orienteering Championships. Nearby Rocky Mountain House, a fur trading post from 1799 into the 1870s, was settled around 1900. Claire is from Québec; Larry grew up in the area (his parents were trappers). Originally they ranched and farmed; they still run a few cattle along creek bottoms, valleys, clearings, and boreal forest.

Address: Box 1636, Rocky Mountain House, AL T0M 1T0
Tel/fax: (403) 845-6786; fax: (403) 845-2444
e-mail: terratima@ccinet.ab.ca
Internet: www.tamarac.com/terra
Location: West-central Alberta
Airport: Calgary and Edmonton, each 150 miles
Train: Red Deer, 60 miles
Memberships and Awards: Cross Country Ski Areas Association; finalist, Alberta Tourism Small Business Award
Medical: Rocky Mountain House Hospital, 16 miles
Accommodations: Terratima possesses remarkable lodging variety, from rustic chalets (bring bedding, bathhouse across the way) to handsome Wolf Willow Lodge, designed for groups and meeting, with library and fireplace. All ski-in/ski-out. Non-smoking lodges. Two-night minimum in cabins.
Guest capacity: 65
Conference Capacity: 30-plus

Rates: $–$$ (Wolf Willow Ski Week includes all meals, hot tub, ski trails, afternoon tea, cake and cookies)
Credit cards: Visa, MasterCard, JCB
Season: Mid December–April 1; annual snowfall 100"
XC Skiing: Terratima trails spread over more than 2,000 acres: 75% Easier, 20% More Difficult, 5% Most Difficult. Larry maintains 40 kms by snowcat, including a taste of everything: single track and skating, double track and skating, single track, and double track. Much is one-way. The single longest trail is 18 kms; 2 kms lighted. Daily trail fee. Altitude range 3,100'–3,900'. You'll find abundant signs of wildlife—rabbit, deer, coyote, moose, and the odd elk, lynx, and wolf.
Maps: The trail map is most useful for skiing close to Terratima.
Activities and Entertainment: On-site: snowshoeing, ice skating, ice fishing, sleigh rides behind Belgian draft horses, skijoring, dog sledding by request, Finnish sauna, massage, outdoor hot tub; sometimes classical guitar before dinner. Nearby: alpine (Red Deer), ice climbing, snowmobiling.
Children's programs: Limited.
Dining: Meals are served in the Goldfinch Dining Lodge, complete with stained glass windows. Classic dishes include medallions of tenderloin beef served with butternut squash and cilantro chutney. Licensed dining room at Sees-the-Sun Lodge, set above Prairie Creek.
Special Nordic Distinction: Terratima is an ideal beginner destination. A short ski north along wooded trails leads to a meadow to greet sunrise. Ski to the Indian grave site on a ridge for views of grand peaks to the west, or visit the old Glacier schoolhouse, which still contains blackboards, desks with ink wells, and an ancient but functioning stove.
Summary: Wonderfully warm and genuine hosts, the Kennedys present fine food, modest lodging, and above all harmony with man and nature.

Big Bar Guest Ranch
Jesmond, Clinton, British Columbia

British Columbia has a fair sprinkling of guest ranches, but only a few stay open in winter, and only two are seriously committed to nordic skiing. Big Bar, in the southern Cariboo, lies in a valley of the Marble Range, with outlooks toward 7,400-foot Mt. Bowman. It's near The Hills as the crow flies, but a dimension away in pace and landscape. Peaks stand above, trails lie below, in rolling hills, open grasslands, or on mountain flanks among pine and fir. The relaxed, family atmosphere makes it a favorite drop-in for neighbors, and it's not unusual to find local cowboys sipping coffee and telling tales. Western Canadians enjoy the ranch, but mighty few American skiers know of it. It's a stiff drive from the highway, so a four-wheel-drive vehicle is a good investment.

Address: P.O. Box 27, Jesmond, Clinton, BC V0K 1K0
Tel/fax: (250) 459-2333
e-mail: info@bigbarranch.com
Internet: www.bigbarranch.com
Location: South-central British Columbia
Airport: Kamloops, 120 miles (shuttle available)
Train: Clinton, 40 miles (shuttle available)
Medical: Ashcroft Hospital, 60 miles
Accommodations: Guests are offered options among 11 private rooms with bath or four cozy log cabins with kitchens, fireplaces, and full bath, resting above a creek. Handsome new six-bedroom Coyote Lodge is designed for groups, with fireplace, kitchen, two bathrooms, and large living area. Ski-in/ski-out. No smoking in guest rooms or dining room. Minimum stay varies.
Guest Capacity: 50
Conference Capacity: 50
Rates: $$ (most packages include meals, use of trails)
Credit Cards: Visa, MasterCard
Season: December 1–March 15; annual snowfall 48"
XC Skiing: The ranch snowmobile-grooms 30 kms of double-tracked trail; 50% Easier, 45% More Difficult, 5% Most Difficult. If you're a little unsure about technique, it's wisest to ski upper trails clockwise to minimize downhill thrills; if you enjoy an adrenaline rush, reverse the process! One novelty: pets are permitted on the trails. Limited rentals. Altitude range 3,200'–3,800'—in other words, you get the vistas without paying in altitude exhaustion.
Maps: There's a succinct photocopied hand-drawn handout; no difficulty ratings, but you get a good feel for where hills and forest lie.
Activities and Entertainment: On-site: snowshoeing, dog sledding, sleigh rides, lighted ice skating, ice fishing, toboggan runs, billiards, stargazing from the hot tub, snowmobile tours. Big Bar is the only Canadian ranch offering winter horseback riding (50 kms of trail). Nearby: hiking and gold panning along the Fraser River, Big Bar XC trails (nope, a different network entirely, near Highway 97).
Children's Programs: Babysitting can be arranged, equipment, snow play.
Dining: The homey Wagonwheel Dining Room is licensed, offers Western fare with special care for guests with vegetarian needs or with allergies.
Special Nordic Distinction: The vast stretches of land and changes in terrain allow Big Bar to specialize in different activities in different areas. Thus skiers, horseback riders, and snowmobilers can all enjoy this grand countryside.
Summary: As in so much of Canada, keynotes are wonderful landscape, fine skiing, hospitality, and unbelievably inexpensive fun. It's a wondrous thing to ski in the morning, ride in the afternoon, then relax in the big outdoor hot tub, gazing at black mountain profiles and the northern lights at play.

Emerald Lake Lodge
Field, British Columbia

Emerald Lake Lodge is only 40 kilometers by highway from Château Lake Louise, and it's in the midst of magnificent mountains. But in other senses they are worlds apart. It's not simply a matter of provincial boundaries or crossing the Continental Divide—it's the human factor. Emerald Lake lies at the base of the stunning Presidential Range, whose highest peak reaches almost 9,000 feet. Mornings after a good snow, you may stand outside your cabin with only a breeze as company—then see and finally hear the echo of an avalanche pouring down steep-walled peaks and ridges. The historic lodge is a 13-acre property, 10 kilometers off the Trans-Canada Highway. The lake was discovered in 1882, the first guest house built 20 years later by the Canadian Pacific Railway. (It's fun to muse on the role of the rails in exploration and development of the West, including Izaak Walton Inn.) New cabins follow the architectural style of the lodge, renovated in 1986. It's unlikely that Parks Canada will permit further growth, so it seems Emerald Lake will remain a place of private magic in winter, in contrast to the bustle of Banff and the enormous scale of Château Lake Louise.

Address: P.O. Box 10, Field, BC V0A 1G0
Tel/fax: (800) 663-6336 or (604) 343-6321; fax: (403) 609-6158
e-mail: info@crmr.com
Internet: www.crmr.com
Location: Southeastern British Columbia
Airport: Calgary International, 125 miles
Train: None nearby
Medical: Lake Louise Family Health Center, 15 miles
Accommodations: Emerald Lake has 24 "cabins" (no suggestion of the spartan here!). Except during holidays and weekends, winter occupancy is well below that of summer. Ski-in/ski-out. One-night minimum.
Guest Capacity: 200
Conference Capacity: 160

Rates: $$–$$$ (includes use of trails; winter packages available)
Credit Cards: Visa, MasterCard, American Express, Diners En Route
Season: Early December–early April; annual snowfall 180"
XC Skiing: 40 kms are groomed by snowmobile. 50% Easier, 30% More Difficult, 20% Most Difficult. Some afternoons you can ski through mist rising from the lake, running into pockets of cloud and re-emerging into brilliant sun—spellbinding beauty! Group instruction and backcountry guided tours available by reservation. Rentals at Emerald Sports. Altitude range 3,800'–4,200'.
Maps: Greatly improved version now available; complimentary to guests.
Activities and Entertainment: On-site: snowshoeing, ice skating and broomball, sleigh rides at Christmas, games room (huge billiards table), clubhouse (hot tub, sauna, exercise room). Nearby: alpine (complimentary shuttle to Lake Louise), heli-skiing, dog sledding, snowmobiling; and *really* near, the tiny town of Field.
Children's Programs: Equipment only.
Dining: Specialty is "Rocky Mountain Cuisine," including game such as caribou, venison, and duck. Full license to admire the bar.
Special Nordic Distinction: Guests can ski on a groomed trail to Field, passing a natural bridge carved by the Kicking Horse River. In town you'll find the Yoho National Park Visitor Center as well as Velvet Antler Pottery and a general store, The Siding. The latter has good coffee and deli(sh) sandwiches. For a wonderful but lengthy backcountry tour, secure a guide and head for 1,248' Takkakaw Falls, the highest in the Canadian Rockies. Complimentary weekly escorted tours on the trail to field in company of lodge managers; return transportation.
Summary: Emerald Lake's setting may be equaled in the Rockies, but it seems impossible to better it. The splendid scenery on the way from Calgary alone justifies a visit.

Emerald Lake Lodge, British Columbia

Douglas Peebles

Helmcken Falls Lodge
Clearwater, British Columbia

Joyce Harrington has a great warm chuckle, and guests hear it frequently. Though originally from Massachusetts, she has easily assumed Western Canadian ways—instead of "New England brisk," you feel welcomed to her home. (This is, of course, no less than the literal truth. And since she's everything from chef to CANSI-certified instructor, you're likely to meet her in a variety of situations.) The lodge was built in 1949 and later renovated; Joyce purchased the property in 1990. It's set beside the forest on the edge of a vast wilderness (Wells Gray Provincial Park is almost twice the size of Rhode Island). From near the lodge you can see 8,455-foot Trophy Mountain in the Cariboos. Begin skiing beside the Lodge or drive up to two small trailheads within Wells Gray. B.C. Parks emphasizes "preservation rather than recreation," so trails are wooded promenades rather than city boulevards; forest gives excellent wind protection. And the centerpiece awaits: a backcountry day tour to spectacular ice-draped 450-foot Helmcken Falls—fourth highest in Canada, over twice the height of Niagara. It is *spectacular*!

Address: Wells Gray Park, P.O. Box 239, Clearwater, BC V0E 1N0
Tel/fax: (250) 674-3657; fax: (250) 674-2971
e-mail: helmfall@mail.wellsgray.net
Internet: www.profiles.net/helmcken
Location: South-central British Columbia
Airport: Kamloops, 100 miles
Train: Clearwater, 22 miles
Medical: Clearwater Medical Center, 22 miles
Accommodations: Joyce welcomes guests to 11 rooms in the chalet block, or 8 even more comfortable rooms in two log buildings, all with private bath and shower. (Alas, the fine old pioneer cabin doesn't cope well with the cold.) Ski-in/ski-out. One-night minimum.
Guest Capacity: 57
Conference Capacity: 28
Rates: $$ (includes meals)
Credit Cards: Visa, MasterCard, American Express

Season: December 20–March 31; annual snowfall 80"
XC Skiing: 35 kms of double track are snowcat-groomed by the Wells Gray Outdoors Club. (These folks are responsible for maintaining several networks some distance apart, so they can't always get to the lodge trails immediately after a storm.) 20% Easier, 35% More Difficult, 45% Most Difficult. Groomed downhill practice area. Two warming shelters. Daily instruction in classic style. Snowshoes and older-line equipment available for rent. Daily trail fee. Altitude range 2,070'–2,950'—enough vertical change to make skiing exciting, not enough altitude to dramatically tax your respiratory system.
Maps: The photocopied handout doesn't give a great deal of detail.
Activities and Entertainment: On-site: snowshoeing, special photography seminars, Elderhostel, music workshops (songwriting, voice, and guitar). Nearby: alpine (Clearwater Ski Hill), heli-skiing, ice skating and fishing, dog sledding, sleigh rides, indoor skating and curling, snowmobiling. Hut-to-hut skiing along the Trophy Mountains is something rare and wonderful; it's also Joyce's favorite spring tour.
Children's Programs: Kids are welcome, but there are no special facilities or programs, and happily, not even TVs.
Dining: The copious buffet tends toward the gourmet, with home-made breads and soups. The fully licensed dining room carries B.C. wines, among the best in the world.
Special Nordic Distinction: Who says gambling doesn't pay? Funding for the grooming snowcat comes from the B.C. lottery!
Summary: Most Americans and Eastern Canadians know of Banff and Jasper but have never heard of Wells Gray, far less visited in winter. No crowds, no glitter, just comfort, in country where you may see wolves, moose, and possibly even caribou in bottom lands.

The Hills Health Ranch
100 Mile House, British Columbia

British Columbia's Cariboo region still tastes like the frontier. It's big, rolling country that's sparsely settled. The whole South Cariboo region has a deep commitment to nordic skiing. Part of the motive for this is, of course, economic, but part is real enjoyment of the sport. The Hills is a 350-acre resort perched on a promontory among 20,000 acres of skiable terrain—meadow, lake, and forest. More accurately, it's a ranch, spa, and wellness center as well as the region's XC showpiece. Owners Pat and Juanita Corbett opened The Hills in 1985, offering the first year-round health and fitness vacation resort in Canada; today they draw winter weekend visitors from as far away as Seattle. There's a racing history with the Cariboo Marathon, while the ranch has also hosted the Canadian and Australian National Teams, but most trails are fine for the inexperienced. The world's longest skis (11 meters) are on display just a few miles south, outside the Information Centre in downtown 100 Mile House. (They need new bindings.)

Address: Box 26, 108 Ranch, BC V0K 2Z0
Tel/fax: (250) 791-5225; fax: (250) 791-6384
e-mail: thehills@bcinternet.net
Internet: www.grt-net.com/thehills/
Location: South-central British Columbia
Airport: Williams Lake Municipal, 60 miles
Train: 100 Mile House, 9 miles
Memberships and Awards: Cross Country Ski Areas Association
Medical: 100 Mile Hospital, 9 miles
Accommodations: Guests can choose from rooms in a new lodge, or among 20 handsome three-bedroom, two-level chalets with kitchen facilities. Ski-in/ski-out. Mostly nonsmoking rooms. No minimum stay.
Guest Capacity: 230
Conference Capacity: 200
Rates: $ (remarkable multi-day packages include breakfast, dinner, sleigh ride, pool and fitness facilities, use of trails)
Credit Cards: Visa, MasterCard, American Express

Season: Early December–mid-March; annual snowfall 60"; up to 25 kms have snowmaking from a mobile system.
XC Skiing: 150 kms are groomed by snowcat, with a smorgasbord of single track, double track, single with skating, and double with skating. 20 kms are on the ranch; the rest is contiguous. 40% Easier, 40% More Difficult, 20% Most Difficult. 8 kms lighted next door at 108 Ranch Resort. Groomed downhill practice area. Biathlon range. Three warming shelters. Daily instruction in skating, classic, and now, telemarking. Excellent rentals and retail available through Gunner's Ski Shop. Daily trail fee. Altitude range 3,100'–4,100'.
Maps: The Hills provides a simple handout; map of their own trails on one side and the entire 100 Mile/108 Ranch network on the other.
Activities and Entertainment: On-site: alpine with night skiing, snowboarding, snowshoeing, dog sledding (learn mushing!), sleigh rides, ice skating and broomball, curling, tobogganing, tubing, snowmobiling, two hot tubs. The spa includes pools, saunas, exercise equipment, massage, reflexology, aromatherapy, herbal wrap, and tranquility classes staffed by a physiotherapist, physician, nurse, and fitness instructors. Nearby: alpine (Mt. Timothy).
Children's Programs: Instruction, equipment, pulks.
Dining: The Hills has two menus, one of gourmet ranch fare, the other a low-fat spa alternative. Both chef and nutritionist on staff.
Special Nordic Distinction: With a new tow for their 145' hill, snowmaking, and state-of-the-art grooming equipment, it's easy to consider this the cutting-edge XC area in B.C. The resort is also home to World's Fastest XC Skier Race. There's a new day lodge with restaurant, lounge, and Victorian tea parlor.
Summary: Distinguished skiing, and a lot of it—but still more attractive, the Cariboo remains frontier-friendly.

See color photos, page 104

Manning Park Resort
Hope, British Columbia

When Vancouverites make a three-hour drive to spend a weekend XC skiing, it's not necessarily because they dislike the home trails at Cypress Bowl or Whistler. Nor is it entirely the beautiful drive to Manning Park Resort or transcendent architecture exuding aesthetic magnetism. Simply, it's the skiing—drier snow and a longer season than along the coast, plus comfortable lodgings. The resort's address may be Hope, but it's actually the better part of an hour's drive to the east, far removed from the temptations of civilization. These mountains are part of the Cascades, more rounded than the steep-sided Rockies but nonetheless impressive; views become more expansive as you ski up the valley toward the alpine hill. There's opportunity to drive about halfway, parking at Lightning Lake, skipping a Black Diamond section between the lodge and lifts. Most of the terrain swings only gently uphill or down, ideal for beginners and intermediates.

Address: P.O. Box 1480, Hope, BC V0X 1L0
Tel/fax: (250) 840-8822; fax: (250) 840-8848
e-mail: info@manningparkresort.com
Internet: www.manningparkresort.com
Location: Southwestern British Columbia
Airport: Vancouver, 170 miles
Train: Hope, 40 miles
Memberships and Awards: Cross Country Ski Areas Association
Medical: Hope, 40 miles
Accommodations: Visitors can choose between cabins, chalets (some with kitchens), or motel-type units in the lodge. If you can swing it, book cabin #16, a luxury unit, but it's not likely to be available weekends. Ski-in/ski-out. Two-night minimum weekends.
Guest Capacity: 452
Conference Capacity: 120
Rates: $–$$ (includes use of trails and ski school discount); very inexpensive for groups
Credit Cards: Visa, MasterCard, American Express
Season: December–March; annual snowfall

214". The region had an excess of the white stuff in late December '96—avalanches closed western access via Allison Pass for several days, but the skiing was *great*.
XC Skiing: The resort has 17 kms of two-way double track and skating, groomed by snow-cat. 55% Easier, 25% More Difficult, 20% Most Difficult. Several road crossings. XC manager Donna Hays and helpful staff offer daily instruction in skating, classic, and telemarking, with a neat little practice hill near the center. Saturday waxing clinics. Guided snowshoe tours Saturdays. Good rentals. Daily trail fee. Altitude range 3,900'–5,000'.
Maps: XC is on the flip side of the alpine map. A multi-color illustration shows more about mountains than trails.
Activities and Entertainment: On-site: snowshoeing, lit ice skating, sleigh rides, saunas; snow play and alpine skiing 10 kms up the road (the bottom of a little handle tow at Gibson Pass is the highest point on the XC system—a fine downhill-on-skinny-skis practice-and-play area!). A complimentary shuttle makes several stops between the alpine area and the lodge.
Children's Programs: Day care (at alpine area, 6 miles), excellent instuction program for ages 7 up, pulk, tobogganing.
Dining: There are not many alternatives to eating at the café (breakfast, lunch) and restaurant, but food is quite good (the baked lasagne and stir-fries are fine, and the hybrid bumbleberry pie, excellent); service is friendly and efficient. The non-smoking Bear's Den lounge has handsome murals.
Special Nordic Distinction: The Nordic Center was built in 1987 as a school class project. Classic-only Cascade Cup race in early March.
Summary: Other than a fair number of folks from Washington and several from Oregon, Americans seem never to have heard of the resort. It's great fun to enjoy Manning, then head northeast to Silver Star.

Silver Star Mountain Resort
Vernon, British Columbia

Though well known in Europe, Silver Star is not yet a household name, even among Canadian skiers. This is a serious oversight because the area provides one of the most comfortable blends of alpine and cross-country skiing anywhere. Hotel staff, ski instructors, and shopkeepers are invariably friendly; Gaslight Era architecture in the pedestrian village works beautifully; dining is unpretentious and excellent; weather is usually moderate; and skiing is exceedingly entertaining. Silver Star is remarkably unassuming and intimate for an area that sees 200,000 alpine skier visits annually; and XC feels like a partner rather than the second fiddle familiar at most alpine resorts.

Address: Box 3002, Silver Star Mountain, BC V1B 3M1
Tel/fax: (800) 663-4431 or (250) 542-0224; fax: (250) 542-1236
e-mail: star@junction.net
Internet: www.silverstarmtn.com
Location: South-central British Columbia
Airport: Kelowna, 36 miles
Train: Salmon Arm, 50 miles
Memberships and Awards: Cross Country Ski Areas Association
Medical: Vernon Jubilee Hospital, 16 miles
Accommodations: While visitors can stay in anything from vacation homes to condos, the rooms above the Chilcoot Conference Centre are particularly pleasant. Smoke-free environment. Ski-in/ski-out. Minimum stay varies with holidays.
Guest Capacity: More than 1,000
Conference Capacity: 400
Rates: $$
Credit Cards: Visa, MasterCard, American Express
Season: Early November–mid-April; annual snowfall 225"—and when it falls, it stays dry!
XC Skiing: While Silver Star hosted World Cup races in 1991, most of the trails are gentle to moderate, and all are wide enough to accommodate two major snowcats grooming double track and skating lane. Over 85 kms of trail, with a mix of one- and two-way routes, including the Silver Star system and the adjoining Sovereign Lake network. Two chairlifts to the summit connect to trails to the village. 34% Easier, 28% More Difficult, 38% Most Difficult; 4 kms lit. Good range of rentals. There are terrific views west to the Okanogan Valley and east to the Monashee range. Best trail to see the sunset: Sidewinder. Daily trail fee. Altitude range 4,200'–6,800'.
Maps: The clear and concise map relates Silver Star trails to the overall resort; on the reverse, a map of Sovereign Lake XC area and upper trails.
Activities and Entertainment: Don't bother leaving Silver Star! On-site: downhill, snowshoe tours, sleigh rides, nature trail, indoor swimming pool, outdoor hot tub, ice rink, dog sledding—plus the National Altitude Training Centre. Enjoy live evening performances at the Vance Creek Saloon. Then there's the famous Best Boxer Shorts contest. . . .
Children's Programs: Day care, special instruction, snow play, pulks.
Dining: There are six restaurants to choose from, including exceptional Italian food with generous portions at Lucciano's Trattoria. Try local Okanogan Valley wines; they compare to some of California's best vintages.
Special Nordic Distinction: Long-time XC director Howard Maddex does everything—grooms, instructs, even chats with visitors about local animal life (he's seen a bear strolling through the village in early morning). Starting mid-November, Silver Star has outstanding fall camps with Marty Hall, former U.S. *and* Canadian XC team coach—ideal not for just accomplished racers, but also for pure beginners. There are special women's camps, too.
Summary: If you're an alpine skier, in this setting cross-country may prove tempting; if you're a nordic enthusiast, trying a day of downhill is well-nigh irresistible. The staff are among the most amiable and entertaining you'll meet at any resort, anywhere.

Hardwood Hills Cross Country Ski Centre
Oro Station, Ontario

During the decade following its founding in 1983, Hardwood Hills had the reputation as southern Ontario's high-tech XC day area—a great place to race and train. Trails ran over glacial moraines—no huge or prolonged climbs but a lot of up and down. Owners Dave and Kim Viney introduced big-snowcat grooming and snowmaking, and they continue to run the finest retail operation in the province. Since 1995 they have fundamentally restructured the center, expanding services and facilities and adding over 7 kilometers of easy trails. Hardwood is now very attractive to less experienced skiers.

Address: R.R. 1, Oro Station, ON L0L 2E0
Tel/fax: (705) 487-3775, (800) 387-3775 for retail/catalog sales; fax: (705) 487-2153
e-mail: hardwood@bconnex.net
Internet: www.hardwoodhills.on.ca
Location: South-central Ontario
Airport: Toronto International, 60 miles
Train: Barrie or Orillia, 12 miles
Memberships and Awards: Cross Country Ski Areas Association, Ontario Ski Resort Association
Medical: Royal Victoria Hospital, 12 miles
Accommodations: Plan to stay on-property at The Inn at Hardwood Hills. Five pleasant rooms; #2 is the pick, with king-sized bed and gas fireplace. Outdoor hot tub. Package includes hearty country breakfast, preferred parking, washer and dryer (!), discounted trail fee, and conversation with owner/innkeeper Janet Gates, herself a vital force in Canadian XC skiing and a nutritionist. Ski-in/ski-out. Non-smoking environment. Two-night minimum weekends.
Guest Capacity: 12 at Inn at Hardwood Hills
Conference Capacity: None
Rates: $
Credit Cards: Visa, MasterCard, American Express, Debit cards
Season: Mid-November–end March; 120" annual snowfall; up to 7 kms of snowmaking
XC Skiing: Trails are divided into three networks: Meadowlands (for never-evers), the Recreational System, and the Olympic System. Forty-two kms are spread over a half-dozen complex loops, groomed lovingly. 30% Easier, 50% More Difficult, 20% Most Difficult, though Hardwood has its own criteria: Physical Difficulty and Technical Difficulty. Everything is maintained for both track and skating, mostly double track set side by side; virtually everything is one-way. Three groomed instruction areas. 1.5 kms night skiing. Despite the name, evergreens and meadows do appear. Dogs, pulks, snowshoers, and even hikers are welcome on the ungroomed 6-km Wilderness Trail loop. Daily trail fee. Altitude range 1,050'–1,230'.
Maps: Incorporated into brochure and separate, more detailed version.
Activities and Entertainment: On-site: sleigh ride from parking to the Chalet. Nearby: alpine skiing, Simcoe County Museum in Minesing (an indoor Victorian village), and the Ontario Provincial Police Museum in Orillia; symphony in Barrie; casino near Orillia.
Children's Programs: With the introduction of babysitting weekends, pulks, and snowshoes on the Meadowlands loop, the center has become much more attractive to families. Rentals, instruction.
Dining: Head into Barrie to Graydon's Spirits and Grill (15 minutes), where you can sit on chairs or loll on couches, enjoying artwork and dining alike. Vast tureens of tasty soup; excellent pasta and memorable chocolate mousse.
Special Nordic Distinction: Hardwood offers a "natural skiing program" under former Olympic coach Jack Sasseville—outstanding introduction for beginners, too. "Rent to buy" program deducts rental fee from same-day equipment purchase.
Summary: The Vineys have surveyed visitors and responded to their requests. Still evolving as a destination, Hardwood Hills has expanded skiing and widened its appeal from "hot Lycra" to "come as you are, who e'er you be."

Hiawatha Highlands
Sault Ste. Marie, Ontario

To most Americans, the small city of Sault Ste. Marie, Ontario, is part of the mysterious Great White North, though it's only a bridge away from Michigan. The area has some fame as the home of Roberta Bondar, Canada's first female astronaut (herself a XC skier). Near neighbor Stokely Creek Lodge has an international reputation. But Hiawatha Park, on the city's outskirts, remains sadly unsung despite excellent skiing, handsome views, and colorful winter entertainment in the region. Trails are largely the legacy of local skiers, particularly a strong Finnish contingent. Restaurant, bar, rentals, and banquet area are located on site, and a motel is in the works.

Address: Economic Development Corporation, P.O. Box 580, Sault Ste. Marie, ON P6A 5N1

Tel/fax: (800) 461-6020 or (705) 759-5432; fax: (705) 759-2185

Internet: www.sault-canada.com

Location: Northeastern Ontario

Airport: Sault Ste. Marie, 10 miles

Train: None nearby

Memberships and Awards: Cross Country Ski Areas Association

Medical: Plummer Memorial Hospital, 10 miles

Accommodations: Glenview Vacation Cottages caters to XC skiers and has its own (ungroomed) nature trail. It's five minutes from Hiawatha, 15 minutes from Stokely or downtown. About half the one- and two-bedroom cabins are non-smoking; 10 have wood stoves; all have fridges and stoves. Sauna, whirlpool, coin laundry, waxing room. Two-night minimum on weekends. 2611 Great Northern Road, Sault Ste. Marie, ON P6A 5K7; (800) 668-3100 in Canada and some states, or (705) 759-3436.

Guest Capacity: 160 at Glenview Vacation Cottages

Conference Capacity: Recommended site is Algoma's Water Tower Inn, 15 minutes away, owned by Jim Hilsinger, the Soo's leading entrepreneur (also an avid XC skier); (705) 949-8111.

Rates: $

Credit Cards: Visa, MasterCard, American Express, Discover, Diners En Route

Season: Mid-December–late March; annual snowfall 170"

XC Skiing: 35 kms snowcat-maintained in three networks, spread over 3,000 acres, winding through hardwoods and pine plantations on 12 trails. Another 50 kms of trail lies half an hour away at Searchmont Resort. Prettiest routes pass by Crystal Creek. All trails are double-tracked; two of three trail systems have skating. Long, gentle views over the city to the St. Marys River and Michigan. Instruction by arrangement. Rentals available. Daily trail fee. Altitude range 708'–962'.

Maps: Simple maps are available for each system, relating trails to the base area.

Activities and Entertainment: On-site: snowshoe trail plus rentals, alpine skiing at Landslide (tiny but steep). Nearby: the engrossing Canadian Bushplane Heritage Centre, Bon Soo Winter Carnival, Agawa Canyon Snow Train (wonderful eight-hour excursion—valleys, cliffs, frozen waterfalls!), curling, ice skating, downtown shopping in Queenstown, casino in Sault Ste. Marie, Michigan, ice fishing, and omnipresent Ontario snowmobiling.

Children's Programs: Very limited for non-residents, though local interest borders on the hyperactive.

Dining: The Soo's Italian community is nobly represented at Giovanni's Family Restaurant, with lively staff and pleasant decor. The wide-ranging menu covers everything from ribs to Sicilian pasta; veal dishes are particularly tasty. Visit Paul's Bakery for delicious fruit pastries.

Special Nordic Distinction: Hiawatha is supposed to be particularly suited for intermediates, but there's a surprising amount of mild terrain.

Summary: Hiawatha deserves attention, both for its own attractions and as a complement to Stokely Creek.

Highlands Nordic
Duntroon, Ontario

Some XC areas are ungainly giants (which are naturally skipped over in this book); Highlands is a small, multifaceted gem, with trails beckoning skiers from the modern-looking chalet (actually rebuilt barns) into rolling wooded hills. Lying along the top of the Niagara Escarpment, trails receive a fair share of moisture coming off Lake Huron's Georgian Bay. Once based at a golf course clubhouse, the current network has been developed entirely for skiing. Co-owner Larry Sinclair is a former coach and administrator, with a very unbureaucratic sense of fun. Highlands' entrance is unobtrusive, due to environmental strictures by a government agency that ironically has permitted a multi-acre limestone quarry next door. To give an idea of the diversity in ski program available, the area has hosted both the 1999 Canadian Senior Championships and the 1997 World Special Olympics—300 athletes from 25 countries taking part in XC and snowshoe events.

Address: P.O. Box 110, Duntroon, ON L0M 1H0
Tel/fax: (800) 263-5017; fax: (705) 444-5017
e-mail: skiinfo@highlandsnordic.on.ca
Internet: www.highlandsnordic.on.ca
Location: South-central Ontario
Airport: Toronto International, 60 miles
Train: Barrie, 30 miles
Memberships and Awards: Cross Country Ski Areas Association, Ontario Ski Resorts Association, Fischer Race Centre dealer
Medical: Collingwood General Marine Hospital, 8 miles
Accommodations: On-site lodging is provided by a delightful renovated 75-year-old farmhouse. Guests rent the entire rustic building, which contains three bedrooms, seven-bed loft, showers (no baths), full kitchen, wood stove, living room, coin-operated sauna, washer and dryer. Smoke-free environment. Ski-in/ski-out. No minimum stay.
Guest Capacity: 16
Conference Capacity: None

Rates: Low $
Credit Cards: Visa, MasterCard
Season: December–March; annual snowfall 120", with limited snowmaking
XC Skiing: Highlands uses a big 'cat on the scale of Hardwood Hills' to groom 16 kms of single track with skating lane, 1.5 km lighted. 10% Easier, 80% More Difficult, 10% Most Difficult. A number of university and high school teams train here, but inexperienced skiers often do better than they anticipate because routes are wide, with good visibility— very desirable, since the highest point in this part of Ontario is a stone's throw away. From the system's crest, views stretch over 20 miles west to Georgian Bay. Instruction is available every day, with occasional special programs (Women's Day, telemarking). Both rental and retail selection are wide-ranging. Daily trail fee. Altitude range 1,400'–1,700'.
Maps: On the tiny side, with no contour indications.
Activities and Entertainment: Nearby: alpine skiing, dog sledding, snowmobiling, Creemore Springs Brewery tour, Collingwood Museum, Blue Mountain Bingo Parlor, Grandma Lambe's (good home-made pies), and a variety of shopping from hand-painted decoys to antiques.
Children's Programs: Indoor play area, rentals, instruction, small obstacle course, pulks.
Dining: Most guests do their own cooking at the Farmhouse (Highlands even keeps the spice cupboard stocked). For variety, pop down to the Duntroon Arms for fish and chips, steak and kidney pie, British ales, and a game of darts; or try Mylar and Loretta's in nearby Singhampton.
Special Nordic Distinction: A jewel of a trail system, and the only cross-country area that operates as a Haunted House at Halloween.
Summary: Highlands mixes pure skiing pleasure with good humor. Larry anticipates building additional trails and adding, ice skating, a snow play area, and more plantings to create windbreaks and mute buildings' visual impact.

Horseshoe Resort
Barrie, Ontario

Horseshoe is primarily an alpine ski area named for the shape of surrounding hills, but the XC operation has considerable stand-alone stature. One of the oldest operations in Canada, it has an excellent range of services (fine instructional program, modern rental fleet, upstairs cafeteria) based in a two-story building across the road from the resort proper. It's a comfortable place, more popular with the knicker-clad than Lycra-wearers. Horseshoe remains committed to classic skiing more than skating. It's remarkable for forest variety and for a taste of history—you can ski by farmers' stone fences and see the finely laid rock foundation of a 200-year-old house, now surrounded by lilac bushes.

Address: P.O. Box 10, Horseshoe Valley, R.R. 1, Barrie, ON L4M 4Y8
Tel/fax: (800) 461-5627 (lodging) or (705) 835-2790; fax: (705) 835-6352
e-mail: hsvalley@barint.on.ca
Internet: www.horseshoeresort.com
Location: South-central Ontario
Airport: Toronto International, 60 miles
Train: Barrie, 20 miles
Memberships and Awards: AAA and CAA Four-Diamond Inn, RCI Gold Crown Resort
Medical: Royal Victoria Hospital, 13 miles
Accommodations: The Inn at Horseshoe has very attractive loft suites, including a sitting room downstairs, upstairs bedroom, huge bathroom, Jacuzzi, and views north to the Medonte Hills. Ski-in/ski-out. Smoke-free rooms available. No minimum stay.
Guest Capacity: 510
Conference Capacity: 150
Rates: $ (XC package includes lodging, breakfast, and trail pass)
Credit Cards: Visa, MasterCard, American Express, Diners En Route
Season: Mid-December–end March; annual snowfall 120"; some snowmaking may be added
XC Skiing: Trails change slightly some years as the resort expands, but the network should remain at about 35 kms, maintained by snow-cat, on 11 trails. 20% Easier, 50% More Difficult, 30% Most Difficult. Customarily the North Trails are double-tracked with no skating; South Trails have no track; and West Trails are a mix. The only two-way sections are tiny connectors. The nicest beginner loop is West Yellow, beginning beside the chalet. Longest trail is 12 kms. Tree plantations of oak and pine march in measured cadence. From the lookout/rest area on advanced North Red, you can see west to Georgian Bay. It's remotely possible visitors will see a wolf. Orienteering course. Moonlight tour each month. Be cautious crossing busy road between South and other trail systems. Daily trail fee. Altitude range 918'–1,325'.
Maps: One map is unwieldy in size but gives excellent detail; the other is easier to read but depends on trail signage for clarity.
Activities and Entertainment: On-site: snowshoeing, alpine skiing, ice skating, sleigh rides (Christmas only), piano lounge; sports center with fitness room, indoor pool, squash court, aerobics, tanning bed, sauna, whirlpool, massage. Nearby: snowmobiling, home of humorist Stephen Leacock, Orillia Opera House, shuttle to casino.
Children's Programs: Instruction, rentals, day care, pulks.
Dining: Silks offers fine dining (wild boar!), but the Go West Grille is a lot livelier, really hopping on weekends. Good Italian dishes (choose among "Spaghetti Westerns"); eclectic menu includes Buffalo-style wings and deep-fried alligator.
Special Nordic Distinction: Try a Nature Ski, learning about serene 4,500-acre Copeland Forest. Artist Ernie Somer can tell you about winter mushrooms or snow fleas, and charm wild birds out of the trees.
Summary: Perhaps because it's not a major alpine area, Horseshoe has maintained a pleasant, relaxed atmosphere. Telemarking seems almost unknown.

Stokely Creek Lodge
Goulais River, Ontario

Stokely Creek is legendary among Midwestern skiers. It's easily accessible by highway yet thoroughly secluded—in fact, one of the few XC destinations accessible only over snow (though a mere .5 km). Trails enjoy early snow, encompass 11,400 acres, and explore a land of lakes and spectacular granite bluffs of the Canadian Shield, the latter all that remains of a vast mountain range crushed and eroded by glaciers thousands of feet thick. Owner Chuck Peterson, a chemical engineer, spent years searching for the ideal snow and topography before settling on Stokely in 1977. He hopes to incorporate most of his own 8,400 acres into the Algoma Highlands Conservancy, dedicated to protecting the land in a wild natural setting.

Address: R.R. 1, Goulais River, ON P0S 1E0
Tel/fax: (705) 649-3421; fax: (705) 649-3429; free video
Internet: www.stokelycreek.com
Location: Northeasernt Ontario
Airport: Sault Ste. Marie, 30 miles
Train: None nearby
Memberships and Awards: Cross Country Ski Area Association, Great Lakes Nordic Ski Council, *Outside* magazine's 100 Best Getaways
Medical: Plummer Memorial Hospital, 25 miles
Accommodations: Diversity is the story here. The Peter Kalm Chalet contains four rooms with private baths and a common living area, with small refrigerator and microwave. Smoke-free environment. Ski-in/ski-out. Two-night minimum weekends and holidays.
Guest Capacity: 75
Conference Capacity: 50
Rates: $–$$
Credit Cards: Visa, MasterCard
Season: December 15–third Sunday in March; annual snowfall 200" ("snow all winter, *every* winter!")
XC Skiing: There are a total of 120 km: 82 km double-tracked, 50 km for skating, 40 km of backcountry skiing. 30% Easier, 40% More

Difficult, 30% Most Difficult. Instruction available daily, including telemarking and guiding. Best view is from the Hanggliders' Platform over the Goulais River Valley to Lake Superior. Close to 1,000' of vertical and plenty of flow between high and low points, but at day's end you always ski downhill to the lodge. Talk with Stokely staff about where to find old-growth white pine; check on the lodge board for recent animal sightings; ski to Norm Bourgeois' Cabin for tea or to a local tavern on Lake Superior. Rentals available on the drive from town at the Old Ski House. Daily trail fee. Altitude range 825'–1,880'.
Maps: Multi-color map in brochure; separate handout gives more detail.
Activities and Entertainment: On-site: two saunas, massage, ping-pong, nature and ski video library, special presentations (example: an introduction to peregrine falcons). Few civilized vices—not even phones or TVs in rooms—but city attractions are only 30 minutes away. Guests customarily retire around 9:00 p.m.
Children's Programs: Babysitting, recreation room, instruction, snow play, pulks.
Dining: Dinners feature several devastating all-you-can-eat entrées (one always vegetarian), served family style. The chef also creates great breads and pastries. B.Y.O.B.
Special Nordic Distinction: Stokely Creek is a beneficiary of the "Lake Superior snow machine," such as the 5' storm of December '95. The Wabos Loppet is a unique non-competitive event that includes a chartered train ride, 27 kms of skiing, and a barbecue.
Summary: The lodge is particularly attractive for food lovers, couples, and more experienced skiers. For the ideal, combine all three qualities; you'll find like-minded fellow guests. What other area has inspired a 70-page trail guide by a longtime friend? This is one of the great destinations in North America.

See color photos, page 105

Stokely Creek Lodge, Ontario

Bill Howe

©Anne Peterson

Wigamog Inn Resort
Haliburton, Ontario

Wigamog Inn Resort, on the north shore of Kashagawigamog Lake (Algonquin for "long and winding waters"), is a major player in the huge but little-known Haliburton Nordic Trails system. The area is a vast, high, rugged plateau, famous in summer for wild beauty, lakes, rivers, forested ridges, and granite outcroppings. A diffuse trail network was built in the mid-'80s, intended to serve everyone from beginners to World Cup events. Initial emphasis lay on inn-to-inn skiing. The concept didn't meet expectations, largely because grooming was inconsistent, and distances between some accommodations (as much as 25 kilometers) were intimidating. But trail maintenance has improved, facilities are more sophisticated, and visitors are coming to recognize that individual destinations merit prolonged tasting.

Address: R.R. 2, Haliburton, ON K0M 1S0
Tel/fax: (800) 661-2010 or (705) 457-1962; fax: (705) 457-1962
e-mail: wiggyone@halhinet.on.ca
Internet: www.wigamoginn.on.ca
Location: South-central Ontario
Airport: Toronto International, 150 miles
Train: None nearby
Memberships and Awards: Cross Country Ski Areas Association
Medical: Haliburton Hospital, 5 miles
Accommodations: Cabins have deceptively simple white clapboard exteriors but exceedingly comfortable living space. Several suites have fireplace, king bed, lake views, couples Jacuzzi (*and* smoked-glass mirror). Ski-in/ski-out. No minimum stay except holidays.
Guest Capacity: 200
Conference Capacity: 200
Rates: $$–$$$ (package includes breakfast and dinner, trail use, waxing, instruction)
Credit Cards: Visa, MasterCard, American Express
Season: Christmas holidays–mid-March; annual snowfall 80"
XC Skiing: Wigamog borders Haliburton's most popular loops: Boundary, Allsaw, and Slipper. Trails on the 160-km network are double-tracked by snowcat; skating is limited. 20% Easier, 47% More Difficult, 33% Most Difficult—the Wigamog locale has the region's heaviest concentration of beginner/recreational routes, though there are some substantial drops such as Suicide Hill, doing double duty as a toboggan run. All trails are two-way. You may see wildlife—there's a deer yard about 3 kms from Wigamog—and you're certain to see birds along the way. Instruction weekends, weekday by reservation. Modern rentals. 2.5 kms lit nearby at Glebe Park. Daily trail fee. Altitude range 1,055'–1,200', but this includes an unusual amount of rise and fall.
Maps: A huge two-sided production relates trails to landmarks (lakes, towns, roads), with an inset on the Wigamog area.
Activities and Entertainment: On-site: tobogganing, ice fishing, ice skating, snowshoeing, dog sledding, sleigh rides, piano bar, indoor pool, sauna, billiards, whirlpool, massage, wine tasting. Nearby: alpine (Sir Sam's), snowmobiling, Haliburton Forest Wolf Centre; visit local artisans (pottery, birdhouses, twig furniture). You can ski from Wigamog to the local historical museum.
Children's Programs: Holiday programming for six age groups, babysitting, rentals, pulks, snow play.
Dining: Copious breakfasts. Dinner offers a choice of three entrées; the moderate-sized wine list is strong on reds, including an Ontario label. Non-smoking dining room. Locally made Beatty's Maple Syrup kindly informs consumers that it contains vitamins, vital minerals, and only 40 calories per tablespoon.
Special Nordic Distinction: Ideal jumping-off point to the Haliburton system; 15-station bird-feeding nature trail.
Summary: Wigamog owners Kimberley and Christopher Grossman and delightful staff run a family-oriented resort perched at the edge of wilderness.

Camp Mercier
Québec City, Québec

If there's snow anywhere in the province of Québec, you're likely to find it an hour north of Québec City at Camp Mercier—not quite a resort but certainly more than a day area. It's a high land, populated with beaver, moose, and rabbit, where hills and long ridges are cut by streams and interspersed with lakes. (There's a spectacular view from Le Pic warming hut into the valley of the Montmorency River.) The rambling day lodge lies just off the highway, on the southern end of a vast undeveloped area (Réserve Faunique des Laurentides). Though the center has been government-run since it opened around 1970, it functions like a friendly full-service private operation—lodging, cafeteria, rentals, retail, waxing room, bathrooms with showers, trail fee, and all. It's one of the few XC centers in the region where English is seldom spoken.

Address: 801 Chemin St. Louis, Bureau 125, Québec, PQ G1S 1C1
Tel/fax: (418) 848-2422, ski condition report (418) 848-1037; fax: (418) 848-0879
Location: South-central Québec
e-mail: laurentides@sepaq.com
Internet: www.sepaq.com
Airport: Québec International, 45 miles
Train: Québec City, 40 miles
Memberships and Awards: Cross Country Ski Areas Association, Association des Centres de Ski de Fond du Québec.
Medical: CLSC La Source, 30 miles
Accommodations: Lodging is very simple—and usually booked months ahead for weekends and holidays. Among the choices: five newish cabins (the Chalets Devlin) on a lake, a moment's drive north of the center but removed from the highway, housing from two to eight. Though there's power, running water, fireplaces, stoves, and refrigerators, guests need to bring both their own groceries and bedding. It's possible to bushwhack to the accommodations, but you have to cross Route 175 in process. Minimum stay two days.
Guest Capacity: 82

Rates: Very low $
Credit Cards: Visa, MasterCard, American Express
Season: Mid-November–mid-April; average snowfall 260"
XC Skiing: Snowcats maintain some 18 trails, 13 for classic, 5 for skating; in all, Camp Mercier grooms close to 200 kms, 20% Easier, 55% More Difficult, 25% Most Difficult. Really energetic visitors can make the 35-km loop to and from Forêt Montmorency. One-way double track predominates, though there are also two-way quadruple-tracked routes. CANSI-certified instruction available by reservation. Six warming huts, all named after birds found locally. More than 200 km of backcountry skiing in Parc de la Jacques-Cartier, with four shelters and nine tent platforms. Waxable classic skis for rent; small retail shop. Daily trail fee. Altitude range 2,200'–3,000'.
Maps: Simple but extremely clear, using contour lines to note valleys, ridges, and peaks.
Activities and Entertainment: When you come to Camp Mercier, it's usually to ski and little else, though all the attractions of an old and great city are conveniently close. Snowshoes can be rented but used only on special trails. A few minutes' drive north is the Forêt Montmorency Experimental Station, owned by the University of Laval, with more XC trails, nature displays, sledding, and ice skating.
Children's Programs: Equipment, pulks.
Dining: Though there's a truck stop 8 miles south, it's more sensible either to cook your own meals or drive to Québec City, where choices are legion.
Special Nordic Distinction: Due to elevation, Camp Mercier has the most reliable *light* snow and longest season of any XC area in Québec.
Summary: Most skiers come for the sport; many return to track ski, for long backcountry tours, and for peace.

Far Hills Inn
Val-Morin, Québec

Far Hills is one of Canada's grand XC destinations and perhaps the oldest in the province; winter here revolves around nordic skiing. Located in the heart of the Laurentians but a mere hour from Montréal, there's no hint of urban proximity. This a place where English speakers and Francophones feel equally at home. The inn is also famous for culinary excellence. Built in 1940, the property was purchased by David and Louise Pemberton-Smith in 1974. They expanded accommodations, built a clubhouse/ski center in 1976, and expanded their private land base to 1,000 acres so as to allow trail expansion. At 1,400 feet, Far Hills is the highest inn in the Laurentians, with panoramic views of lakes and mountains from crests like Mt. Iceberg and Mt. Mustafa. The nearby town of Val-David is renowned for its artists and craftspeople.

Address: 3399 Chemin de Far Hills, Val-Morin, PQ J0T 2R0
Tel/fax: (800) 567-6636 or (514) 990-4409; fax: (819) 322-1995
e-mail: info@farhillsinn.com
Internet: www.farhillsinn.com
Location: South-central Québec
Airport: Montréal Dorval (U.S. connections), 50 miles
Train: Montréal, 50 miles
Memberships and Awards: Cross Country Ski Areas Association, Association des Centres de Ski de Fond du Québec, *Snow Country* magazine's Top 10 XC Centers in Canada, Prix de la Restauration
Medical: St. Agathe, 6 miles
Accommodations: Some of the inn's original pine-paneled rooms tend to be small, but all rooms are well decorated and charming. Cedar and Spruce lodges provide more options, along with conference space. Ski-in/ski-out. No minimum stay.
Guest Capacity: 140
Conference Capacity: 140
Rates: $ (Modified American Plan)—astonishingly attractive to gastronomes!

Credit Cards: Visa, MasterCard, American Express
Season: Mid-December–mid-April; annual snowfall 96"
XC Skiing: This is one of the largest private trail systems in North America, with an equal mix of 15' wide boulevards and 7' private-feeling paths: a total of 100 mostly wooded km, maintained largely by snowmobile (grooming is excellent). Single-tracked trails predominate; about 20 kms double-tracked with skating. 20% Easier, 55% More Difficult, 25% Most Difficult. There are an additional 50 kms of backcountry routes, including the historic Gillespie and Maple Leaf East, best skied with Far Hills Staff. Trails are linked to the popular Parc Linéaire, a railroad bed transformed into a 40-km aerobic skating corridor. Instruction, guide service, and modern rentals. Daily trail fee. Altitude range 1,150'-1,700'.
Maps: The annotated topographic map is one of the best around.
Activities and Entertainment: On-site: swimming, sauna, hot tub, sleigh rides, snooker, and piano bar (flintlocks mounted above the fireplace). Nearby: alpine skiing, ice skating, dog sledding, snowmobiling.
Children's Programs: Equipment, instruction, pulks, snow play area.
Dining: Quality, service, presentation, *and* wine list: Far Hills truly has *haute cuisine Française*, with a chef, seven cooks, an assistant chef, pastry chef, and four dishwashers. It matters little which entrée you order; each is superb. Breakfast crêpes are delectable. Dining room is non-smoking.
Special Nordic Distinction: The ski school has often been called one of the best in Canada. This is definitely a family operation, with the skiing end run by son Michael.
Summary: Far Hills has long been American recreational skiers' favorite XC destination in Québec. As a personal investment, Mr. Pemberton-Smith sacrificed his beloved court to expanding the clubhouse.

Far Hills Inn, Québec

Michel Guertin

Gatineau Park
Québec

A number of national capitals pride themselves on "greenbelts," but only one has the most popular XC area in the country, with 150,000 visitors a year. Proximity to a population approaching one million, right on the eastern edge of Ottawa, is just one of the reason's for Gatineau's winter prominence. There's also the matter of inviting terrain, natural beauty (meadow, forest, and river valley), and that rarity, park administrators who are land *stewards*, passionately committed to public enjoyment of a recreational delight. Ottawans are very conscious of the need for open space, and Gatineau's 88,000 acres provide a haven from urban pressures. Skiing visitors can stay within minutes of the trails, yet benefit from all the attractions of a major city. Founded in 1938, the park is named after the French discoverer of the Gatineau River. Ski up to the Champlain Lookout on Eardley Escarpment, and you'll find breathtaking views over the Ottawa River.

Address: 33 Scott Road, Chelsea, PQ J0X 1N0
Tel/fax: (800) 465-1867 or (819) 827-2020; fax: (819) 827-3337
e-mail: gpvisito@ncc-cnn.ca
Internet: www.capcan.ca/gatineau/winter/english/home.html
Location: Québec/Ontario border
Airport: Ottawa International, 15 miles
Train: Ottawa, 8 miles
Memberships and Awards: Cross Country Ski Areas Association, Association des Centres de Ski de Fond du Québec
Medical: Hull Hospital, 3 miles
Accommodations: Visit Maison Dawn in Old Chelsea, very close to the park. No smoking in the three pretty rooms, new one-bedroom apartment. Innkeepers Garry Dahl and Dawn Bell-Jack were on tour (baritone and wardrobe mistress) before they became hosts. No minimum stay. 253 Old Chelsea Road, P.O. Box S5, Old Chelsea, PQ J0X 1N0; (819) 827-9162.
Guest Capacity: 10
Conference Capacity: None

Rates: $ (includes breakfast, fresh baked goods)
Credit Cards: Personal checks or cash
Season: December 1–early April; annual snowfall 80"
XC Skiing: Gatineau snowcat-grooms 150 kms of trail—single track, double track, *quadruple* track, double track with skate lane. 50% Easier, 25% More Difficult, 25% Most Difficult. Eight day shelters, six overnight cabins. Carman Trails, a remarkable hostel/café/nordic center on Gatineau's northern periphery, offers instruction and rentals. Daily trail fee. Altitude range 250'–1,300'.
Maps: The new bilingual winter map covers trails, services, and resources and is absolutely gorgeous.
Activities and Entertainment: Within the park (remember that there are multiple access points): alpine (Camp Fortune), snowshoeing, kick sledding, walking, dog sledding. Nearby: everything from museums to casinos to watching the performance of national politicians.
Children's Programs: Snow play at visitor's center by Old Chelsea, pulks.
Dining: A multitude of choices, but if you're clever enough to stay at Maison Dawn, then simply cross the street to lively L'Agaric, whose menu changes a little each day but always has mushrooms. The daube de boeuf Arlésienne is extremely tasty.
Special Nordic Distinction: Gatineau is home to the Keskinada Loppet, Canada's most popular race, but it's really a *winter* destination, not a XC ski site alone. The greater part of the park is undeveloped, including 50 kms of ungroomed trail. Despite (because of?) the wild setting, Parliament conducts retreats at Meech Lake.
Summary: This is an instance of market-responsive management by a public land agency to create a "social experience." It works magnificently.

See color photos, page 106

Hôtel l'Estérel
Estérel, Québec

Hôtel l'Estérel is set on the shore of a sizable lake deep in the Laurentians but comfortably close to Montréal. It's a virtual secret to Americans, even those familiar with Far Hills or Mont-Sainte-Anne; in fact, there are more European and *Japanese* visitors than Yanks. Trails run south across Lac Dupuis into heavy forest, or over a golf course to the north. If you're hyperactive or driven to sample all that winter offers, this is the resort of your dreams. No XC destination in North America exceeds the diversity of programs and services; for example, not only is there an ice skating rink but also a 6-kilometer ice trail on the lake, plus ice sculpture and igloo building. Ski legend Bill Deskin is master of nordic ceremonies. He has been a fixture (if that's the appropriate word for someone so lively) among the hotel family since the mid-'70s. Born in Brooklyn, his French accent is remarkable; and he's an inveterate, droll storyteller who rivals Joe Pete Wilson of The Bark Eater.

Address: P.O. Box 38, Estérel, PQ J0T 1E0
Tel/fax: (888) 375-3735 or (450) 228-2571; fax: (450) 228-4977
e-mail: info@esterel.com
Internet: www.esterel.com
Location: South-central Québec
Airport: Montréal/Dorval, 50 miles (transportation available)
Train: Montréal, 55 miles (transportation available)
Memberships and Awards: Cross Country Ski Areas Association, *Snow Country* magazine's Top 10 XC Areas in Canada
Medical: Ste. Adéle Clinic, 10 miles
Accommodations: 135 recently renovated rooms and suites. Ski-in/ski-out. No minimum stay.
Guest Capacity: 300
Conference Capacity: 300
Rates: $$ (upon request, multi-day package includes breakfast and dinner, use of indoor sports facilities and XC trails, and other inducements)

Credit Cards: Visa, MasterCard, American Express, Diners Club
Season: December 15–March 15; annual snowfall 130"
XC Skiing: The hotel grooms as much as 85 kms by small snowcat—70 kms of double track alone, 15 kms double track and skate lane. 50% Easier, 35% More Difficult, 15% Most Difficult. Road crossing. Daily instruction in everything; some fun guided tours such as a round-trip to the town of Entre Lac. Daily trail fee. Altitude range 500'–700'. A trail now connects to skiing on Le Petit Train du Nord, a former railroad line that is immensely popular in all seasons and over 120 miles long.
Maps: It's not elaborate and lacks contour lines, but then, trails don't have dramatic vertical change.
Activities and Entertainment: On-site: snowshoeing, ice skating, ice fishing, fur trapping (not a hit with U.S. visitors), kite flying, dog sledding, sleigh rides, hot dog parties, snow play, aerial tours of the Laurentians, snowmobiling. Indoors: swimming pool, saunas, whirlpool, gymnasium, jogging track, games room. On request: wine tasting, cooking classes, fashion show. Nearby: seven alpine areas.
Children's Programs: Babysitting on request, instruction, equipment, pulks, toboggan slide.
Dining: Five minutes from l'Estérel, Le Bistro Champlain displays both fine art and wine art. The walls carry paintings by Jean-Paul Riopelle, the cellar holds more than 2,000 different wines, and the table has been rated among the 100 finest in Canada.
Special Nordic Distinction: Skiing across the lake can be a windy experience. Dog sledding and snowmobiling are important to the hotel's solvency and are just as popular as XC.
Summary: Hotel l'Estérel's character might be described as "amiable elegance." Bill Deskin has assured that it's very comfortable for beginners.

La Montagne Coupée Country Inn and Resort
Saint-Jean-de-Matha, Québec

La Montagne Coupée is next door to tiny Saint-Jean-de-Matha, an hour north of Montréal. It's delightful to ski or relax at the elegant seven-year-old, 50-room inn, which also houses an indoor pool, saunas, and fitness station. True to Québecois tradition, cuisine is of a high order. The resort's name ("The Cut Mountain") comes from the abrupt 350-foot cliff a few steps out the back door, from whose top you can see Montréal's highest buildings, 45 kilometers away along the horizon. Owner Réjean Gadoury and wife Simone ("the real boss") run the inn portion of the resort; daughter Martine and her husband, Denis Vincent, own and operate the ski center itself. The separate, older full-service XC building is a little distance away from the inn (*definitely* downhill) and contains a cafe and lounge. Over 60 kilometers are groomed for skating—a reflection of the Gadourys' commitment to race training. Trails are predominantly rated "difficult" (roughly equivalent to intermediate terrain), running through beautiful countryside—a favorite route parallels the Assomption River. As at Far Hills, snow is usually reliable, but M. Gadoury is considering supplemental snowmaking.

Address: 1000 Chemin de la Montagne Coupée, Saint-Jean-de-Matha, PQ J0K 2S0
Tel/fax: (800) 363-8614 or (450) 886-3891; fax: (450) 886-5401
e-mail: info@montagnecoupee.com
Internet: www.montagnecoupee.com
Location: South-central Québec
Airport: Montréal/Dorval, 60 miles
Train: Montréal, 45 miles
Memberships and Awards: Cross Country Ski Areas Association, Association des Centres de Ski de Fond du Québec, *Snow Country* magazine's Top 10 XC Areas in Canada
Medical: Clinique Médical de Saint-Jean-de-Matha, 3 miles
Accommodations: Lodging is first class. In particular, the 11 suites are roomy, with fireplaces

and double whirlpool baths. Ski-in/ski-out. No minimum stay.
Guest Capacity: 180
Conference Capacity: 150
Rates: $$ (includes breakfast and dinner, use of indoor facilities, ski trails)
Credit Cards: Visa, MasterCard
Season: Mid-December–March 31; annual snowfall 40"
XC Skiing: Denis uses a major snowcat to maintain 65.5 kms of double track plus skate lane (the entire system is 85 kms), with a mix of one- and two-way. 22% Easier, 43% More Difficult, 35% Most Difficult. One warming shelter. Three groomed instruction areas. Daily instruction in track and skating. First-class rental and retail shop; all waxable skis. (There's a separate waxing building. Area operators in this part of Canada detest non-wax skis; on the other hand, they'll often volunteer to do the waxing for you.) Daily trail fee. Altitude range 375'–1,050'.
Maps: Simple but clear on ratings, lengths, and skating/classical.
Activities and Entertainment: On-site: snowshoeing, indoor swimming pool, sauna, massage by appointment. Nearby: alpine (Val St.-Côme), sleigh rides, ice skating, dog sledding, tubing, snowmobiling.
Children's programs: Instruction, equipment, snow play.
Dining: Martine has a small restaurant specializing in crêpes and fondues just across from the center. The inn's dining room presents regional cuisine such as rabbit anthime in rhubarb sauce; desserts are rich surprises. Full license.
Special Nordic Distinction: By Québec standards, a very high percentage of trails have skating. M. Gadoury expects to have the first lighted trail in the province, taking off near the inn. There's a very strong youth racing program.
Summary: La Montagne Coupée and Far Hills are Québec's only luxury destinations devoted to nordic skiing.

Le Château Montebello
Montebello, Québec

Château Montebello hosted world leaders in 1981 for the G7 economic summit, but there's more substance to this grand lodge than the gourmet jellybeans in the mini-bars that President Reagan so enjoyed. This is not simply the largest log building in the world, located on the site of a seventeenth-century *seigneurie*; equally impressive, it was erected in 1930 in only 90 days. Built of red cedar, it's an imposing and complex structure (six fireplaces in a central chimney) on the Ottawa River. Originally a private club, then purchased in 1970 by Canadian Pacific Hotels, the Château is convenient for skiers flying into either Ottawa or Montréal (figure an hour from the former, 15 minutes more from the latter). Skiing is surprisingly varied. Two trails on the grounds are gentle indeed. But cross the highway and head up granitic Westcott Mountain, and terrain changes immediately, like Cordillera redefining "golf course skiing."

Address: 392 Notre Dame Street, Montebello, PQ J0V 1L0
Tel/fax: (819) 423-6341; fax (819) 423-5283
e-mail: aratel@lam.mobs.compuserve.com
Internet: www.chateaumontebello.com
Location: Southwestern Québec
Airport: Ottawa International, 55 miles
Train: Ottawa, 55 miles
Memberships and Awards: Association des Centres de Ski de Fond du Québec, Mobil Four-Star, Pinnacle Award, five stars Hébergement Québec
Medical: Montebello Clinic, 5 miles
Accommodations: The Château has 210 rooms, including six executive suites with Jacuzzi. Other rooms are nicely appointed but have changed little since 1930, other than updated bathrooms. Ski-in/ski-out. Half of all rooms are non-smoking. No minimum stay.
Guest Capacity: 420
Conference Capacity: 450
Rates: $$–$$$ (includes breakfast, use of all trails, use of indoor pool, tennis and squash courts)

Credit Cards: Visa, MasterCard, American Express, Diners Club, Discover, JBC
Season: December 20–March 24; annual snowfall 87"
XC Skiing: The Château uses a small snowcat to maintain 28 kms, but there are connectors to another 60 kms. There's some skating, but double tracks predominate. For the whole network: 24% Easier, 39% More Difficult, 37% Most Difficult. 1 km lighted nearby. Several road crossings; the one near the Château is intimidating. Instruction in classic and skating by reservation; guided trips to nearby 65,000-acre Kenauk Preserve. Equipment is not particularly up to date. Daily trail fee. Altitude range 147'–689'.
Maps: The English version is on one side, French on the other. Difficulty ratings give a hint about ups and downs.
Activities and Entertainment: Cross-country is one element among many. On-site: snowshoeing, ice skating, ice fishing, curling, sleigh rides, dog sledding, indoor pool, exercise room, indoor tennis, squash, health club (mud, massage, and all), tobogganing, snowmobiling. Nearby: alpine skiing (Mt. Tremblant), historic trapping tours, Parc Oméga (1,500-acre wild animal park—moufflon, bison, ibex), Hull Casino, and antique store La Vieille Commode.
Children's Programs: Babysitting by arrangement, instruction, gear, snow play, crafts.
Dining: Aux Chantignoles, the main dining room, changes its menu constantly; buffets are splendid (crème brulée with blueberries is unforgettable). Bistro-Bar La Seigneurie offers lighter fare. Formidable wine list.
Special Nordic Distinction: Wintering at the Château seems hardly known outside of Québec, though there's more trail than at *confrère* Jasper Park Lodge and better grooming than at Château Lake Louise.
Summary: Like other regal Canadian Pacific hotels in winter, Château Montebello is surprisingly inexpensive. You can walk the estate and taste history.

Mont-Sainte-Anne
Beaupré, Québec

Although there's lively debate as to who is number 2 among Canadian XC areas, Mont-Sainte-Anne is usually accorded the premier position by acclamation. This reflects its skiing and grooming quality rather than a remarkable range of programs (Hotel l'Estérel) or wonderful support facilities (La Montagne Coupée). Which isn't to say that skiers exist here by trails alone—there's a full-service day lodge (the Chalet du Rang Saint-Julien) and a trailside B&B, plus a huge alpine parent area. Simply, this is wonderful skiing, with a lot of short loops near the base and longer loops further out. The staging area is separate enough from the main resort to have its own character. For cultural relief, consider Québec City, 30 minutes away.

Address: P.O. Box 400, Beaupré, PQ G0A 1E0
Tel/fax: (800) 463-1568 or (418) 827-4561; fax: (418) 827-3121
e-mail: info@mont-sainte-anne.com
Internet: www.mont-sainte-anne.com
Location: South-central Québec
Airport: Québec International, 50 miles
Train: Québec City, 30 miles
Memberships and Awards: Cross Country Ski Areas Association, Association des Centres de Ski de Fond du Québec, *Snow Country* magazine's Top 10 XC Areas in North America, National Team Development and Training Center
Medical: Ste.-Anne-de-Beaupré Hospital, 3 miles
Accommodations: L'Auberge du Fondeur is a famous but not fancy B&B. Shared rooms, sauna, wine and coffee bar, evening kitchen privileges. Ski-in/ski-out. Non-smoking environment. No minimum stay. Inquiries can be made through the main resort phone numbers.
Guest Capacity: 26 at L'Auberge du Fondeur
Conference Capacity: 26
Rates: $ (includes breakfast, use of trails)
Credit Cards: Visa, MasterCard, American Express

Season: Early December–end March; annual snowfall 180"
XC Skiing: The resort grooms an amazing 223 kms (by snowcat, natch), almost all of which has track, and 125 kms of which has skating; mostly one-way. 29% Easier, 40% More Difficult (i.e., not all that altitude is gained in one swoop), 31% Most Difficult. Seven warming shelters, including two with lodging. High quality rentals. Daily CANSI-certified instruction in skating and classic; guide service. Ski patrol on duty at all times. Daily trail fee. Altitude range 575'–2,475'.
Maps: An excellent aerial/graphic approach shows both the lay of the land and the magnitude of this huge network.
Activities and Entertainment: At resort (either on-site or at the alpine base area, several minutes away—weekend shuttle): snowshoeing, alpine, ice skating, dog sledding, paragliding. Further: snowmobiling (trails come to the resort); the historic and beautiful city of Québec.
Children's Programs: Day care (at alpine area), special trails, instruction, equipment, pulks. The latter have been designed by Pierre Harvey, formerly Canada's top male racer, who lives beside the trail system.
Dining: La Camarine is about ten minutes by car from the *auberge*, but it's a different world—suavely delicious yet not outrageously expensive. *Gourmet* called it a "world-class establishment." It's a delightful postulate worth testing.
Special Nordic Distinction: A true nordic skiing destination. There are also some memorable multi-day backcountry tours, though the famous connector to Camp Mercier is no longer available.
Summary: Count the areas that began with a racing ethos—Giants Ridge, Canmore, Craftsbury. All of them have diversified in response to changing skier needs, and Mont-Sainte-Anne has been among the leaders.

Mont-Tremblant Region
Mont-Tremblant, Québec

Mont-Tremblant is the highest peak in the Laurentians, which helps dictate the character of XC skiing locally—there are blacks and several double blacks; but most of the really precipitous trails are limited to the mountain. Greens and blues run through forested hills and valleys and over lakes. Though the alpine slopes receive most press attention and most use, there's a very extensive community-supported XC network with European touches. For instance, it's thoroughly decentralized; walking trails are interspersed with ski trails (some shared routes); and the pedestrian Village, with period architecture and vivid colors, is designed to resemble eighteenth century France. (It comes off very well, perhaps because the whole thing is human-sized rather than overwhelming.)

Address: Case Postale 203, Mont-Tremblant, PQ J0T 1Z0
Tel/fax: (819) 425-5588 or (819) 425-2434; fax: (819) 425-2434
e-mail: info_tremblant@intrawest.com
Internet: www.tremblant.ca
Location: Southwestern Québec
Airport: Montréal/Dorval, 75 miles (shuttle)
Train: Montréal, 75 miles
Memberships and Awards: Association de Centres de Ski de Fond du Québec
Medical: Clinique Saint-Jovite, 6 miles
Accommodations: While there are all kinds of lodging at this burgeoning resort, Le Johannsen offers a little nostalgia—named for Jackrabbit Johannsen, the father of XC skiing in Eastern North America. Studio, one- or two-bedroom arrangements, with fireplace, fully equipped kitchen. Great access to the Village but not to trails. Some non-smoking rooms. Two night minimum holidays. Station Mont-Tremblant, 3005, chemin Principal, Mont-Tremblant, Québec J0T 1Z0; (800) 461-8711.
Guest capacity: 200-plus at Le Johannsen
Conference Capacity: Available at neighbor Château Mont-Tremblant
Rates: $–$$$$

Credit cards: Visa, MasterCard, American Express, Diners En Route
Season: Early December–end March; annual snowfall 150"
XC Skiing: You'll find 100 kms on 26 trails; "boulevards" are groomed by snowcat, narrower paths by snowmobile; mostly two-way double track, 12 kms of skating. 30% Easier, 25% More Difficult, 25% Most Difficult, 20% Extreme. If it just snowed, check which trails are being groomed first. Multiple road crossings. Two warming shelters. Daily instruction in all disciplines; guide service. Daily trail fee. Altitude range 800'–1,600'.
Maps: It's an entrancing product, using symbols rather than trail names. Best viewpoints are marked. There are even distance explanations for each segment of trail.
Activities and Entertainment: The Québecois are a lively people. In addition to alpine skiing at Mont-Tremblant and Gray Rocks, there's strolling the Village (best guess: 500,000 cobblestones, but who's counting?), sleigh rides, dog sledding, horseback riding, deer observation, ice skating-climbing-carving-fishing, star gazing program, snow volleyball, snowmobiling. Nearby: Jackrabbit Museum, hut-to-hut trips on groomed trails in Parc du Mont-Tremblant.
Children's programs: Day care, instruction, snow play (luge), magic show, Ciné-Youth.
Dining: Try the pastries at La Chouquetterie; for dinner, visit Aux Trouffes for fresh foie gras, fowl, venison, and (*bien sûr*) truffles. Eat at Mexicali Rose to commit culinary heresy.
Special Nordic Distinction: A new golf clubhouse is now the trail nexus. For equipment, see Yves et Yves in Mont-Tremblant. For easiest trails, head first to the Domaine St. Bernard; you can quickly reach a skating loop, see many birds and sometimes a monk skiing.
Summary: The Laurentians are a particularly beautiful part of this huge province. The $467 million recently invested in Mont-Tremblant's infrastructure has helped create new trails and upgraded grooming.

Ripplecove Inn
Ayer's Cliff, Québec

Ripplecove Inn's self-description—"elegant, intimate, exclusive"—isn't a Madison Avenue catch phrase. Founded in 1945, the *auberge* was completely rebuilt and expanded after a devastating fire in 1979. It's run by Jeffrey and Debra Stafford—his father built the resort, and brother Stephen owns and operates neighboring Hovey Inn. The 12-acre estate has stately trees, Victorian decor, antiques, and paintings hung on paneled walls. Ripplecove staff are bilingual, in part because of the inn's location in the English portion of the Eastern Townships (many families descend from British Loyalists). Some of the best views are of Mt. Orford, to the northwest, and across Lake Massawippi (Abenaki for "lake of deep water"). Set on Massawippi's southeastern border, once ice sets up and snow falls, guests can head out across to the western shore. Unique to the region is the Skiwippi program, a multi-day inn-to-inn adventure in which Ripplecove is the southern extremity. (Cost is astoundingly reasonable.) It's 18 forested kilometers west and north to Hovey Inn, with a stop for lunch at the summit, then 2 kilometers to the Hatley Inn. Seventy neighbors cooperate to provide land for the trail, open only in winter.

Address: 700 Ripplecove Road, Ayer's Cliff, PQ J0B 1C0
Tel/fax: (800) 668-4296 or (819) 838-4296; fax: (819) 838-5541
e-mail: ripcove@abacom.com
Internet: www.ripplecove.com
Location: Central far-south Québec
Airport: Dorval, 80 miles
Train: Magog, 10 miles
Memberships and Awards: AAA Four-Diamond
Medical: Magog, 10 miles
Accommodations: The inn has 25 rooms, suites, and chalets; the most luxurious possess fireplace, whirlpool bath, and private balcony. Some non-smoking rooms. Ski-in/ski-out. No minimum stay.
Guest Capacity: 50

Conference Capacity: 50
Rates: $$–$$$ (includes breakfast, dinner, ice skating, use of trails)
Credit Cards: Visa, MasterCard, American Express
Season: December–late-March, annual snowfall 150"
XC Skiing: Ripplecove Inn, Hovey Manor, and Hatley Inn maintain 50 kms of track, grooming with snowmobiles (some trails are too narrow for big machines). 25% Easier, 50% More Difficult, 25% Most Difficult. Two warming shelters. Instruction available every day in skating, classic, and telemarking; guide service. Daily trail fee. Altitude range 900'–1,800'.
Maps: Good contour presentation but not much character.
Activities and Entertainment: On-site: snowshoeing, ice skating, sleigh rides, ice fishing, snow play. Nearby: alpine (Mt. Orford, Mont-Sutton), horseback riding at Turtle Hill Farm (both Western and English), antique shops, the wonderful Galerie Jeannine Blais in North Hatley (specializes in Naive Art), the Gorge of Coaticook (sightseeing, power-tubing!), snowmobiling. There's a double-tracked 7-km converted railroad bed a few minutes away.
Children's Programs: Day care, snow play.
Dining: Award-winning cuisine, Québec elegant (rack of lamb, an enchanting crème brulée)! The inn also has a deep wine cellar.
Special Nordic Distinction: Sadly, it seems that inn-to-inn skiing in New England has died in the past few years, so it's delightful to see an experience of this quality evolve in Québec. The mostly double-tracked connector trail isn't always easy (there are downhills, narrow spots, and turns, and they can coincide), and you gain 1,000' in elevation. But guides are first rate, and the hostelries are of the same caliber. New cooperative inn program includes dog sledding, snowshoeing, snowmobiling to the famous Bombardier Museum.
Summary: Ripplecove is just over the Vermont border, accessible via Interstate 91; Boston is less than four hours away. Irresistible!

APPENDIX

Resources

Sometimes it seems impossibly difficult to find out where to cross-country ski. There's no comprehensive list for North America; what information is available tends to be factual rather than descriptive or evaluative. I've found a number of state, provincial, and regional books, but they concentrate on trails rather than "context." Contacting state tourism agencies for information can elicit anything from real help to a giggled "Cross whaaaa?" Canadian provinces do a bit better.

But be of good cheer: One can assemble knowledge from several storehouses (in addition, of course, to this modest tome). There are three good print sources on a continental scale that can be used together. The first is *Cross Country Skier* magazine (612/361-6760); the second is *Ski Trax* magazine (416/977-2100). I subscribe to both and find them extremely informative on destinations, events, and equipment.

The third is *The Best of Cross Country Skiing*, the directory of Cross Country Ski Areas Association (603/239-4341, www.xcski.org), an industry trade group. The pamphlet provides a succinct introduction to over 200 areas in Canada and the United States, broken down by region, then by state/province. While the areas listed are limited to CCSAA members, they are definitely the cream of the XC crop.

An excellent, wide-ranging Web site is www.xcskiworld.com. Check them out for information on events, places, personalities, controversies, and more.

Ski Museums

Colorado Ski Museum
P.O. Box 1976
Vail, CO 81658
(970) 476-1876

Ketchum-Sun Valley Heritage and Ski Museum
P.O. Box 2746
Ketchum, ID 83340
(208) 726-8118

New England Ski Museum
P.O. Box 267
Franconia, NH 03580-0267
(603) 823-7177

U.S. National Ski Hall of Fame and Museum
P.O. Box 191
Ishpeming, MI 49849
(906) 485-6323

Western SkiSport Museum
P.O. Box 729,
Soda Springs, CA 95728
(916) 426-3313

Specialty Cross-Country Equipment Catalogs

Akers Ski
P.O. Box 280
Andover, ME 04216
(207) 392-4582
fax (207) 392-1225

Cross Country Ski Shop
P.O. Box 749
Grayling, MI 49738
(800) 889-7456

Eagle River Nordic
P.O. Box 936
Eagle River, WI 54521
(800) 423-9730
(715) 479-7285

Fitness Fanatics
12425 E. Trent
Spokane, WA 99216
(800) 786-9796
(509) 922-6080

Gunner's Cycle & X-Country Ski
Box 515, 108 Mile Ranch
BC V0K 2Z0
(250) 791-6212

New Moon Ski Shop
P.O. Box 591, Hwy. 63 North
Hayward, WI 54843
(800) 754-8685
(715) 634-8685

Nordic Equipment
P.O. Box 980250
Park City, UT 84098
(800) 321-1671

Reliable Racing Supply
643 Upper Glen St.
Queensbury, NY 12804
(800) 517-7555

Sports Rack
315 W. Washington St.
Marquette, MI 49855
(800) 775-8338

Wild Rose
702 3rd Ave.
Salt Lake City, UT 84103
(800) 750-7377
(801) 533-8671

Pulks and Kicksleds

If you're looking for the best way to introduce a youngster to winter, here are sources for specially designed pulks (child sleds) and kick sleds (with runners, designed for a packed surface).

Baby Glider
Le Groupe CH2, Inc.
480, rg. St.-Antoine
St.-Ferréol-le-Neiges, PQ,
Canada G0A 3R0
(418) 826-0900,
fax (418) 826-0901
harveyco@microtec.ca

CrosSled
CrosSled North America
Ltd.
4981 Highway 7, Suite 241
Markham, ON, Canada
L3R 1N1
(877) 276-7753,
fax (905) 940-6739
www.crossled.com

Fridtjof Nansen Kicksled
Nordic Pursuits
P.O. Box 3764
Bozeman, MT 59772
(406) 586-9705,
fax (406) 586-9706
wyntrking@aol.com

Mountainsmith
18301 W. Colfax Avenue
Heritage Square, Bldg. P
Golden, CO 80401
(800) 426-4075,
(303) 279-5930,
fax (303) 278-7739
service@mountainsmith.com
www.mountainsmith.com

Nordic Lynx
True North Enterprises
203 Vancouver Avenue
Medford, OR 97504
(800) 803-6196
www.nordiclynx.com

Ridge Runner
P.O. Box 270373
Fort Collins, CO 80527
(970) 282-8785
ridgerunner@bwn.net
www.bewellnet.com/
ridgerunner

Tow-Boggan
Ziffco Outer Limits
1301 W. Walnut St.
Compton, CA 90220
(800) 532-2242, (310)
631-3452,
fax (310) 631-4175
ziffco@ix.netcom.com
www.ziffco.com/olimits.htm

State and Province Departments of Tourism

Some states and provinces produce extensive winter guides annually, including directories of places to cross-country ski. They do not necessarily distinguish between groomed and ungroomed trails.

Alaska
(907) 465-2010
fax (907) 465-2287

California
(916) 322-2881
(800) 862-2543
fax (916) 322-3402

Colorado
(303) 832-6171
(800) COLORADO
fax (303) 832-6174

Idaho
(208) 334-2470
(800) 635-7820
fax (208) 334-2631

Maine
(207) 623-0363
(800) 533-9595
fax (207) 623-0388

Massachusetts
(617) 727-3201
fax (617) 727-6525

Michigan
(517) 373-0670
(888) 784-7328
fax (517) 373-0059

Minnesota
(612) 296-2755
(800) 657-3700
fax (612) 296-7095

Montana
(406) 444-2654
(800) VISIT-MT
fax (406) 444-1800

New Hampshire
(603) 271-2666
fax (603) 271-6784

New Mexico
(505) 827-7400
(800) 733-6396
fax (505) 827-7402

New York
(518) 474-4116
(800) CALL-NYS
fax (518) 486-6416

Oregon
(503) 986-0000
(800) 547-7842
fax (503) 986-0001

Utah
(801) 538-1030
fax (801) 538-1399

Vermont
(802) 828-3237
fax (802) 828-3233

Washington
(360) 753-5600
(800) 544-1800
fax (360) 753-4470

Wisconsin
(608) 266-7621
(800) 432-TRIP
fax (608) 266-3403

Wyoming
(307) 777-7777
(800) 225-5996
fax (307) 777-6904

Alberta
(403) 427-1905
fax (403) 427-9127

British Columbia
(604) 387-1642
fax (604) 356-8246

Ontario
(416) 314-0944

Québec
(514) 873-2015
fax (514) 864-3838

Ski Events

A decade ago, almost every cross-country area held at least one race a month. Today, competition has largely given way to "fun events"—some of them strange and wonderful indeed. Many are dining-oriented, such as Garland's Zhivago Nights, Royal Gorge's Fête du Printemps, and Stokely Creek's Wabos Loppet.

Listing individual events here would be an intriguing exercise in futility, as literally hundreds are added or dropped each year. A new Web source for every type of ski and snowshoe event is www.nordicalliance.org, with a searchable database.

The North American Ski Fest is an ongoing happening, held at over 100 Canadian and American sites every January. Designed to encourage first-timers to try the sport, participants receive free instruction and opportunity to play with the latest in demo equipment. Depending on the area visited, you can anticipate virtually anything entertaining and legal—clowns, reindeer, snowshoe games, guided tours, sleigh rides, snow and ice sculpture contests, and roast pig barbecues. For an updated list of participating areas, contact Cross Country Ski Areas Association, 259 Bolton Road, Winchester, NH 03470; (603) 239-4341, ccsaa@xcski.org, www.xcski.org.

Women's Programs

Christal McDougall offers America's leading camps and clinics, designed for women by women. The *Ski For Yourself!* series is usually held in five locations from coast to coast. Emphasis is on skiing, bonding, fun, and fulfillment. Contact Women's Sports Works, 6204 Simmons Drive, Boulder, CO 80303; (303) 499-0436; e-mail wsw@indra.com.

SPECIAL FEATURES DIRECTORY

Airport Within 50 Miles

Alaska
Anchorage Region

California
North Lake Tahoe Region
Northstar-at-Tahoe
Royal Gorge Cross Country Ski Resort
Tahoe Donner

Colorado
Aspen/Snowmass Region
Beaver Creek Cross Country Ski Center
Cordillera
High Meadows Ranch
The Home Ranch
San Juan Guest Ranch
Vista Verde Ranch

Idaho
Sun Valley Nordic
Sun Valley Region
Teton Ridge Ranch

Maine
Smiling Hill Farm

Massachusetts
Cranwell Resort & Golf Club

Michigan
Crystal Mountain Resort
Shanty Creek

Minnesota
Bemidji Region
Maplelag

Montana
Lone Mountain Ranch

New Hampshire
Woodbound Inn

New York
Salmon Hills

Oregon
Mt. Bachelor Cross Country Center

Utah
Sundance

Vermont
Green Mountain Ski Touring Center
Green Trails Cross Country Ski Center
Ole's (Inn at the Round Barn)
Trapp Family Lodge
Woodstock Inn & Resort

Washington
Sleeping Lady

Wisconsin
Eagle River Nordic
Justin Trails Nordic Ski Center
Mecan River Outfitters & Lodge
Minocqua Winter Park Nordic Center
The Springs Golf Club Resort
Palmquist's "The Farm"

Wyoming
Jackson Hole Region

British Colombia
Silver Star Mountain Resort

Ontario
Hiawatha Highlands
Stokely Creek Lodge

Québec
Camp Mercier
Far Hills Inn
Gatineau Park
Hôtel l'Estérel
Mont-Sainte-Anne

Associated with Alpine Skiing

California
Kirkwood Ski & Summer Resort
North Lake Tahoe Region
Northstar-at-Tahoe
Tahoe Donner
Yosemite National Park

Colorado
Aspen/Snowmass Region
Beaver Creek Cross Country Ski Center

Idaho
McCall Region
Sun Valley Nordic

Maine
Sugarloaf Ski Touring Center

Michigan
Boyne Nordican
Crystal Mountain Resort
Gaylord Region
Shanty Creek

Minnesota
Bemidji Region
Giants Ridge

New Hampshire
The Balsams Wilderness
Bretton Woods Resort
Loon Mountain
Waterville Valley

Oregon
Mt. Bachelor Cross Country Center

Utah
Sundance

Vermont
Woodstock Inn & Resort

Wyoming
Jackson Hole Region

British Columbia
The Hills Health Ranch
Manning Park Resort
Silver Star Mountain Resort

Ontario
Hiawatha Highlands
Horseshoe Resort

Québec
Gatineau Park
Mont-Sainte-Anne
Mont-Tremblant Region

Babysitting/Day Care

California
Kirkwood Ski & Summer Resort
Montecito-Sequoia Nordic Resort and
   Winter Sports Center

Northstar-at-Tahoe
Royal Gorge Cross Country Ski Resort
Yosemite National Park

Colorado
Aspen/Snowmass Region
Beaver Creek Cross Country Ski Center
C Lazy U Ranch
Cordillera
The Home Ranch
Snow Mountain Ranch
Vista Verde Ranch

Idaho
Sun Valley Nordic
Sun Valley Region

Maine
Sugarloaf Ski Touring Center

Michigan
Boyne Nordican
Crystal Mountain Resort
Gaylord Region
Shanty Creek

Minnesota
Bemidji Region
Giants Ridge
Maplelag

Montana
Rendezvous Ski Trails

New Hampshire
Bretton Woods
The Balsams Wilderness
Jackson Ski Touring Foundation
Loon Mountain

New York
Mohonk Mountain House
Mountain House

Oregon
Mt. Bachelor Cross Country Center

Utah
Sundance

Vermont
The Equinox

Washington
Methow Valley Sport Trails Association
Sun Mountain Lodge

Wisconsin
Justin Trails Nordic Ski Center

Wyoming
Jackson Hole Region

Alberta
Château Lake Louise
Jasper Park Lodge

British Columbia
Manning Park Resort
Silver Star Mountain Resort

Ontario
Hardwood Hills Cross Country Ski
    Centre
Horseshoe Resort
Wigamog Inn Resort

Québec
Mont-Sainte-Anne
Mont-Tremblant Region
Ripplecove Inn

Bed and Breakfasts On-Site

Colorado
San Juan Guest Ranch

Maine
The Birches Resort

Michigan
LakeView Hills Country Inn Resort

Minnesota
Pincushion Mountain Bed & Breakfast

Vermont
Green Trails Cross Country Ski Center
Hazen's Notch Cross Country Ski Center
Ole's (Inn at the Round Barn)
Viking Ski Touring Centre

Wisconsin
Justin Trails Nordic Ski Center
Trail Farm

Ontario
Hardwood Hills Cross Country Ski
    Centre

Québec
Mont-Sainte-Anne

Dog Sledding

Alaska
Anchorage Region

Colorado
Aspen/Snowmass Region
C Lazy U Ranch
Cordillera
Latigo Ranch

Idaho
Sun Valley Region
Teton Ridge Ranch

Minnesota
Giants Ridge

Montana
Rendezvous Ski Trails

New York
Salmon Hills

Oregon
Mt. Bachelor Cross Country Center

Utah
Sundance

Wyoming
Jackson Hole Region

Alberta
Château Lake Louise
Terratima Lodge

British Columbia
Emerald Lake Lodge (Christmas)
The Hills Health Ranch

Ontario
Wigamog Inn Resort

Québec
Le Château Montebello
Far Hills
Gatineau Park
Hôtel l'Estérel
La Montagne Coupée Country Inn and
    Resort
Mont-Sainte-Anne
Mont-Tremblant Region

Dog Trails

Alaska
Anchorage Region

California
Bear Valley Cross Country
Kirkwood Ski & Summer Resort
Royal Gorge Cross Country Ski Resort

Colorado
Aspen/Snowmass Region
Devil's Thumb Ranch
Snow Mountain Ranch

Idaho
McCall Region
Sun Valley Nordic
Sun Valley Region

Maine
The Birches Resort
Smiling Hill Farm
Sunday River Cross Country Ski Center

New York
Salmon Hills

Oregon
Mt. Bachelor Cross Country Center

Utah
Ruby's Inn Nordic Center

Wisconsin
Justin Trails Nordic Ski Center
Minocqua Winter Park Nordic Center
Trail Farm

British Columbia
Big Bar Guest Ranch

Ontario
Hardwood Hills Cross Country Ski
    Centre

50+ Kilometers Groomed

Alaska
Anchorage Region

California
Bear Valley Cross Country
Kirkwood Ski & Summer Resort
North Lake Tahoe Region
Northstar-at-Tahoe
Royal Gorge Cross Country Ski Resort
Tahoe Donner

Colorado
Aspen/Snowmass Region
Devil's Thumb Ranch
Latigo Ranch
Snow Mountain Ranch

Idaho
Sun Valley Region

Maine
Sugarloaf Ski Touring Center

Michigan
Gaylord Region

Minnesota
Bearskin Lodge
Bemidji Region
Cascade Lodge
Golden Eagle Lodge & Nordic Ski Center

Montana
Lone Mountain Ranch

New Hampshire
The Balsams Wilderness
Bretton Woods Resort
Jackson Ski Touring Foundation
Norsk Cross Country Ski Center
Waterville Valley

New York
Garnet Hill Lodge
Lake Placid Region

Oregon
Mt. Bachelor Cross Country Center

Vermont
Blueberry Hill Inn
Burke Cross Country Ski Area
Craftsbury Outdoor Center
Highland Lodge
Mountain Top Inn and Resort
Ole's (Inn at the Round Barn)
Trapp Family Lodge
Woodstock Inn

Washington
Methow Valley Sport Trails Association
Sun Mountain Lodge

Wisconsin
Eagle River Nordic
Minocqua Winter Park Nordic Center
Paust's Wood Lake Resort

Wyoming
Jackson Hole Region

Alberta
Canmore Nordic Centre
Château Lake Louise

British Columbia
The Hills Health Ranch
Silver Star Mountain Resort (in
  conjunction with Sovereign Lakes)

Ontario
Stokely Creek Lodge
Wigamog Inn Resort (Haliburton
  Highlands)

Québec
Camp Mercier
Le Château Montebello
Far Hills Inn
Gatineau Park
Hôtel l'Estérel
La Montagne Coupée Country Inn and
  Resort
Mont-Sainte-Anne
Mont-Tremblant Region
Ripplecove Inn

Fly-Fishing

California
North Lake Tahoe Region

Colorado
Vista Verde Ranch

Idaho
Sun Valley Region

Montana
Lone Mountain Ranch

Utah
Sundance

Horseback Riding

Alaska
Anchorage Region

California
Northstar-at-Tahoe

Colorado
C Lazy U Ranch
Vista Verde Ranch

Massachusetts
Cranwell Resort and Golf Club (nearby)

Montana
B Bar Guest Ranch

New York
The Bark Eater
Lake Placid Region

Vermont
Burke Cross Country Ski Area (nearby)
The Equinox (nearby)
Ole's (Inn at the Round Barn) (nearby)

British Columbia
Big Bar Guest Ranch

Québec
Mont-Tremblant Region
Ripplecove Inn (nearby)

Lighted Trails

Alaska
Anchorage Region

California
Tahoe Donner

Colorado
Snow Mountain Ranch

Idaho
McCall Region

Maine
Sunday River Cross Country Ski Center

Michigan
Boyne Nordican
Cross Country Ski Headquarters
Crystal Mountain Resort
Garland
Gaylord Region
Shanty Creek

Minnesota
Bearskin Lodge
Bemidji Region
Giants Ridge
Golden Eagle Lodge & Nordic Ski Center
Pincushion Mountain Bed & Breakfast

Montana
Izaak Walton Inn

New York
Garnet Hill Lodge
Lake Placid Region
Lapland Lake Cross Country Ski &
   Vacation Center
Salmon Hills

Utah
Sundance

Vermont
Viking Ski Touring Centre

Washington
Sleeping Lady

Alberta
Canmore Nordic Centre
Terratima Lodge

British Columbia
The Hills Health Ranch (next door)
Silver Star Mountain Resort

Ontario
Hardwood Hills Cross Country Ski
   Centre
Hiawatha Highlands
Highlands Nordic

Québec
La Montagne Coupée Country Inn and
   Resort

Over-Snow Access

California
Royal Gorge Cross Country Ski Resort

Montana
Wade Lake Resort

Ontario
Stokely Creek Lodge

Passenger Train Access within 20 Miles

California
North Lake Tahoe Region
Northstar-at-Tahoe
Royal Gorge Cross Country Ski Resort
Tahoe Donner

Colorado
C Lazy U Ranch
Devil's Thumb Ranch
Snow Mountain Ranch

Maine
Smiling Hill Farm

Massachusetts
Bucksteep Manor
Cranwell Resort & Golf Club

Minnesota
Maplelag

Montana
Izaak Walton Inn

New York
Mohonk Mountain House

Vermont
Blueberry Hill Inn
The Equinox
Grafton Ponds Cross Country Ski Center
Green Mountain Ski Touring Center
Green Trails Cross Country Ski Center
Ole's (Inn at the Round Barn)
Trapp Family Lodge
Woodstock Inn & Resort

Washington
Sleeping Lady

Alberta
Jasper Park Lodge

British Columbia
Helmcken Falls Lodge
The Hills Health Ranch

Ontario
Hardwood Hills Cross Country Ski
  Centre
Horseshoe Resort

Québec
Gatineau Park
Ripplecove Inn

Ranches

Colorado
C Lazy U Ranch
Devil's Thumb Ranch
High Meadows Ranch
The Home Ranch
Latigo Ranch
San Juan Guest Ranch
Vista Verde Ranch

Idaho
Teton Ridge Ranch
Wapiti Meadow Ranch

Montana
B Bar Guest Ranch
Lone Mountain Ranch

British Columbia
Big Bar Guest Ranch
The Hills Health Ranch

Real Estate Element

California
Kirkwood Ski & Summer Resort
Northstar-at-Tahoe
Tahoe Donner

Colorado
Beaver Creek Cross Country Ski Center
Cordillera

Maine
Bethel Inn & Country Club
Sugarloaf Ski Touring Center

Michigan
Boyne Nordican
Crystal Mountain Resort
Garland
Shanty Creek

Minnesota
Giants Ridge

New Hampshire
Bretton Woods Resort
Loon Mountain
Waterville Valley

New York
Salmon Hills (yurts!)

Utah
Sundance

Vermont
Green Mountain Ski Touring Center
Trapp Family Lodge

Wisconsin
The Springs Golf Club Resort

British Columbia
Silver Star Mountain Resort

Ontario
Horseshoe Resort

Romantic Getaways

California
Royal Gorge Cross Country Ski Resort
Yosemite National Park

Colorado
Cordillera
High Meadows Ranch
The Home Ranch
Latigo Ranch
Vista Verde Ranch

Idaho
Teton Ridge Ranch
Wapiti Meadow Ranch

Massachusetts
Cranwell Resort & Golf Club

Michigan
Garland
Marsh Ridge (Gaylord Region)

Minnesota
Beltrami Shores Bed & Breakfast (Bemidji
  Region)
Bearskin Lodge
Golden Eagle Lodge & Nordic Ski Center
Maplelag (cabooses!)
Pincushion Mountain Bed & Breakfast

Montana
B Bar Guest Ranch
Izaak Walton Inn (more cabooses!)
Lone Mountain Ranch

New Hampshire
The Balsams Wilderness

New York
The Bark Eater
Friends Lake Inn
Mohonk Mountain House
Salmon Hills

Utah
Sundance

Vermont
Blueberry Hill
The Equinox
Grafton Ponds Cross Country Ski Center
  (The Old Tavern)
Green Mountain Ski Touring Center
Green Trails Inn
Mountain Top Inn and Resort
Ole's (Inn at the Round Barn)
Trapp Family Lodge
Woodstock Inn & Resort

Washington
Freestone Inn (Methow Valley)
Sun Mountain Lodge
Sleeping Lady

Wisconsin
Justin Trails Nordic Ski Center
The Springs Golf Club Resort
Trail Farm

Alberta
Château Lake Louise
Jasper Park Lodge
Terratima Lodge

British Columbia
Big Bar Guest Ranch
Emerald Lake Lodge

Ontario
Stokely Creek Lodge

Québec
Le Château Montebello
Far Hills Inn
La Montagne Coupée Country Inn and
  Resort
Ripplecove Inn

Ski Regions

Alaska
Anchorage

California
North Lake Tahoe

Colorado
Aspen/Snowmass

Idaho
McCall
Sun Valley

Michigan
Gaylord

Minnesota
Bemidji

New Hampshire
Jackson Ski Touring Foundation

Washington
Methow Valley Sport Trails Association
Sleeping Lady (Leavenworth)

Wyoming
Jackson Hole

Ontario
Wigamog Inn (Haliburton Highlands)

Sleigh Rides (Horse-Drawn or Reindeer On-Site)

California
Kirkwood Ski & Summer Resort
Northstar-at-Tahoe

Colorado
Aspen/Snowmass Region
C Lazy U Ranch
Cordillera
Devil's Thumb Ranch
The Home Ranch
San Juan Guest Ranch
Snow Mountain Ranch
Vista Verde Ranch

Idaho
McCall Region
Sun Valley Region
Sun Valley Nordic
Teton Ridge Ranch

Maine
Bethel Inn & Country Club
Smiling Hill Farm
Sugarloaf Ski Touring Center
Sunday River Cross Country Ski Center

Massachusetts
Bucksteep Manor

Michigan
Crystal Mountain Resort
Garland
Shanty Creek

Minnesota
Giants Ridge

Montana
B Bar Guest Ranch
Lone Mountain Ranch

New Hampshire
Bretton Woods Resort
The Franconia Inn
Jackson Ski Touring Foundation
Waterville Valley

New York
The Bark Eater
Friends Lake Inn (Christmas)
Lake Placid Region
Lapland Lake Cross Country Ski &
   Vacation Center

Utah
Ruby's Inn Nordic Center
Sundance

Vermont
Burke Cross Country Ski Area
Green Trails Cross Country Ski Center
Mountain Top Inn and Resort
Trapp Family Lodge
Woodstock Inn & Resort

Washington
Methow Valley Sport Trails Association
Sun Mountain Lodge

Wisconsin
Palmquist's "The Farm"
Paust's Wood Lake Resort

Wyoming
Jackson Hole Region

Alberta
Château Lake Louise
Jasper Park Lodge

British Columbia
Big Bar Guest Ranch
Emerald Lake Lodge (Christmas)
The Hills Health Ranch
Manning Park Resort

Ontario
Hardwood Hills Cross Country Ski Centre
  (limited)
Horseshoe Resort (Christmas)
Wigamog Inn Resort

Québec
Far Hills Inn
Hôtel l'Estérel
Ripplecove Inn
Mont-Tremblant Region

Snowmaking

Alaska
Anchorage Region

California
Royal Gorge Cross Country Ski Resort

Maine
Sugarloaf Ski Touring Center

Massachusetts
Cranwell Resort & Golf Club

Michigan
Boyne Nordican
Cross Country Ski Headquarters

Minnesota
Giants Ridge

Montana
Lone Mountain Ranch

New York
Lake Placid (Mt. Van Hoevenberg)

Vermont
Grafton Ponds Cross Country Ski Center
  (The Old Tavern)
Mountain Top Inn and Resort

Alberta
Canmore Nordic Centre

British Columbia
The Hills Health Ranch

Ontario
Hardwood Hills Cross Country Ski Centre
Highlands Nordic

Spas

Colorado
Cordillera

Michigan
Shanty Creek

New York
Mohonk Mountain House

Vermont
The Equinox

Wisconsin
The Springs Golf Club Resort

British Columbia
The Hills Health Ranch

INDEX

Guidebooks that really *guide*

City•Smart™ Guidebooks

Pick one for your favorite city: *Albuquerque, Anchorage, Austin, Calgary, Charlotte, Chicago, Cincinnati, Cleveland, Denver, Indianapolis, Kansas City, Memphis, Milwaukee, Minneapolis/St. Paul, Nashville, Pittsburgh, Portland, Richmond, Salt Lake City, San Antonio, San Francisco, St. Louis, Tampa/St. Petersburg, Tucson.*
US $12.95 to 15.95

Retirement & Relocation Guidebooks

The World's Top Retirement Havens, Live Well in Honduras, Live Well in Ireland, Live Well in Mexico.
US $15.95 to $16.95

Travel•Smart® Guidebooks

Trip planners with select recommendations to *Alaska, American Southwest, Arizona, Carolinas, Colorado, Deep South, Eastern Canada, Florida, Florida Gulf Coast, Hawaii, Illinois/Indiana, Kentucky/Tennessee, Maryland/Delaware, Michigan, Minnesota/Wisconsin, Montana/Wyoming/Idaho, New England, New Mexico, New York State, Northern California, Ohio, Pacific Northwest, Pennsylvania/New Jersey, South Florida and the Keys, Southern California, Texas, Utah, Virginias, Western Canada.* US $14.95 to $17.95

Rick Steves' Guides

See *Europe Through the Back Door* and take along guides to *France, Belgium & the Netherlands; Germany, Austria & Switzerland; Great Britain & Ireland; Italy; Scandinavia; Spain & Portugal; London; Paris;* or *Best of Europe.* US $12.95 to $21.95

Adventures in Nature

Plan your next adventure in *Alaska, Belize, Caribbean, Costa Rica, Guatemala, Hawaii, Honduras, Mexico.*
US $17.95 to $18.95

Into the Heart of Jerusalem

A traveler's guide to visits, celebrations, and sojourns.
US $17.95

The People's Guide to Mexico

This is so much more than a guidebook—it's a trip to Mexico in and of itself, complete with the flavor of the country and its sights, sounds, and people. US $22.95

JOHN MUIR PUBLICATIONS
P.O. Box 613 ◆ Santa Fe, NM 87504

Available at your favorite bookstore.
For a catalog or to place an order call 800-888-7504.

John Muir Publications' guides are available at your favorite bookstore

The 100 Best Small Art Towns in America 3rd edition
Discover Creative Communities, Fresh Air, and Affordable Living
U.S. $16.95

Healing Centers & Retreats
Healthy Getaways for Every Body and Budget
U.S. $16.95

Cross-Country Ski Vacations, 2nd edition
A Guide to the Best Resorts, Lodges, and Groomed Trails in North America
U.S. $15.95

Gene Kilgore's Ranch Vacations, 5th edition
The Complete Guide to Guest and Resort, Fly-Fishing, and Cross-Country Skiing Ranches
U.S. $22.95

Yoga Vacations
A Guide to International Yoga Retreats
U.S. $16.95

Watch It Made in the U.S.A., 2nd edition
A Visitor's Guide to the Companies That Make Your Favorite Products
U.S. $17.95

The Way of the Traveler
Making Every Trip a Journey of Self-Discovery
U.S. $12.95

Kidding Around®
Guides for kids 6 to 10 years old about what to do, where to go, and how to have fun in *Atlanta, Austin, Boston, Chicago, Cleveland, Denver, Indianapolis, Kansas City, Miami, Milwaukee, Minneapolis/St. Paul, Nashville, Portland, San Francisco, Seattle, Washington D.C.*
U.S. $7.95

JOHN MUIR PUBLICATIONS
P.O. Box 613 ◆ Santa Fe, NM 87504

For a catalog or to place an order call 800-888-7504.

ABOUT THE AUTHOR

Jonathan Wiesel had expected to teach Contemporary Latin American Military History but instead drifted into the cross-country ski business. Since 1971, he has worked variously as a ski shop employee, retail and rental manager, ski patrolman, trail groomer, ski area gofer, resort owner, and international trip leader. His only racing accomplishments are bronze and silver medals in the 1996 World Winter Tourism Games in Austria against competition ranging from "never-evers" to a former World Champion (she waxed the field).

A graduate of Dartmouth College and the U.S. Forest Service National Avalanche School, Jonathan currently works as a journalist, ski guide and instructor, and resort consultant. He is devoted to winter, Newfoundlands, and appallingly rich desserts. An inveterate traveler who has lived in seven snowbelt states and three European countries, he resides near Bozeman, Montana, and has been unerringly described as "a man of few words who uses them often."